Knowing What We Know

Knowing What We Know

AFRICAN AMERICAN WOMEN'S EXPERIENCES OF VIOLENCE AND VIOLATION

GAIL GARFIELD

RUTGERS UNIVERSITY PRESS

New Brunswick, New Jersey, and London

LIBRARY OF CONGRESS CATALOGING-IN-PUBLICATION DATA

Garfield, Gail, 1964–
   Knowing what we know : African American women's experiences of violence and violation / Gail Garfield.
     p.   cm.
   Includes bibliographical references and index.
   ISBN-13: 978-0-8135-3659-0 (hardcover : alk. paper)
   ISBN-13: 978-0-8135-3660-6 (pbk. : alk. paper)
   1. African American women—Violence against. 2. African American women—Crimes against. I. Title.
   HV6250.4.W65G37 2005
   362.82'92'08996073—dc22
                                 2005004830

A British Cataloging-in-Publication record for this book is available from the British Library

Manufactured in the United States of America

I dedicate this book to the memory of my friend Doris Denice Taylor. Her legacy of compassion, commitment to the wellness of the human body and spirit, and dedication to the possible, lives on in the many lives she touched.

Contents

Acknowledgments *ix*

Preface *xi*

Introduction I

1 *Becoming* 42

2 *Lessons to Learn* 83

3 *The Worlds of Men* 115

4 *The Worlds of Women* 150

5 *She Works* 206

Conclusion 244

References 253

Acknowledgments

MANY WISE and supportive people have contributed to the making of this book to whom I am deeply grateful.

To the nine African American women who generously shared their life histories, I offer my deepest gratitude. Your unforgettable stories are now a part of me and my life is forever changed and enriched by your experiences.

This book began as my dissertation and the thoughtful comments of William Kornblum and Hester Eisenstein early on proved invaluable. But Barbara Katz Rothman, my dissertation chairperson, mentor, and friend continues to provide unwavering support, guidance, and a belief in me for which I am sincerely grateful.

For their help in reading, providing needed dialogue, and pointing me in the right direction with their suggestions and ideas, I would like to thank Patricia Yancey Martin, Clifton Gail Mitchell, Marie Littlejohn, Beth Richie, Natalie Sokoloff, Heather Dalmage, Angelique Harris, and Rossetta Morris.

I thank Catherine Pierce and Nadine Neusville of the U.S. Department of Justice Office on Violence Against Women for their untiring and relentless efforts to do the right thing in the face of tremendous challenge.

I am grateful to my editor, Kristi Long, who immediately got what I was trying to achieve by guiding me in a way that respected me as an author and the women's stories as important text. To the anonymous reviewers who helped to shape this book and the staff at Rutgers University Press who guided the manuscript through the production process.

And finally, for simply being my friends and close confidants, I thank Linda Goode Bryant, Sandra Morales-DeLeon, Dana Ain Davis, Angela Dews, Priscilla Simons, and Dahlia Norman, all of whom had no doubts that I could write this book.

PREFACE

In the fall of 1981, I was approached by a group of women who asked me if I would work with them to develop the first battered women's shelter for Latina women in Minnesota. The idea of working cross-culturally with women appealed to me. I was also interested in providing technical support that could help develop and strengthen community-based organizations. This was an interest wholly consistent with my understanding that one avenue toward community empowerment is the creation of self-sustaining organizations that can effectively respond to the unmet needs of community residents. So, over many dishes of red beans and rice, we defined a plan of action that laid out what needed to be done to make Casa de Esperanza a reality.

I busied myself with the mechanics of the project: identifying potential sites, negotiating financial arrangements, and setting up administrative protocols for operating a battered women's shelter. I intentionally stayed away from policy and programmatic decisions: these were areas I thought could best be handled by other team members who were battered women advocates, who knew what they wanted, and who had more knowledge of the issues involved. At the time, my understanding of domestic violence, spousal abuse, family violence, battering, and sexual assault,—violence against women, in general—was quite limited. These were all new terms to me, and they appeared to have their own particular set of meaning within the anti-violence movement.

One day, several members of the team, on their way to the hospital to visit a woman who had been beaten by her husband, asked me to join them. The woman had received an order of protection against her husband for prior assaultive acts, but he broke into her house and beat her anyway. I was not prepared for what I saw upon entering her hospital room. I had never seen a person so thoroughly brutalized. There was an immediate disconnect. I could not grasp how someone who would probably profess some form of affection for this woman could be so brutal toward her. In offering explanations, the advocates talked about broad issues like male "power, control, and domination" that seemed abstract and inadequate to explain the deeply personal level of brutality this woman experienced.

My experiences with the women of Case de Esperanza marked an important professional and political turning point in my life. Even though I was far from being an advocate and becoming an activist was even farther removed, the issue of violence and its particular significance for women's lives began to take shape in my consciousness. I started attending conferences, forums, and workshops, and I listened to testimonials of women's experiences. Slowly, I began to accept the explanations offered by advocates for the disruption that could force some women to flee their homes in fear of losing their lives and the destruction that left some women physically and emotionally scarred for life. They were convincing in arguing that violence against women is a manifestation of male dominance. Accordingly, violence represents an attempt by men to exercise some form of power and control over women's lives, to assert their will over women's lives in ways that could result in harm, injury, and even death.

As a fundamental premise, the advocates' explanations finally made sense to me. But I began to remember and encounter new situations that did not fit neatly within the boundaries of those explanations: situations where the complexities and contradictions of women's lives included those explanations but also said something different about women's experiences of violence. My evolving understanding of the role of violence in women's lives only generated new issues for me to ponder and posed important questions for which I had no answers. My experiences with the women of Casa de Esperanza forced me to reflect upon situations that I had long ago dismissed as interesting but not necessarily insightful, important, or connected to anything in particular. To me, such situations were just mere occurrences in my life that I had not bothered to name.

Growing up in rural Georgia in an all-female household, male violence was simply not an issue for me as a child, or so I thought until I remembered a male cousin, who seemingly every weekend would have a fight with his wife. He would always end up at our house either on Saturday or Sunday morning because his wife would chase him away with a gun. Their actions were expected and accepted as part of our community lore. Influenced by my family opinions, my cousin was seen as hard working and his wife as mean spirited. So, as a child, I understood that whatever my cousin did to his wife, she deserved it because she was evil and disliked. Upon reflection, I thought that surely, if I felt physically threatened, would I not attempt to defend myself? My cousin's wife reaction did not seem unusual to me, but somehow it did not seem to fit the paradigms that were beginning to shape my understanding of violence against women. And it seemed contrary to the experiences of the other women I had been listening to, who saw themselves as victims, did not take self-assertive actions to defend themselves, and who were the ones that were forced to leave their homes out of fear in search of the safety of a battered women's shelter.

I also recalled a fight between two high school girls, one of whom was popularly known as a bully. As we stood and watched this fight, the bully was slashed in the face with a razor blade. Blood was everywhere, and she needed sixty-four stitches to close her wounds. But none of us who watched the fight had any compassion for her pain because, after all, she was an intimidating bully whom we feared. This situation too seemed far removed from the experience of the woman I had met in the hospital. This fight was a public spectacle that was not played out in the privacy of a home. There was no male to blame this violence on. So what role did notion of male "dominance, power, and control" play in this situation? It was unclear to me how to position this incident, but somehow it seems relevant to any discussion of women's experiences of violence.

My guilt and shame will never allow me to forget yet another situation that did fit quite neatly into my fledgling understanding of violence against women. While I was in graduate school, there was a woman who was an undergraduate, an acquaintance, who had married a Nigerian student. It was rumored that they had gotten married so quickly because he wanted to become a U.S. citizen. Maybe three months after their marriage, her husband threw battery acid in her face while she was taking a shower. The burns were so severe that her facial tissue was destroyed and doctors could not perform plastic surgery, so she would forever live with her scars. Her husband was convicted of criminal charges and imprisoned.

At the beginning of my last semester in college, I was sitting with other students in the grill, where, to my surprise, she entered while wearing a full-faced clear plastic mask designed to protect her damaged skin from the harsh cold of the Minnesota winter. It was a surreal sight, and everybody stared. She came over and sat at our table, and it was the first real conversation that I can recall ever having with her. Her enormous courage and the strength it took for her to show her deeply scarred body day after day, as she was determined to get her college degree, will forever remain a part of my memories. I will also never forget that I did not visit her as she lay for months recovering in the hospital or provide her with any meaningful support as she struggled to reclaim her sense of self.

Along with past reflections, I also encountered situations in the 1980s and 1990s that introduced other issues and questions for me to consider in my attempts to understand the role that violence plays in women's lives. I began to realize that broad cultural and social arrangements influenced by gender, race, and class relations—even though these influences are not necessarily predicated on notions of male dominance—could shape women's experiences of violence. This realization was revealed in my work as a researcher in the area of child welfare, after moving to New York City. I examined the unexpected and rapid increases of children entering New York City foster care system and how the city was responding to this growth.

I entered the bizarre world of an entrenched city bureaucracy in the form of the Child Welfare Administration, as it faced the world of drug addiction that was stimulated in large part by the crack cocaine epidemic of the mid-1980s. These worlds are linked together by the presence of poor, often black, mothers and their children. I found that the controlling institutional arrangements questioned the maternal adequacy of poor mothers and could legally separate some of them from their children, forever. I witnessed the effect of physical and emotional abuse and sometimes the total abandonment rendered by mothers on their children, owing in large part to their insatiable drug addiction. I also observed the effects of physical and sexual abuse, criminal activities, and the exploitation of women involved in the crack cocaine drug culture. From my widening perspective, all these social arrangements largely depended upon the interpretations of women's experiences of violence.

In 1984, I participated in my first protest march against police brutality. It was over the killing of a sixty-seven-year-old black grand-mother, Mrs. Eleanor Bumpers, who was to be evicted from her apartment because she was behind in rent. Three police officers alleged that an arthritic and overweight Mrs. Bumpers lunged at them with a knife and the only way they could protect themselves was to shoot her dead. Speaker after speaker at the City Hall protest framed Mrs. Bumper's murder as another incident of police brutality. Although I refused to believe that I was the only person in the crowd of thousands who saw what I thought to be an obvious connection, not one speaker ever drew the connection between police brutality and the issue of violence against women. I cannot say that it was intentionally excluded from their analysis of what happened to Mrs. Bumpers; instead, I think that it was simply not seen as an important connection to make.

For me, the issues of race, gender, and violence collided around Tawana Brawley four years later, and I could not privilege one of these issues as more significant than the other; they were all tightly knotted and intersected. But the issue of her silence resonated for me. The fifteen-year-old high school student's advisers and supporters told of her kidnapping, rape, and physical assault by several white men who were believed to be cops. It was obvious to me that something terrible had happened to this child, but the political circus that was created and played out between her largely black male advisers and the largely white male politicians and government officials made a public mockery of her experience. And Tawana refused to speak. I wondered why? Was her silence generated by shame and humiliation? Was her silence based on the fear of being called a liar and the additional burden of not being taken seriously if she spoke? Was her silence an intentional act of defiance? Or, was her silence rooted in the belief that others could best give voice to and articulate her unspeakable experience?

Certainly, black cultural sentiments that I grew up with seem to complicate the issue of violence against women for me. I know, from experience, that you are not supposed to wash your dirty laundry in public, especially for white folks to see. For me, I also know that my old school "race woman" tendencies will easily surface when I perceive white folks acting in blatantly unjust ways to black folks. Both realities impacted my understanding of Tawana Brawley's story as well as the overlapping stories surrounding the Rodney King incident. Members of the Los Angeles police force, their brutality captured on video and shown on every major news network around the country, were acquitted of criminal charges for beating Rodney King.

A riot that many blacks called a rebellion broke out all over Los Angeles County. Then Rodney King made the pathetic plea before national news cameras when he asked, "Can we all just get along"? In the aftermath of the police acquittal and rebellion, his wife made an emergency telephone call to the police, and Rodney King was once again arrested for beating her up. Many in the black community, who had been so vocal about the injustice Rodney King suffered at the hands of white cops, were silent at the injustice his wife had suffered at the hands of Rodney King. I waited for comments, but the silence was deafening, and then I realized that this was simply not a topic for public discussion.

Male dominance, institutional arrangements, due process, cultural sentiments, public voice, private suffering and all within the working of race, gender, and class relations unexpectedly burst into my consciousness during a three-day period in 1991. Violence against women was simultaneously positioned as a backdrop and as a central issue in an internationally publicized hearing. The Senate Judiciary Committee interrupted its confirmation hearing on Clarence Thomas's nomination to the Supreme Court to hold a special hearing on allegations of sexual harassment made against the nominee by Anita Hill. It was high drama, worthy of popcorn, and I was glued to my television set. I had never witnessed such a spectacle before, and at the heart of this television drama was a lone middle-class black woman attempting to convey to an international audience her experiences at the hands of a lone middle-class black man, who used his positional power to abuse her. After the testimony of the "pubic hair" on the coke can, a friend called from London to ask if we in this country had lost our collective minds.

Yet I continued to watch as scores of white men, white women, and black men sat as analysts before television cameras claiming and disclaiming Anita Hill's experience. I was both amazed and amused at their attempts to frame and interpret for me this drama that I was watching, while I wondered on what television channel the black women analysts were sequestered, because I could not seem to find their commentary. Even though I recognized what was unique about this drama, I saw what can happen to a black woman who dares to speak publicly about her private pain and the attacks upon her personhood as result of giving voice to her experience. I learned that there are important implications to a public fight and that a lone black woman is extremely vulnerable to additional violence.

A variation on this theme became real for me in the summer of 1995. I was attending a meeting on violence against women in Washington, D.C.; and upon returning to my hotel room I had telephone messages from coworkers and friends telling me that the front-page story in the *New York Amsterdam News* was the welcome home celebration to be held in Harlem in honor of Mike Tyson, the former heavyweight boxing champion who was being released from prison. Many well-known black male activists, business leaders, politicians, and church leaders comprised the welcoming home committee. The only woman on the committee was Roberta Flack, who was scheduled to provide entertainment for an affair at the historic Apollo Theater. It was unacceptable to me that the leadership of this black community, my community, would publicly embrace and give accolades to a convicted rapist.

Mike Tyson was convicted of raping Desiree Washington, a black beauty queen contestant. His defense attorney conceded that Mike Tyson was a brute and acknowledged that there was a long and public history of reported accounts where Tyson had violated women in his past. His defense was that Desiree Washington should have known not to go to Mike Tyson's hotel room alone, especially in the early morning hours. Many in the black community, particularly women, supported Mike Tyson and professed his innocence while vilifying Desiree Washington as a "gold digger." His generosity was exemplified by rumors of a Rolex watch he had given to Tawana Brawley and Christmas turkeys he distributed to the needy in Harlem. I had watched the evening news and read in the newspapers that celebrities such as Whitney Huston and public figures like Betty Shabazz visited Mike Tyson in prison.

Rushing back to New York City, I found that a coalition had already been formed to stop the Tyson celebration. Our position was clearly articulated: we believed that Mike Tyson deserved a second chance, but he did not deserve to be welcomed as a hero in the black community. Hero status must be awarded to the black women who had survived male violence. We decided to hold a candlelight vigil on 125th Street in the heart of Harlem the day before the welcoming parade to call attention to misplaced sympathies. But prior to this, we also created quite a political ruckus. We protested the city awarding a parade permit to the welcoming committee and got it withdrawn; we lobbied members of the committee, particularly politicians, who were more receptive to our concerns, for they understood political consequences; we wrote editorials and appeared on television and radio; and we organized for the vigil. For this, members of our coalition were harassed, and some even received death threats from Mike Tyson's supporters. As we stood with our candles lit in support of the value of black women's lives, an organized group of black women stood across the street in front of the Apollo Theater with their placards heckling, harassing, and threatening us. Some of whom, I felt, would have surely approached in an aggressive manner, if the police and their barricades had not been there to "protect" us from injury and harm.

With all the complexities, conflicts, contradictions, commotion, and at times just plain ugliness I have engaged in during my attempts to understand how women experience violence, two fundamental questions continue to linger for me. What is the meaning of violence in women's lives, especially given the different layers and dimensions that are insinuated into their experiences? And, more important, how do I position black women's, as well as my own, experiences of violence into this understanding?

This book represents my continuing search for answers to these questions. It is about violence and the ways it is experienced by nine African American women as they engage the process of living. This book offers a different dialogue on women's experiences of violence, in that it explores what happens when women's agency come into conflict with cultural and social constraints that are imposed on their everyday lives. The main argument is that when this occurs, violence is sometimes insinuated into their lives. And women experience this violence as a violation to their sense of personhood. Their sense of violation shapes the meaning they give to their experiences of violence, and that meaning, in turn, shapes how they see themselves as human beings. How these nine African American women maintain, sustain, and in some instance regain their sense of human worth as a result of their experiences of violation in the context of violence, is the focus of this book.

Based on life history interviews, this book places the women's varied experience in the context of history: not only the history that is imposed

on them as black women, but also the history they make in their struggles to give value to this identity. Covering more than forty years of lived
experiences, it follows the course of the women's lives as children to that
of mature adults to see what is revealed when agency and constraints collide. Over time, change and continuity are salient features of the women's
experiences. For change and continuity rearticulate not only the dynamic relationship between agency and constraints but also the significance of violence and violation in their lives. What make the women's
stories compelling are not the decisions and actions of others in shaping
their experiences, although this is an important consideration; rather, the
decisions and actions that the women take on behalf of their own needs,
interests, and aspirations provide texture and complexity to their experiences. As such, this book provides an understanding of how history is
made in the lives of nine African American women, and how violence
and violation become an integral part of that history.

Knowing What We Know

Introduction

FOR MORE than twenty years, anti-violence advocates shaped the discourse on violence against women. Rooted in the contemporary women's movement, their perspectives and activism influenced our understanding of both the cause and the nature of violence against women. Whether they either argued that violence against women stems from the workings of patriarchy or offered a more structural explanation for the role that violence plays in women's subordination and oppression, the advocates' seemingly different ideological and political stances ultimately ended up in the same place: Fingers were pointed at what men do as a way of imposing their will on women's lives.

The discussions, debates, and disagreements over male "power, control, and domination" as introduced by the anti-violence movement of the 1970s, established the foundation for the discourse on violence against women. This advocacy-led discourse emphasized strategies for *women's empowerment*. Under its influence women-centered programs were developed over a broad spectrum of service delivery areas. Also, women from different cultural and social backgrounds—sometimes together but oftentimes not—held rallies, vigils, and marches and engaged in other forms of direct action that demanded *women's safety*. And, this advocacy-led discourse called for an *end to male violence* by proposing important legislative and policy changes—at the local, state, federal levels of government—that would hold men accountable for their bad behavior toward women.

The persistent activism of the anti-violence movement paid off. In 1994, Congress passed the Violence Against Women Act, this landmark legislation is widely known as VAWA. Under VAWA statutory provisions a new discourse on violence against women emerged. We now have what I call the government-sponsored discourse on violence against women.

In replacing the advocacy-led discourse, a major shift in the conceptual, programmatic, and political landscape occurred that dramatically alters how our society interprets and responds to violence against women.

VAWA was enacted as Title IV of the 1994 Crime Control and Law Enforcement Act. With the passage of VAWA, the federal government assumes an obligation to insure women's safety as a matter of both justice and criminal jurisprudence. The legislative intent is to hold male *perpetrators* legally accountable for specific acts of violence against women. Under VAWA statutory provisions violence against women is defined primarily as acts of domestic violence and sexual assault. These acts provide an important point of reference for women's experiences of violence, regardless of history or cultural and social context. Through tougher criminal sanctions that encourage arrest, prosecution, and *victims'* involvement in these legal processes, the underlying assumption of VAWA is that an increase in the conviction and punishment of men who perpetrate violence against women will result in safer women.

With a crime-and-punishment focus the federal government, largely through the U.S. Department of Justice Office on Violence against women, assumes a major role in interpreting and implementing the statutory provisions of VAWA. To assist in this effort, this office draws on a broad and diverse body of professional experts who come from academia, law enforcement, legal advocacy, health and human services, victim services, professional associations, and public policy organizations. These experts are not staff; rather, they are paid consultants. What do these experts do? They are instrumental; the experts shape the very character of the government-sponsored discourse by establishing the conceptual and programmatic frameworks for interpreting women's experiences of violence. Specifically, they assist in documenting and analyzing issues, assess models for best practice approaches, influence funding decisions through peer review, evaluate program development, and frame the discussions by defining the parameters of the public debate through forums, seminars, workshops, and conferences.

The experts give form and texture to the disposition of the government-sponsored discourse. However, they do not provide the day-to-day response to women's experiences of violence; this response rests largely in the hands of local agencies. By asserting administrative and fiscal authority granted under VAWA, the Office on Violence Against

Women implements a system that is called a "coordinated community response." In this system local victim services, law enforcement, prosecutors, and courts are required to work together in fashioning a response to domestic violence and sexual assault, if they are to receive federal funding under VAWA.

For the past ten years, the development of this well-crafted and largely bureaucratic government-sponsored discourse has established the standards across the country for communities' interpretation of and response to violence against women. As a result, violence against women has gained increased recognition, acceptability, and credibility as a legitimate social problem that demands a public response. To achieve this public acknowledgment anti-violence advocates made important compromises, concessions, and trade-offs. The price of government's increased participation was high: anti-violence advocates lost control over the discourse. Ten years prior to the enactment of VAWA Susan Schechter, historian and activist of the anti-violence movement, cautioned that with government's increased involvement the anti-violence movement risks relinquishing its principles (Schechter 1982). In many important ways this is precisely what has happened. The ideological, political, strategic vision as well as the activism of the anti-violence movement no longer guides the focus and direction of the public discourse on violence against women.

With enormous achievements and needed structural changes that have established violence against women as a social priority, what has this shift from an advocacy-led to a government-sponsored discourse meant for how women experience violence in their lives? In other words, as VAWA enters its ten-year anniversary, I pose an important question: Are women's experiences of violence limited to and can they be addressed solely by a crime-and-punishment model as embodied in the statutory provisions of VAWA and as implemented by the government-sponsored discourse?

I LOVE THE sense of freedom I get from riding commuter trains, especially America's version of the "bullet train," the Acela Express. Increasingly this is true in the aftermath of 9/11. Maybe it is because the direction I am traveling is unambiguous, uncomplicated, and unchallenged. Even though my black woman's baggage is weighted down with contradictions, ambiguities, and frustrations it is overhead, out of sight, and for a brief moment out of mind. There are neither fears nor anger. I can relax and let my mind wander unencumbered by expectations, and beyond simple acts of common courtesy I do not feel the need to explain who I am, why I am there, or where I am going. Once again, I am on the Acela Express, leaving New York City's Pennsylvania Station heading toward Washington, D.C., to attend another meeting on violence against women sponsored by the U.S. Department of Justice Office on Violence Against Women.

Upon arriving, I enter an/other world, one that is largely white, administrative, and formal. It is a world that social philosopher Nancy Fraser would characterize as the "expert needs discourse." But in this instance, I call it the government-sponsored discourse on violence against women. In this particular discourse professional experts provide the critical link between the politicized needs identified by advocates of the anti-violence movement and government's response to those needs. They bring to the discourse specialized skills that are "associated with professional class formation, institution building, and social problem-solving" (Fraser 1989). With their ideas, statistics, research, strategies, rhetoric and obscure vocabularies the experts' role is to reinterpret, redefine, and reposition women's needs in ways that can be institutionalized. At some point within this largely bureaucratizing or problem-solving process they have reshaped women: Women are now *victims* who are "rendered passive, positioned as potential recipients of predefined services rather than as agents involved in interpreting their needs and shaping their life conditions" (Fraser 1989).

Over the years, I have participated in more policy, program, research, funding, and training meetings in this government-sponsored discourse than I can recall. Admittedly, the reasons why I find myself in these gatherings are riddled by contradictions, ambiguities, and frustrations. Why am I invited? Why do I attend? And, more important, what is accomplished by my forays into these select and mostly white gatherings?

I do not assume that I have been selected to participate in these meetings because I possess rare credentials or special expertise that other similarly positioned African American women do not have. I know that it is not my self-perception, but the perception of others that make me appear more acceptable or worthy of an invitation to these select gatherings.

Why, then, do I venture beyond the black community to participate in these meetings, when there is an obvious need for activism, to get "the community" to acknowledge the importance of and respond to African American women's experiences of violence?

My answer is quite simple: I reject the either/or assumption that is implicit in my own question. I participate because I believe African American women have a stake in the issue of violence against women. Their needs, interests, and aspirations are not isolated to the black community, separated from the white discourse, or limited by a lack of struggle in both of these arenas. I know that through the daily acts of living, violence extracts an immeasurable toll on African American women's lives. Whether they are devalued, deprived, or demeaned by cultural and social conditions and practices of uneven relations of power, or whether they are stabbed in their homes, shot while working behind a desk, or strangled in a darken alley by a stranger imposing his will, the cost to their humanity is too high a stake to simply ignore. I believe that the integrity of African American women's physical, personal, and social lives is at stake, and for this reason the question of why I participate in the discourse is resolved.

However, what is accomplished by my participation in this government-sponsored discourse on violence against women is an issue that is far from resolution and far more difficult to answer.

As I sit in meeting after meeting among the experts, I realize that in such gatherings the thorny issue for me is one of inclusion. Admittedly inclusion is seductive. But in such gatherings it poses a challenge. Often I find myself confronting the tensions, dilemmas, and contradictions that are produced by strategies to include African American women into *the process*. The meaning that lies beneath the inclusion is of concern; in this instance that meaning tells me how African American women's experiences are interpreted, and it holds important implications for how their experiences of violence are positioned within *the process*. As a principle, inclusion is fundamental to me. As a practice, inclusion raises a fundamental question: Does the meaning of inclusion challenge or reproduce established patterns of uneven relations of power? I am ever confronted with this question as I engage the conceptual, programmatic, and political dimensions that encompass the government-sponsored discourse.

The legislative provisions of VAWA frame the government discourse.

But professional experts interpret, establish, and convey the meaning of its statutory requirements. They focus our attention on what is common to women's experiences. Indeed, it is difficult to argue that domestic violence and sexual assault are limited to a particular group of women's experiences. By tacitly agreeing that this is *true*, we come to accept the narrow parameters that now establish the reference for what constitutes violence against women. In our acceptance, we too limit our perspective to individual bad male behavior, acts of battering and rape in particular, and physical harm and injury as the critical markers for authenticating women's experiences of violence. Implicit in this reference is the presumption that a crime has occurred, and this opens up the possibility of holding male *perpetrators* legally accountable for their bad behavior against women. In an ironic way, one might reasonably find that this narrow conceptual reference also opens up the possibility for greater inclusion.

By limiting the meaning of violence to what men do to women important barriers to inclusions are removed. Of importance in the government-sponsored discourse is a common ground upon which to link all women's experiences of violence. To establish this link, cultural and social distinctions are ignored by the experts. Distinctions such as race, gender, and class in particular become ambiguous, if not completely obsolete, in the experts' interpretations. But as we see later, precisely those cultural and social distinctions, which the experts attempt to disregard, give meaning to and contextualize women's experiences of violence.

No matter how skillfully the experts attempt to silence and devalue cultural and social distinctions, they impose a powerful reality. They not only play a critical role in shaping women's experiences of violence, but they also penetrate the very conceptual, programmatic, and political foundation of the discourse itself, regardless of lacking recognition or resistance to their importance. Nevertheless, within the government discourse, race, gender, and class distinctions are seen as barriers to inclusion: distinctions decenter women, reinterpret experiences, and refocus uneven relations of power. Indeed, those particular distinctions limit possibilities for inclusion, especially when such inclusion is based on what appears to be common among all women's experiences of violence.

In principle cultural and social distinctions are not denied, but in practice they are simply deemphasized. In the government-sponsored discourse domestic violence and sexual assault are acts of violence; the government discourse sees these acts, in particular, as crossing cultural and social boundaries to construct what appears to be a share reality for all women's experiences. Indeed, these incidents of violence do appear to be common among women's experiences, and they provide an important baseline for our general understanding and knowledge of violence against women. This shared reality is authenticated and verified by the similarities in the resulting physical harm and injury that is inflicted on women by men. Within this narrow realm of reality, a powerful argument can be made that no important cultural and social distinctions exist. Conceptually, the absence of cultural and social distinctions eliminates barriers to inclusion, while the discourse appears almost commonsensible and rational in its interpretation and response to violence against women. Therefore, commonality of experiences establishes a strong practical and rational basis for inclusion that is difficult to simply ignore.

However, if this is so, why then do I encounter *special categories* that are established for certain groups but not for other groups of women's experiences within the government-sponsored discourse?

Even though the cause and nature of violence against women is seen as the same for different groups of women's experiences regardless of social and cultural distinctions, VAWA provisions suggest that there are "traditionally underserved communities" of women. They are underserved due to impediments that inhibit greater participation. These impediments are deeply rooted in precisely those same cultural and social distinctions that the experts would like to ignore when it comes to interpreting and responding to women's experiences of violence. But in affirming a commitment to inclusion, historical patterns of discrimination against particular groups of women must be acknowledged. For these impediments are seen as barriers inhibiting access. The experts have devised useful strategies to address these barriers. They have created categories of inclusion that acknowledge historical impediments.

Special categories are established to specifically address barriers to access. Yet those categories neither challenge nor provide an oppositional meaning for violence against women within the discourse. To the contrary, they reflect important ideological and political perspectives that on the surface *special categories* conceal: "The acts of judgment entailed in classifying are masked by the uses of categories, particularly in scientific contexts, which more often than not treat (or appear to treat) categories as if they were commonsensical reflections of the natural world." In the government-sponsored discourse the development of *special categories* is seen as an obvious way to address historical impediments that inhibit greater inclusion. Instead, they really are "humanly created conceptual boxes" based on ideas and politics that structure women's realities (Yanow 2003). Hence, the categories conform to normative interpretations thereby reinforcing what is thought to be a common reality for women's experience of violence. As a consequence, the experiences of women placed into *special categories* are in fact viewed as the same as those who are not: for they are all positioned as female *victims* who are potential recipients of predetermined services.

I sit in meetings knowing that African American women's experiences are included in the government-sponsored discourse. I also know that at some point, regardless of the specific topic, the *special categories* will appear in the discussion: as if, on cue, the "women of color," "marginalized communities," "diverse and special populations," or "the underserved populations" take their places in the dialogue. Presumably, somewhere within these abstracted categories that contain the anonymous experiences of women is the presence of African American women's experiences of violence. Often, I am reminded of sociologist Patricia Hill Collins's observations that, "concrete experience effectively destabilized seemingly scientific categories when such categories appeared unable to explain Black women's experiences and when Black women refused to accept the authority of those categories to explain their lives" (Collins 1998).

Inclusion in the context of *special categories* offers little satisfaction. In fact, it is simply not good enough because they do not "explain black women's experiences," and I do not "accept" their authority. African American women's inclusion as well as my own participation in the government-sponsored discourse does not challenge, but in many ways our presence contributes to reproducing established patterns of uneven power relations. The meaning of our inclusion makes me question what is accomplished by my participation, for my experience, knowledge, and professional judgment will not allow me to sit in meetings and pretend that those categories are limited to strategies of inclusion: the judgments upon which they are constructed are not concealed.

For me those categories incorporate meaning where cultural and social distinctions are given a particularity that is measured against a white, often middle-class, normative standard, and for those experiences that fall outside of that norm inclusion becomes synonymous with accommodation. I call this accommodation the "make it fit" approach for those "other" experiences of violence that appears to be a bit odd, unique, or, dare I say the word, different. Differences do not fit neatly in the presumed normative patterns of violence against women. The *special categories* include the experiences of women whose race is also an important marker for their experiences of violence and the experiences of women whose culture and class positions mark the dimensions of violence against women in distinct ways. This includes women who live in poverty, those who are substance abusers, prostitutes, newly arrived and undocumented immigrants, lesbians, and those who have physical and mental disabilities, and criminal histories. Too often the particularities of these women's experiences of violence are not just disregarded; rather, their experiences of violence are fragmented and distorted beyond recognition in this "make it fit" process of accommodation. But on the surface what counts in the government discourse is that all women's experiences, regardless of history or context, are included into the process. What lies beneath the surface is not openly discussed, debated, or offered for disagreement in the discourse.

African American women's experiences do destabilize the "conceptual boxes," the seemingly scientific or rational categories. Their experiences reveal the tensions, contradictions, and dilemmas that lie beneath the dominant norms, explicit assumptions, and structural arrangements that now influence how we should view violence against women. Yet the tensions, contradictions, and dilemmas do not arise because African American women's experiences appear to be different from, while also appearing to be the same as, other women's experiences. Their experiences of violence are what they are: they are neither more typical or exceptional, authentic or specious, nor vested with a greater or lesser degree of complexity than other women's experiences. Indeed, African American women's experiences are what they are. But in the particularities of history that shape the cultural and social context of their lives and give meaning to their experiences of violence. Yet such history and context remains unrecognized in the government-sponsored discourse.

The difficulties in trying to make experiences fit established paradigms and models do not rest with African American or any other particular group of women's experiences of violence. Rather, the difficulties
lay in the experts' attempts to homogenize, systematize, and standardize
all women's experiences of violence based on the appearance of com-
monalities or essential truths. Guided by the provisions of VAWA, the
government-sponsored discourse has effectively reduced women's experiences to incidents of domestic violence and sexual assault, created a
system of response that respects these boundaries, placed conceptual
blinders on our thinking by skillfully silencing opposing perspectives
through the use of authoritative voices, and thawed political activism
with a seemingly commonsensible or rational approach to violence against
women. This narrowing by the government-sponsored discourse not
only distorts all women's experiences but also marginalizes the meaning
of violence in their lives. I contend that physical violence as a result of
bad male behavior does not constitute the total sum of African American—
or any other particular group—women's experiences of violence. Nor
are women's needs, interests, and aspirations limited to or able to be addressed solely by a crime-and-punishment model.

But I digress. Let me return specifically to the issue of inclusion, for
it continues to be my thorny issue. Unresolved for me is whether the inclusion of African American women's experiences is well meaning; for
instance, is inclusivity offered as an appeasement to stem perceptions of
racism, aimed at coopting or appropriating experiences, used in attempts
to fend off potential political backlash, or employed as a combination of
some or all of these reasons. Whatever the logic, I know that the blatant exclusion of African American women's experiences from the
government-sponsored discourse is not a viable option, politically or
otherwise. Women's experiences of violence in all of their similarities,
differences, and complexities establish the political currency by which
the government-sponsored discourse assumes its legitimacy, and violence
against women acquires its status as a social problem that necessitates a
public response.

Toward that end, what am I to make of my inclusion into the discourse? I have no illusions about what is accomplished; unfortunately
both the content and the process are all too familiar. Of course, my activist sensibility continues to tell me that the discourse must be held

accountable, but my common sense asks of me, to what effect? I am well aware that African American women's experiences, like my own participation, provide only a token presence in the discourse, and accountability cannot be demanded through tokenism. Audre Lorde aptly reminds me of this fact when she said: "The tokenism that is sometimes extended to us is not an invitation to join power; our racial 'otherness' is a visible reality that makes that quite clear" (Lorde 1984). And the important implication, as Kimberle Crenshaw tells me, is that "tokenistic, objectifying, voyeuristic inclusion is at least as disempowering as complete exclusion" (Crenshaw 1994).

So, after being simultaneously included and excluded from the government-sponsored discourse on violence against women, I take my black woman's baggage, weighted a bit heavier by "the paradox, the dichotomy, the schism," and catch a taxi to the Washington, D.C., Union Station and board the Acela Express to return to New York City.

In my departure, I know that to reclaim the humanity within African America women's experiences of violence, to attach a human face to their existence, a different dialogue is needed. But this dialogue requires another shift in the discourse, for the conversation must be framed from the perspectives of women's lives. This book seeks to begin this dialogue by exploring violence and the ways it is experienced by women as they engage their cultural and social worlds.

AFTER PARTICIPATING IN the advocacy-led and government-sponsored discourses on violence against women, I have come to realize that another important dialogue awaits. In this conversation a male-centered focus— that is, what men do as a way of imposing their will—is not the only reference for understanding women's experiences of violence. Therefore, the dialogue that I propose moves beyond the limits of violence against women and a focus on women's relationship to men. Instead, it introduces a conversation that focuses on the ways violence is experienced by women as they engage their cultural and social worlds. As a starting point, this dialogue requires that women's lives are brought to the forefront of their own experiences by exploring what they think, feel, and do as they engage conditions and practices that shape their everyday existence.

Before turning specifically to how violence is experienced by women, several underlying issues give significance to women's lives that must be taken into consideration. First, it is important to consider how women's experiences are created. In so doing, let us start from the perspective that women are active participants in the process of living. Teresa De Lauretis argues that as participants, women's experiences are "produced not by external ideas, values, or material causes, but by one's personal, subjective, engagement in the practices, discourses, and institutions that lend significance to the events of the world" (De Lauretis 1984).

De Lauretis's perspective suggests that women's experiences are created through their interactions with their cultural and social environments. Through those interactions women come to know their experiences and the meaning they give allow them to interpret and define their reality as they perceive it to be. Importantly, their perceptions inform how they respond to that reality and how they see themselves as a result. Through actively engaging the process of living, women come to know the significance of their subjective experiences: not just by what is done, by whom, and with what purpose; but also by what they think, feel, and do as they interact with their environments. As such women's experiences are not purely personal, created by their actions, nor wholly universal, shaped by cultural and social conditions and practices. Rather both dimensions are inextricably linked to produce women's subjective experiences.

Through the process of living, women engage the conditions and practices of their cultural and social environments. Their interactions construct meaning about the world and how they see themselves within and against that meaning. With this view in mind, let us consider the importance of how women are positioned in their interactions with their environments; for this also contributes to the meaning they give to their subjective experiences. Eduardo Mendieta uses the term "positionality" (Alcott and Mendieta 2003). This is not just the variety of roles and statuses that women assume in the process of living, although this is implied. Instead, the various cultural and social locations women occupy in their interactions are created by ever-changing historical circumstances that position their experiences. This perspective recognizes that cultural and social conditions and practices have histories, and women's interactions do not simply occur in isolation or outside of that history. Rather, their interactions are located within and against cultural and social arrangements formed by that history. The positions women come to occupy in the process of living give texture and shape to their subjective experiences.

However, the reality of women's lives suggests that they are not all positioned in the same ways as they engage the process of living. There is unevenness in the ways women are positioned vis-à-vis cultural and social arrangements that makes their experiences different from one another. That difference reflects uneven power relations. Here, uneven power relations are seen as constraints upon women's self-defined needs, interests, and aspirations. Those constraints are manifested in hierarchical social interactions, but they also circulate in women's personal and physical interactions. Kimberle Crenshaw suggests that the social, personal, and physical dimensions of uneven power relations intersect rather than stand as isolated or discrete relations (Crenshaw 1994). And through this intersection, differences are created that give texture and shape to women's day-to-day experiences. The intersection of gender, race, and class are among the important markers for the particular ways women are positioned differently in their interactions with their cultural and social environments.

To appreciate how women experience violence as they engage their cultural and social worlds, it is important to consider how meaning, positionality, power, and difference are created, circulate, and change as they shape women's subjective experiences. Within and against these complex influences violence is insinuated into women's lives. And, within and against these same influences women respond to the conditions and practices that threaten, jeopardize, and compromise their sense of being.

As I see it, these influences provide an important reference for looking at the complexities that make up women's experiences of violence. With this in mind, violence is seen as relational; as such, a dual reference shapes women's experiences. I contend that women's experiences of violence refer to what they think, feel, and do when cultural and social conditions and practices threaten, jeopardize, and compromise their sense of personhood. But their experiences of violence also refer to what is done, by whom, and for what purpose when cultural and social arrangements place constraints on their needs, interests, and aspirations as human beings. This dual reference is essential for positioning women's experiences of violence; for the former acknowledges the importance of women's agency, and the latter recognizes that agency occurs within and against structures of constraint. I believe that the ways agency and constraint intersect bring us closer to an understanding of how violence is experienced by women.

To acknowledge women's agency within and against structures of constraints does not somehow diminish, undermine, or distort their experiences of violence. Rather, agency allows us to appreciate the importance of their struggle. In that struggle women are neither totally helpless nor fully autonomous. In other words, they are not simply passive *victims*, which "imply the one-way exercise of power, harm without strength." Nor are they solely agents exercising free will over their lives, which suggest "freedom from victimization" (Mahoney 1994). Instead of looking at women in one way or the other, we should look at what happens to women as they engage their cultural and social worlds in the process of living. The consequences when agency and constraint collide reveal the ways violence is experienced by women.

I CONTEND THAT, when women's needs, interests, and aspirations come into conflict with cultural and social constraints, sometimes violence occurs. This violence is experienced as a violation to women's physical, personal, and social self. The nature of this violation is revealed in the degree of disrespect engendered to women's sense of human integrity. Social philosopher Axel Honneth's analysis of the relationship between "disrespect and human integrity" is useful to understanding the specific nature of this violation: we implicitly owe our integrity to the respect we receive from others. As such, "individuals who see themselves as victims of moral maltreatment" assign meaning to such treatment that reveals the degree of insult and disvalue, which are related forms of disrespect. Honneth argues the significance of disrespect:

> [It] characterize[s] a form of behavior which does not represent an injustice solely because it constrains the subjects in their freedom from action or does them harm. Rather, such behavior is injurious because it impairs these persons in their positive understanding of self—an understanding acquired by intersubjective means. There could be no meaningful use whatsoever of the concepts of "disrespect" or "insult" were it not for the implicit reference to a subject's claim to be granted recognition by others. (Honneth 1995)

In considering how disrespect affects human worth, Honneth has identified three areas that are injurious to the physical, personal, and social self. The first type of disrespect pertains to physical integrity, where the body is injured. For him, physical maltreatment represents disrespect whenever the body is controlled against one's will; regardless of the intent, humiliation and shame occurs. It is not the "raw pain experienced by the body"; rather, the "coupling of this pain with the feeling of being defenseless" has a "destructive impact on an individual's practical relationship to self."

The second area of disrespect is personal and affects a person's "normative understanding of self." Honneth positions this form of disrespect in the context of structural exclusion "from the possession of certain rights" as a member within a given community or society. The defining features of this kind of disrespect, "typified by the denial of rights or by social ostracism, thus lie not solely in the comparative restriction of personal autonomy, but in the combination of these restrictions with the feeling that the subject lacks the status of a full-fledged partner in interaction who possesses equal moral rights."

And, the last area is social disrespect that entails "negative consequences for the social value of individuals or groups." Social disrespect denigrates "individual or collective lifestyles" and is signified by "the degree of social acceptance." The downgrading of "forms of life and convictions as being inferior or deficient" robs individuals and groups of "every opportunity to accord social value to their abilities." This "devaluation" is depriving of social recognition, depriving of worth and esteem.

Physical, personal, and social disrespect speak to degrees of moral indignation that affect how women view themselves as a result of the violation rendered through their experiences of violence. Drawing on Honneth's basic premise, I maintain that violations to women's humanity—disrespect to their integrity as human beings in ways that threaten, jeopardize, and compromise their sense of personhood—are critical to understanding how violence is experienced by women.

Violation in the context of violence and the disrespect that results are important markers for looking at what happens in women's lives. As a framework for analysis, I offer for consideration three prominent and overlapping areas that threaten, jeopardize, and compromise women's personhood: violations to the physical self that demean the integrity of the body; violations to the personal self that disregard individual human worth; and violations to the social self that systematically devalue the individual as reflected in a collective or group experience. Whether occurring together or separately, these dimensions of violation function to disrespect the human worth of women. They can and do evolve from women's direct interactions, interactions that they witness, or through interactions of their own instigation.

In this proposed framework, violence and violation coexist within a complex nexus of uneven social and cultural arrangements and though they often appear to be one and the same, there is an important distinction to be made. Unlike the real or tangible evidence of violence usually associated with physical injury and harm when we consider markers for women's experiences, violation is primarily *intuitive*; it is about feelings that affect what women think and do when they perceive their personhood threatened, jeopardized, and compromised. Their sense of violation rests largely on the meaning women give to their experiences.

What is and is not a violation to women's sense of personhood depends largely on their perceptions of the situation at hand. Women may or may not perceive all incidents of violence as violations that disrespect their sense of being. Furthermore, the degree or magnitude of disrespect experienced can range from the mundane to the extreme, and this too is largely dependent on women's perceptions. In other words, what is done, by whom, and with what purpose may or may not be important given the particular cultural and social contexts in which women's experiences arise? And what women feel, think, and do is also contextualized. My point is twofold: violence is not always accompanied by a sense of violation; yet a sense of violation is inextricably linked to physical, personal, and social violence.

I recognize that the complicated dynamics between violence and violation pose an interpretative challenge, for we must rely in part on women's perceptions to expose this distinction. In women's telling of "what really happened" their sense of violation and the disrespect that results is revealed. But, are women's perceptions of their reality reliable? In answering this difficult question, I believe too often we easily dismiss women's perceptions and rely instead on what appears to be tangible or physical evidence to document and authenticate their experiences of violence. I argue that women's perceptions are as reliable as our own theoretical analysis. It is not just what they tell us that is revealing or even *true*, but it is also what their experiences suggest in that telling, which provides grounding for our analysis.

In our conversation some may not consider women's sense of violation and the disrespect engendered as "real evidence" of violence, no matter how severe the resulting injury and harm to their sense of personhood. However, for me, their sense of violation cannot be easily dismissed. Quite the contrary, I believe that women's interpretations of their experiences offer important perspectives and critiques that are critical for our analysis, and their interpretation of "what really happened" must be respected. I agree with Satya Mohanty's contentions that "subjective, particular perspectives often contain deep sources of information and knowledge or even alternative theoretical pictures and accounts of the world we all share. An appreciation of such 'particular' perspectives and viewpoints make possible a richer general picture, a deeper and more nuance universalist view of human needs and vulnerabilities, as well as—by implication—human flourishing" (Mohanty 2003).

I am by no means suggesting that our analysis of women's experiences should be limited to their perceptions of reality or saying that we should give uncritical acceptance, suspend all judgment, or have absolute agreement on the nature of their experiences. I am saying, however, that we should respect the fact that there are other valid ways of knowing the world besides our own. Women's perceptions of reality may not fit neatly into our preconceived theoretical boxes. Yet I believe that women's perceptions are instrumental to any discussion about their experiences.

Women's self-reflective critiques provide important contributions that can open up and extend our analyses to new areas of consideration. Having said this, I know that their perceptions as well as experiences, in and of themselves, "do not have self-evident meaning, for they are in part theoretical affairs." As such, their perceptions and experiences, not unlike our own analyses, are highly "dependent on social narratives, paradigms, and even ideologies" (Mohanty 2003). But, what would occur if the two explanations of "what really happened" in women's experiences of violence are blended? Would a fuller and more grounded picture of the significance of violence in women's lives emerge?

My aims are similar to those articulated by the author Alice Walker: "the truth about any subject only comes when all the sides of the story are put together, and all their different meanings make one new one. Each writer writes the missing parts to the other writer's story. And the whole story is what I'm after" (Walker 1983). Surely, we can agree that in our conversation broadening our base of knowledge is a good thing. In presuming that this is true, let me share with you my conversations with African American women as they discussed violence and the ways it is experienced, as they engage their cultural and social world.

MY CONVERSATIONS WITH African American women about their experiences of violence differ greatly from those that I have with advocates and professional experts. Generally, in the telling of their stories some conversations are driven by crisis and the immediacy of the moment, others are given as matter-of-fact accounts, and some are slow, hesitant, and searching. Nevertheless, they give voice to their experiences, and depending on the cultural and social patterns of their individual lives African American women's stories are very similar to, yet significantly different from, one another.

Their stories are messy, and in too many instances quite bloody as a result of a busted lip, broken jaw, blackened eye, or a bruised vagina ripped and torn apart by forced penetration. These incidents reflect what we are more accustomed to when we think about violence against women, for there are obvious physical markers of injury and harm. However, physical injury and harm do not reveal the full scope of their experiences; they do not reveal what happens to African American women's sense of being as a result of those experiences. Furthermore, their experiences are not limited to physical violence; they include personal and social violence as well. Hence, African American women's stories are scattered all over the intimate and public spaces of their lives, where at times they are deeply wounded, scarred, beaten down with spirits broken. But physical injury and harm, as markers for violence against women, do not provide an adequate explanation for understanding the full dimensions of their experiences of violence. To understand how they experience physical and personal as well as social violence, we must look to their sense of violation and the disrespect that results, for this will tell us what happens in African American women's experiences of violence.

In telling their stories, I find that African American women do not bother with naming, sorting, cataloguing, and then placing their experiences into conceptual paradigms where experiences are neatly fitted, tidied up, comprehensible, however fragmented and distorted. They do not deny parts of their being, but often recognize that the obvious and the insidious forms of violence blended together to impose its own reality on their lives. Rarely, if ever, have I heard the words "patriarchal" or "structural" violence uttered from their mouths in offering a theoretical explanation for what happened. Yet, their experiences of violence and the interpretations African American women give do offer an important version of history. Their theories of "what really happened" are rooted in their sense of violation for which disrespect becomes an important part of their stories.

History provides the social and cultural context for the ways positionality, power, and difference intersect to shape the broad but also particular meaning women attach to their experiences. I say that African American women's experiences are neither small nor one-dimensional. They are not fixed in time and place. And, they are not monolithic as characterized by a single defining moment or dramatic incident that may appear to constitute the totality of a life. In saying this, I argue that to understand "what really happened" in their stories requires that we accept their experiences on their own historical terms by examining the cultural and social context in which they arise. This presupposes a willingness to look at the fullness of African American women's experiences. Of significance are not only those experiences that they own but also those experiences that they disown. And, those experiences that assume ownership over them, regardless of their views. Only then are we able to preserve the integrity of their experiences with an understanding that African American women are who they are because of their subjective experiences.

This book is about the specific conversations I had with nine African American women, who generously offered their reflections on what they know to be *true* about their lives. Through life history interviews, they framed their perceptions of reality within the context of daily life. Their particular narratives of "what really happened" are inexplicably linked to what it means to be black-and-female in America. This understanding is marked by their struggle to retain a sense of personhood within and against cultural and social conditions and practices that threaten, jeopardize, and compromise that identity. As such, our conversations traveled along many different cultural and social paths and across many different times and places. This allowed the women to reflect on and describe who they have been and who they have become. In the telling of their stories, the dimensions of their physical, personal, and social lives transform over time. Violence and violation also evolve, circulate, and change to become an integral part of that process of transformation. To provide background for the nine women's circuitous journey, as they actively participate in the process of living, an accounting of their historically positioned experiences is presented.

IN THE TELLING of their life stories, the nine African American women of this study reconstruct a past that places them at the center of history. In their mind's eye, they see themselves as the subject of their experiences. They do not speak as the voice of a generalized "other," but as individuals who offer an interpretation of reality based on what they know to be *true* about their experiences. They do not simply provide a narrative of defining moments or significant events that have occurred over the course of their lives, although such accounts are essential parts of their storytelling. Rather, they provide a fluid historical accounting. In multiple layers of reality, their past is offered as a continuous and connected process to their understanding of who they have been and who they have become. History, then, provides a powerful context for positioning the women of this study as historical subjects. As such, their stories are not just about the history that is imposed on them as black women, but they are also about the individual life histories they make in their struggles to give value to this identity.

Their stories begin during the period of World War II, and for some it begins in the immediate aftermath of that war. During the 1940s, as children, the women were born into their unique place in a history where what it means to be black-and-female was already formed and given little cultural and social significance. Through the ever-changing and arduous process of living, however, the women would make their own individual histories. At the center of these histories are their struggles to give value to their sense of humanity. This overarching theme resonates in their reflections as well as in the descriptions they provide of their experiences.

This theme is revealed early on in childhood, as they begin to develop a sense of their own humanity, as they engaged the challenges this posed. In chapter 1, "Becoming," we observe the women as children beginning their life journey. In chapter 2, "Lessons to Learn," we see the important life lessons they are required to learn in order to continue on in their travels. These chapters lay the foundation that allows us to look at their particular childhood struggles as their experiences begin to take shape in the home, neighborhood, community, and the larger society.

In these environments the conflicts between agency and constraints are introduced. This is seen in the ways the women as children grapple with becoming girls, Colored girls, and Negro girls. These identities represent different levels of consciousness for what it means to be black-and-female. These identities are positioned in different environments where different meanings are established for the women's developing sense of self. The women's struggle as children is to navigate within and against the complexities of those meanings.

The development of multiple cultural and social identities is not unique to any particular gender or race of children. But in this instance, what Deirdre Davis calls a "multiplicitous self" shapes the inherent complexities that are part of a black-and-female self-concept (Davis 1997). As the women's reflections and experiences suggest, growing up in a society that offers little value to their existence, they must provide the meaning for their own importance. Thus, they are ever confronted by a dual self-reference. There is the meaning that is imposed through cultural and social expectations by which they are expected to conform. As children, they must figure out the significance of girls, Colored girls, and Negro girls, for these identities represent different levels of cultural and social reality for their experiences. But within and against these same identities, however, the children must claim a sense of personhood. This requires that they make critical decisions about their lives, even as children. For, if they are to know their full humanity, their sense of self-worth, they must determine for themselves what it means to be girls, Colored girls and Negro girls. As we see, the cultural and social meaning of these identities imposes different constraints that at times can threaten, jeopardize, or compromise their childhood sense of self, especially in the absence of a self-definition.

What it means to be black-and-female was a gradual and difficult learning process. In the home and neighborhood the women as children were expected to learn and conform to the gender expectations for girls.

In the black community they were expected to learn and adhere to the color and caste hierarchy for Colored girls. And, as they engaged the larger particularly white society, they were expected to comply with the prevailing racial customs and practices for Negro girls. These seemingly separate and distinct learning experiences as well as different identities intersected as they moved back and forth between their environments. As they sought to claim a sense of self within and against the complexities of their childhood lives, the women learned that the established expectations—who they were supposed to be—imposed significant constraints on their developing image of self.

As the women engaged their cultural and social environments as girls, Colored girls, and Negro girls, violence is sometimes insinuated into their subjective experiences. In their developing sense of violation and the ways their personhood is threatened, jeopardized, or compromised within and against these multiple identities we come to see how they perceived themselves through their childhood experiences. Some experienced corporal punishment and physical fights with other children for breaking household rules and childhood codes of conduct; these experiences demeaned the integrity of their body. Others experienced personal humiliation and shame and were treated with disregard in ways that disrespected their individual worth when they did not or could not adhere to the color and caste hierarchy of the black community. Through their interactions with systemic gender and racial discrimination they experienced a sense of social devaluation, regardless of whether conditions and practices were directly targeted at them or not.

The women's sense of violation and the disrespect engendered is not articulated as such in their reflections of childhood. Rather, what we hear in their reflective telling is how they felt as articulated by "feeling less than," "feeling small," "feeling bad about myself," or "not being good enough" and "not belonging." These perceptions of how they felt, at given moments in time as a result of disrespect, are offered as evidence of violations to their sense of personhood. But their sense of violation is not limited to such feelings; it is also revealed by their childhood actions, which have meaning. In their experiences we see their responses to a sense of violation. Their actions range from acquiescence, to manipulation, to that of resistance as they engage cultural and social conditions and practices that place constraints on their childhood lives.

In the women's reflections and experiences of childhood, they learned an indelible lesson: their subjective self (the person they saw themselves to be) coexisted with an objective self (the person that others supposed them to be). This was often an uneasy and uneven coexistence. As they sought to claim a sense of self within and against the multiple identities imposed on them, one would expect, and indeed it was difficult for, the women as children to sort through and navigate their particular process of becoming. Yet their actions tell us that within and against constraints they asserted agency nonetheless.

Moving from child to adulthood, this lesson continued to have meaning for their experiences. The women's reflections and experiences of adulthood suggest that they were more determined than ever to claim a sense of self in a reified world where what it means to be black-and-female holds little significance. In chapter 3, we watch as they make the transition during the tumultuous period of the 1960s, from adolescence into young adulthood. They entered "The Worlds of Men" for the first time as adult women. In chapter 4 they begin to settle into "The Worlds of Women" during the 1970s, which was called the "decade of the woman."

When the women stepped out of the constraints of childhood they wanted to exercise their independence as adults. We see that both patterns of change and continuity are salient features of their entry into adulthood. After receiving their high school diplomas, the women followed traditional paths into adulthood. Some attended college, others started to work full-time jobs, and several got married, had children, and worked full-time. Even though these paths were traditional, the women's experiences within them were by no means predetermined. For in the 1960s, as young women, they found themselves in the midst of cultural and social transformation. Nowhere was this transformation more profound than in the "rearticulation" of the meaning of blackness in America.

Omi and Winant argues that the civil rights and black movements "redefined the meaning of racial identity, and consequently of race itself, in American society" (Omi and Winant 1994). During the 1960s, Colored and Negro were largely abandoned by blacks as well as by the women as terms of self-identification. But, more important, this "rearticulation" of racial identity infused new meaning into a collective sense of self that offered blacks "a different view of themselves and their world; different, that is, from the worldview and self-concepts offered by the established social order." A new collective consciousness was forged, which created a "new subjectivity by making use of information and knowledge already present in the subject's mind" (Omi and Winant 1994). As young adults, the women of this study were a part of this transformation, which had a critical affect on how they saw themselves. For the first time, unabashedly, they claimed the identity of black women. However, their subjective experiences gave meaning to this new identity they claimed. There was, however, no uniformity in that meaning. Notable during this period were the decisions the women made and the actions they took in giving their own meaning to being black women.

The women's reflections as well as their experiences suggest that they generally embraced a black cultural and social affinity. For those who did, a significant overlap appeared between their collective and individual senses of self during this period. It is important to note that a distinction exists between the two. Hortense J. Spillers tells us that the collective self is mapped onto her world by cultural and social discursive practices, but the individual comes into the realization that she is the "one who counts. This one is not only a psychic model of layered histories of a multiform past, but she is the only riskable certainty" (Spillers 1997). The women fully understand that they are the ones who count; they are the "riskable certainty" as they engage with other blacks during the turbulent climate of the 1960s.

When the women stepped into adulthood life, they were immediately greeted by cultural and social constraints. These constraints, also rearticulated, took on a decisively adult quality, yet they continued to be rooted in the quite recognizable uneven gender, race, and class relations. In many ways, the women found especially gender and racial expectations more rigidly imposed than in childhood. For the cloak of childhood immaturity was removed. Nevertheless, within and against these constraints we watch as the women assert agency. They went about the business of exploring their newfound independence as young black women. For the first time, they had intimate sexual relationships with men; most experimented with alcohol and drugs; several changed their physical persona to accommodate new attitudes; and they all partied to the sounds of the Supremes, the Temptations, Aretha Franklin, and James Brown. Of these and other experiences, the women navigated the treacherous terrain between cultural and social expectations and their own self-defined needs, interests, and aspirations.

In their busy lives as students, full-time workers, wives, and mothers they paid attention to and could not avoid the male-centered politics of the period. Nor could they avoid physical, interpersonal, and political violence of the period. The women came of age in a decade that was predicated on violence. They entered adulthood when America—its people and institutions—was in conflict, particularly with itself. And like all Americans, the women could not avoid the tensions, contradictions, and dilemmas this period of conflict produced. They witnessed excessive and extreme acts of violence, which created deep cultural and social scars upon the landscape of this country. Increasingly, the women's sense of what is and what is not a violation becomes more sharply focused as a result of the disrespect they see.

During this period, only one woman discusses her sense of violation as a result of a physical fight she had with her husband. But several talked about their sense of personal violation, of being disrespected and humiliated: in the context of the uneven gender relations between black men and black women, in getting illegal abortions, or in the continuing struggle against the color and class hierarchy within the black community. Moreover, all the women expressed a sense of social violation and disrespect as they watched paramilitary police tactics in response to marches, sit-ins, and other forms of direct political protests; white supremacists and vigilantes imposing their will on black life; the assassinations, especially of black political leaders; rebellions or riots in black communities; the killing of young black radicals; and the body count produced by the Vietnam War. In these and other instances their sense of violation is expressed in their own reflective telling of "what really happened" as well as through their subjective experiences.

With time, the women's past experiences demanded that they become mature adults. And a part of that maturity is the women's own increasing understanding of what it means to be black-and-female. That meaning becomes more sharply focused. So does their struggle to navigate between their subjective and the objective selves. In their maturity, they establish critical boundaries for themselves that reflect what they will and will not tolerate in their on-going attempts to maintain and sustain their sense of humanity. As they settle into different patterns of life—ironically during the "decade of the woman," the 1970s—violence and the black women's sense of violations become more pronounced in their experiences.

Whether with husbands, boyfriends, or other women, physical fights become more evidence in their experiences. During this period, *fighting* itself becomes an important metaphor for their experiences, and *anger* becomes a sign of their sense of violation and disrespect. Their anger is expressed in their actions, and these actions have meaning. But the women's anger does not simply exist outside the realm of cultural and social reality, and it is neither genetic nor a unique characteristic of African American women's being; instead, their anger evolves from their active engagement with their cultural and social world.

As Satya Mohanty points out, anger represents an alternative account of the "individual's relationship with the world" that is "unavoidably theoretical." For anger represents "notions of what a woman is supposed to be angry about, what she should not tolerate, what is worth valuing, notions that are not merely moral but also social-theoretical in nature" (Mohanty 2003). But the women's anger is not presented merely as a strategy of resistance. As Traci West cautions, "we should not naively or superficially acknowledge anger as a resistance strategy." As in the case of the women of this study, "a tenacious struggle may be demanded of women to elicit and utilize their anger, and even then, their success at doing so will likely be quite costly to them" (West 1999). When they feel disrespected, the moral indignation as expressed through anger represents the women's attempts to defend their sense of being.

In fundamental ways, the women's anger is evident when their sense of personhood is threatened, jeopardized, or compromised. In other words, when they perceive that their established boundaries have in some way been infringed on or breached; when that line has been crossed, they respond in a manner that reflects their understanding of the situation at hand. In so doing, they fight back, literally and figuratively. Although they assert agency, they act on behalf of and in too many instances they act against their self-defined interests, needs, and aspirations. As Beth Richie notes, "some women are coerced or forced by circumstances into doing things they don't want to do." Sometimes this "forces some of us to assume a posture in the world that isn't in our best interest, or we betray ourselves for the good of others by acting in ways or living in relationships that don't serve us well" (Richie 1996). For several of the women this critique becomes notable. There are times when some are unable to fight back. Their reflections and experiences suggest that during these periods, by not fighting back in defense of self they began to lose important pieces of themselves; they lost some of their own sense of value, and their actions become self-destructive.

In the women's struggle, what are and what are not acceptable conditions and practices increasing shape their understanding of what it means to black-and-female. In their insistence on self-value, they no longer simply attempt to navigate between their subjective self and their objective self, as in childhood. Rather, we see their attempts to negotiate within and against cultural and social constraints. Nowhere is human value more revealing, especially in a capitalistic society such as ours, than in the work we do—in what the women do not only to sustain a material foundation for themselves and often for their children but also to make the material conditions of their lives better. In chapter 5, "She Works," we observe the women's attempts to make a living as they negotiate the tensions, dilemmas, and contradictions that arise in different work environments.

For the women both paid and unpaid work is an important aspect of their daily lives. As Sharon Harley and The Black Women and Work Collective tell us, in that endeavor the women find that "work brings pain as well as joy, personal satisfaction as well as anguish, economic success as well as continued poverty, and sometimes all at the same time." Furthermore, they say that in looking at black women's labor it is important to "recognize the connections between their work in the marketplace, in their communities and organizations, and in their homes." And, more important, they tell us that there are critical "connections between work and personal identity, relations with others, and historical and social conditions such as racism and sexism" (Harley and The Black Women and Work Collective 2002). This general description aptly characterizes the women's work histories. Not only do the women's reflections and experiences provide a context for this description, but they also contribute another important layer of complexity as we consider violence and violation in the context of work.

In considering their labor, we see that already a history shapes the women's individual work histories, although the type of work and the circumstances that surround that work differ. The cultural and social conditions and practices under which they perform that work have well-defined boundaries, especially with regard to race and gender relations. These boundaries are more systemic in nature and are manifested through seemingly benign work-related policies, procedures, and practices that are often imparted by coworkers, who bring their own attitudes of gender and race to the process of implementation. I contend that these boundaries mark the presence of the women's experiences of violence. In the context of work, usually we cannot easily point to any physical dimension that validates the presence of violence. Although one could point to workplace sexual harassment that involves complicated patterns of behaviors, it exists on a slippery slope of evidence that ultimately comes down to "she said, he said." This aside, usually the presence of violence is more nuanced and insidious in the workplace presentation, but it is nonetheless injurious and harmful in its affects. In this instance, I believe that women's sense of violation and the disrespect that is engendered become more instructive for looking at their experiences of violence in the work they do.

Even though the women struggle to avoid stereotypical work for black women, in their attempts to do so, they find that they are expected to conform to such roles. What the women do for a living, the established processes and procedures governing that work, and the prevailing attitudes toward race and gender by coworkers provoked a sense of violation that would have an impact on how they viewed themselves, at different times in their working life. Given the degree of voluntariness associated with work relationships, this allowed the women to attempt to negotiate their needs, interests, and aspirations. But more often they found that in many instances it was an uneven negotiation. And they always had the option of quitting. Notable of their experiences is the frequency by which most women changed jobs over the course of their work histories. For some, especially those who left corporate America, they found greater self-satisfaction in creating their own jobs, even though they all failed. Others derived a sense of value from their participation in community work and political activism. But these work experiences did not unfold in the absence of a sense of violation and disrespect, which too would have a defining affect on how they saw themselves. Although several worked as artists, they too had difficulty negotiating the rigidity that race and gender relations imposed on their art. Only one woman continued to create and perform her art.

In placing the women's reflections and experiences in the context of history, these chapters explore several critical questions: How have the women of this study maintained and sustained a concept of self that embraces a sense of human dignity, while also engaging a self that compromises and demeans their sense of being? In other words, what happened when their subjective self collides with their objective self? Does violence occur, and how is it experienced? Moreover, what are the implications of these considerations on how the women see themselves as black women?

To be black-and-female is vested with historical meaning, and the African American women of this study interpret that meaning in their individual ways. In speaking for themselves, they are positioned as self-determining. They navigated within and against cultural and social constraints and when possible negotiated with others as they attempted cope, manipulate, and resist the arrangements under which they acted. They acted in situations as they perceived them, and regardless of the reasons that undergird why they did what they did, their insistence on self-defined action "validates their power as human subjects" (Collins 1991). The women do not view themselves as objects, as things, whose lives are devoid of a sense of dignity, integrity, and humanity, but these powerful impressions impose a particular reality on their lives, nonetheless. As we engage their lives, we see the importance of their struggle. And, in so doing, hopefully we recognize that in many ways their struggle is not particular. For I believe that their struggle is deeply rooted in our own sense of human value, in our own sense of human worth, and this belief provides fertile ground for a different kind of dialogue on women's experiences of violence.

THE SELECTION OF the nine African American women of this study was intentional, rather than based on a random process. Women were recruited from informal networks and through word of mouth. I intentionally did not recruit black women who appeared to fit some specific social demographic category, other than the fact that I wanted to interview women who were at least forty years old. My aim was to interview women who I thought had sufficient life experience to offer reflective knowledge upon their past. The only other criteria was that the women could not have participated with or been involved in what I call the "victim services system," the formal network of human, legal, clinical, and criminal justice organizational services that provide female victims of physical violence with direct assistance.

Through my experience of working with women who are a part of the "victim services system"—as employees, advocates, and clients of services—I have found that for women to be involved in this system, especially those who receive assistance, they must become adept at referencing their experiences according to the institutional definitions and standards imposed on them. As a result, some women often reduce their life experiences to conform to the more narrow male-centered causes of female victimization. In an attempt to avoid this institutional referencing, I decided not to select women who had histories with the system, even though they may indeed reference their experiences in similar ways.

Initially, thirteen women met the limited criteria and were selected for interviews. Based on self-identified social characteristics generated from a semistructured questionnaire, a general profile of the selected participants reveals the following personal descriptions. The women range in age from forty-eight to fifty-eight years, and even though all of them are longtime residents of New York City (twenty or more years), three were actually born and raised in the City, while the others migrated from various parts of the country. Only one of the women was currently married, but she has been separated from her husband for thirty years. Six of the women were married at some point in their lives but are now divorced, one is a widow, and six have never been married. Five of the women have adult children, and two have grandchildren. Six are currently involved in intimate relationships with men, and seven have not been involved in intimate relationships for at least two years. All of the women identified themselves as heterosexual.

In terms of education, one woman holds a master of arts degree, five received a bachelor of arts degree, six obtained a high school diploma or an equivalent degree, and one completed elementary school. The women held an array of jobs and pursued a variety of professions and occupations, and on average they changed employment every three years during their adult life. Only three participants have been at their current employment for seven years or longer, and one has taken an early retirement owing to physical injuries. Most of the women described their economic status as middle class, and only one woman described herself as working class.

Culturally, all the women identified themselves as black, African American, or both. They ranged in skin complexion. Four of the women identified themselves as dark brown skinned, four as brown skinned, and five saw themselves as light skinned. Regarding religious and/or spiritual orientation, the majority of the women identified themselves as Christian, one as Buddhist, one as Yoruba, and two were eclectic and blended several religious faiths.

Of the initial thirteen women who were selected, nine actually completed the interviewing process. During a six-month period, one woman decided not to participate anymore, and three others had scheduling conflicts that prevented their full participation. Interview questions were open-ended and designed to facilitate the women's reflections of their personal histories over the course of their lives. The women preferred to be interviewed at my home, and I offered what John Langston Gwaltney in *Drylongso* calls "amity, security and hospitality" (Gwaltney 1993): I provided a space where they could express themselves in whatever context they deemed appropriate for the telling of their stories. When it was more convenient for the interviewees, we conducted our conversations in their homes.

In general, the interviews were scheduled for five, two-hour sessions, for a total of ten hours with each woman, and on mutual agreement the interviews were usually extended beyond this time. Often, as I listened to each of the women's stories in my living room, the very intimacy of our interaction and my sense of honesty would not allow me to pretend that I was indifferent or far removed from their experiences. As a forty-six-year-old black woman, the women assumed that I had a reference for understanding their stories, and I believed that I did. In the telling of their stories, I usually kept a box of tissues handy for our tears, sometimes we lost control with our laughter, and a hug was not uncommon. I probably crossed the line of "scientific objectivity," but what I gained by venturing beyond the boundary seems more valuable.

All the formal conversations were tape-recorded, and to insure confidentiality I transcribed the interviews myself. As a result, I ended up with almost fourteen hundred single-spaced typed pages of text. The women's life stories are treated as text, and their complete narratives and even their rambling are viewed as important sources of information. I make no judgment regarding the accuracy or inconsistency of the information provided, and I accept the veracity of their interpretations as a given. As text, there are many different ways to read their stories, but I offer no broad theoretical framework within which to place their stories; rather, I choose to place the women's stories alongside what is already known. I read their stories as patterns of everyday life. This involves looking closely at the historical conditions within which race, gender, and class intersect to shape and reshape the women's experiences and, subsequently, how their experiences shape and reshape the ways they see themselves as black women. In essence, I read their stories as a version of how history is constructed through the eyes of a select group of black women.

In my attempts to unravel the complexities of the women's stories and the reflections upon which they are based, I realized that I must accept that their particular version of what is *true* is real to them. This acceptance was critical for me to understand what I was hearing. This brought me to the underlying focus of this book, which centers on the sociology of knowledge and also includes you, the reader. I recognize that in many ways I am asking readers to step back from what they may already know to be *true* about violence against women and consider the possibility of another way of knowing or referencing women's experiences of violence. In so doing, this book falls within and against the debates that define the sociology of knowledge.

As feminist scholar Sandra Harding argues, the sociology of knowledge is a theory of knowledge that "answers questions about who can be *knowers*" (can middle-aged African American women?); "what tests beliefs must pass in order to be legitimated as knowledge" (only tests against men's experiences, white women's experiences, or structural and quantifiable facts); and "what kinds of things can be known" (can *subjective truths* or *lived experiences* count as knowledge?) (Harding 1987). Why is all of this talk about knowledge relevant? As Patricia Hill Collins points out often African American women are not positioned as *knowers* or as *agents of knowledge* (Collins 1990). This book positioned the nine women as such and embraces Berger and Luckmann's contentions in *The Social Construction of Reality: A Treatise in the Sociology of Knowledge*:

> The sociology of knowledge must concern itself with whatever passes for *knowledge* in a society, regardless of the ultimate validity or invalidity (by whatever criteria) of such *knowledge*. And insofar as all human *knowledge* is developed, transmitted and maintained in social situations, the sociology of knowledge must seek to understand the processes by which this is done in such a way that a taken-for-granted *reality* congeals for the man [*sic*] in the street. In other words, we contend that the sociology of knowledge is concerned with the analysis of the social construction of reality. (Berger and Luckmann 1966)

With the sociology of knowledge as a backdrop, in treating what the women know to be *true* about their experiences as valid, I do believe that something important is revealed about the nature of violence in women's lives.

By *Knowing What They Know*, the women's experiences of this study allow us to shift our gaze to the main focus of this book. Their stories allow us to see what violation means in the context of violence. They suggest and their experiences direct us to focus our gaze: Amanda said that we should look at violence as "*any act that attacks a woman's inner core and leaves her dehumanized.*" In similar words, Mary suggests violence should be seen as "*anything that interferes or restricts a girl or a woman, of any age, and breaks their self-confidence in themselves as a human being.*" And Patricia offers a subtle but important distinction for guiding our understanding of the complex ways violence evolves, circulates, and changes: physical violence "*scars a body,*" but violence that demeans and devalues the personal and social self "*scars a life.*"

This book represents my attempt to reclaim African American women's experiences of violence, to put a human face on their experiences by allowing a small group of women to claim their own reality within its pages. Although their experiences reveal the presence of violence and violation, this book is not about black female victimization. Instead, it is about nine black women and the circumstances under which they engage their cultural and social worlds. Their experiences are neither presented nor offered as the experiences of all black women. I recognize that the experiences of any small and select group cannot capture the complexities and varied lifestyles that are of concern to all black women. But I do believe that their particular experiences contribute nine important chapters to the volumes of stories that make up the whole of what it means to be black-and-female in America.

AUTHOR'S NOTE ON THE TEXT
Introducing the Women

The following biographical sketches provide brief overviews of the nine African American women's lives whose stories form the basis for this study. Their names and references to specific places and people have been altered to protect their identities.

Amanda

Amanda, born in 1947, grew up in a predominately black community in New York City. Both parents migrated from the South, where her mother was one of a family of sixteen, and her father and his two sisters were orphaned at an early age. Her parents met at a Harlem nightclub. Her father, thirty years older than her mother, worked as a porter for the railroad. Her mother was a community activist. While in high school, Amanda was discouraged from pursuing college and was told by the only black counselor that "if she insisted on going to college, she should go at night." In 1964, she reenrolled at an historically black college in the South where she was introduced to "black bourgeoisie culture" and what was considered to be proper behavior for a young "Negro" woman of the time. She was also introduced to racial segregation, student protest, sexual politics, and skin color and hair preferences. In 1968, Amanda decided to go to graduate school on the West Coast, where she experienced her "first adult relationship" and a lifestyle that included radical politics, drugs, interracial sex, and physical abuse. Returning to the East Coast in 1978, with a masters degree in social work, Amanda became even more involved in radical political movements, community activism, and union organizing. After the birth of her only child, she moved back to New York City and continued her political activism until she was "purged" from leadership in her base political organization. She regrouped and returned to a "socially committed" life that continues to include her daughter, close familial and intimate relationships, work, and political activism.

Barbara

Barbara, born in 1945, grew up in a large industrial city in the Midwest. Her parents were married in the South and during the war years migrated "up North," where her father worked in a steel factory and her mother worked as a domestic. As a young child, Barbara's father lost his eyesight in an accident at work, but he was also a jazz musician; her family lived on income generated by his music, social security benefits, and her mother's income from cleaning houses. Growing up, she was acutely aware of "poverty and not having." She also hated who she was as a person. "I was dark, I didn't have hair flowing down my back, and I just didn't represent what was attractive." She said, "I had none of the things that would help you to excel." After graduating from high school in 1962, she immediately moved to New York City. To support herself she worked a series of clerical jobs and one eventually lead her to an advertising firm. "I think that's when my life started." During this period, she had her first adult relationship that lasted until she was told, "Barbara, you're too dark for me." After that break-up, she began to "totally change" who she was, and through a series of job promotions her status changed, particularly in relation to whites. She started to date white men exclusively and distance herself from the "black world." She describes her world at the time as "phony." During the latter part of the 1960s, Barbara became addicted to alcohol and prescription drugs. During this period, she married an African, and the marriage lasted for a week. With assistance from a faith-based substance abuse program, she became sober and drug-free in 1979, and for more than twenty years she has attempted to "recover the things that were lost" during her years of addiction.

Sara

Sara was born in 1947, in a small college town in the Midwest. Her father was in the Army, and the family frequently moved around the country living in military housing. The oldest of the five children, Sara recalls a "very protected childhood." By constantly moving from one place to another, she felt different, as if she were a stranger every place she went. Often, her family was either the only black family or one of a very small group of black families living on the base or in small military-dominated towns. But if she ever forgot that she was a "Negro" living with segregation while growing up, "my parents, my peers, white folks would reeducate me. White folks will reeducate you the quickest." In 1961, while in high school, Sara's family moved to Germany where she traveled a lot, formed important friendships with other black military kids, and was introduced to beer. In 1965, over her parents' objections, she enrolled in a historical black college. She fell in love and soon became pregnant. She decided to have an illegal abortion, and a month later her boyfriend, on his way to Vietnam, was killed. "I felt like I was going crazy." During this period, the campus was consumed with Martin Luther King's assassination, the antiwar movement, and the tension between rival black political groups. Although "functioning," she remembers, "I was doing as much drugs and alcohol as I could." She graduated and moved to New York City, enrolling in a local college to become a journalist. While working a series of jobs as a writer with major newspapers and magazines, she got married. The marriage ended in divorce. Recognizing that she had become an alcoholic and addicted to drugs, she became sober in 1980. "It's been nineteen years since I've had a drink." Sara believes that, because she was "self-medicating," alcohol and drugs robbed her of her life. She has now returned to those things that are important to her—family, friends, and intimate relationships as well as writing.

Mary

Mary was born in 1939 and grew up in the rural South. During her early years, she was raised as part of her maternal grandparents' large family, which included their thirteen children. Mary's father was away in the military, and she saw her mother, who was a live-in domestic worker "maybe once or twice a year." She called her grandmother "mama," and it was from her that she learned "stuff like ethics, morals, religion, spirituality in terms of my development." She also learned to keep her distance from her grandfather, who had gotten his fourteen-year-old daughter, Mary's aunt, pregnant. At age twelve, Mary went to live with her mother, and by that time she had six bothers and sisters. Due to her mother's job, Mary became the primary caretaker for her siblings. After graduating from high school, she had dreams of attending college. But her parents had migrated to New York City with the younger children, and Mary followed to help take care of the family. Her boyfriend followed her to the city, and they decided to get married. "I married him because I wanted to get away from parents. I was tired of taking care of everybody, you know." Mary enrolled in secretarial classes and held a series of jobs before she was hired at the telephone company. After two years, she left to give birth to her first child, and she did not return because they would not give part-time work. Eight months later, she became pregnant with her second and last child; her relationship with her husband became abusive and began to deteriorate. She took a job on the night shift at a commercial bank in order to "make ends meet" and to be at home with her young sons during the day. Her boss was hired at another bank and asked Mary to join him, which she did. This was the beginning of her long career in banking. As her children grew, she took an active role in their education, and she eventually became a member of the local school board in 1972. Also during this period she divorced her husband. For the last twenty-five years Mary has focused her attention on her sons' activities, community and citywide politics, work, and intimate relationships.

Anne

Anne, born in 1945, grew up in a small eastern town. Both of her parents had college degrees, and her father was a school principal while her mother held several "professional jobs." Anne's family lived in a black community that she calls a "ghetto." Her parents' emphasized educational achievement. But Anne had difficulties as she competed with a younger sister, who had skipped a grade, and from the time that Anne was in the second grade until she graduated from high school, they were in the same grade and often shared the same classroom. The competitiveness that evolved in childhood between the two sisters continued into adulthood. Anne always felt different because of her "physical size." To deal with being a large-sized girl, she started sewing her own clothes when she was eight years old. But she said, "my mother didn't want her friends to know that I made clothes; that wasn't acceptable." She graduated from high school in 1961 and immediately moved to New York City to attend college, but she "didn't get good grades." Dropping out of college, Anne decided that if she was not going back to school, she still had to get an education. After a series of jobs, she saved her money and traveled extensively abroad. Returning, she got married in 1969, but the marriage did not last because she discovered that her husband was gay. After hitting what she called the "glass ceiling" at a major magazine, Anne attempted to operate her own clothing design company, but it failed. Independently, she now sews and designs clothing for others and hopes that it will be an income-generating enterprise.

Patricia

Patricia was born in 1950, and grew up in a predominately black community in New York City. Her parents migrated from the rural South and married in New York City three years after Patricia was born. Patricia's father worked as a presser and a tailor for a local dry cleaners, while her mother worked for a long time in various garment factories as a piece worker. Her father was "not only an alcoholic, he also had a gambling problem." She describes him as a "functional alcoholic" because he was able to maintain his job until he retired. But he was also extremely physically and psychologically abusive, especially to her mother. Her father's brutality dominated her family life and "terrorized" her throughout her childhood and well into adulthood. "I think these early years were the beginning of my ulcer. I would scream. I would holler. I used to beg my mother to divorce my father." Patricia went to predominantly black public schools, but her teachers were mostly white. Disenchanted, she dropped out but went to night school where she received a high school equivalency degree. She became a secretary and for most of her adult life has worked at clerical jobs. Patricia met her husband at work, but three months after they were married they had a "physical fight," and she left him. "I said, oh God, I've married my father." They tried to make the marriage work, but "alcohol became a part of our relationship." Patricia got pregnant and had her only child, but her husband left before her son was born. After her divorce, Patricia struggled to raise her son and found "courage" when she began to write. She self-published two books of poetry and is "proud of the fact that I'm not the kind of woman that I could've ended up being because certain things intervened at certain times in my life for a reason. I have no doubt about that." Patricia entered her senior year of college in the fall semester of 2003.

Faith

Faith was born in 1951, and although she was born in New York City, she grew up in an urban city in the South. "When I was eight months old, my mother left my dad and she went home." Her mother was a public school art teacher. In 1963, Faith's mother sent her "up North" to a Quaker coeducational preparatory school for her high school years. When she got on campus "there were four black students—three boys and me—and there were four hundred and fifty students altogether. I remember looking around and saying, well, who is going to be my boyfriend?" She found the school academically challenging but managed to hold her own, even though she felt a sense of isolation and loneliness. Faith became interested in theater. "I thought that theater was probably the most powerful thing in the world." After she graduated in 1967, her mother persuaded her to go to college, and she moved to New York City. After graduating from college Faith went on the road with a theater production company, but it "was a mess." She returned to her hometown and worked in a series of acting jobs with local companies before returning to New York City where she took theater classes and whatever acting jobs she could find. Faith had several long-term relationships with men, but she never married or had children. To make "ends meet" she worked a variety of jobs that facilitated her acting career. But she began to assess the "politics of the business" and the kinds of acting roles that were available to her as a black woman. After her mother died, she created a one-woman performance piece based on the life of a controversial black female historical figure. Although she continues to be interested in the arts, and theater in particularly, Faith no longer acts and is attempting to define her life outside of the profession.

Jackie

Jackie was born in 1949, and grew up in a predominantly black community in New York City. Part of Jackie's early years was spent with her paternal grandmother, but she was raised primarily by her maternal grandmother who lived with Jackie and her mother in a public housing complex. She was the only child until the age of eleven, when her mother had three boys and another girl. Jackie describes herself as a mischievous child: "Like the day I tried to burn the school down." She grew up in a large extended family, where many of the members lived in the same housing project. "Even today if we go to a funeral, my family takes up one whole side of the church and then some." She "hung out" with her male cousins and did all of the "boy stuff and I was just as good as they were." But she went to an all-female public high school. Fighting was a part of Jackie's life, and when she was fourteen years old she joined a street gang that was run by her male cousins. She was the "negotiator": the gangs "let me do the negotiating for them in fights, either how the fights were going to happen, where they were going to happen, or if they were going to happen." Jackie met her first "real" boyfriend at church, and they became engaged. He got drafted and was sent to Vietnam where he was injured. He was in the hospital for a year, and their relationship dissolved. In the meantime she had taken a job on Wall Street where she was the only black working in the department and on the entire floor. Also during this period, Jackie reconnected with a childhood boyfriend, and they got married in 1968. By January 1969, she had her first child. Immediately after the birth of her third child she separated from her husband, but they never got divorced. She left her job because she was on the "verge of having a breakdown." During this period she went into a depression: "I literally went to bed." But by the end of the 1970s, "I was looking for something else to do." From that period on, Jackie has worked as a full-time activist in her public housing community.

Sharon

Sharon was born in 1949, and grew up in a predominately white midwestern town. Her parents met while attending separate historically black colleges in the South. They both had masters degrees when they migrated North, where her father worked for the federal government and as a part-time jazz pianist, and her mother stayed home to take care of the family. She grew up in a "very strict" household, and "punishment was mean. It was bang, bang, bang. We got beat up." As a very young child she had to take piano lessons and practice classical music on a daily basis. When Sharon decided to play jazz like her father, "he screamed and hollered me out of all of my creativity." Sharon viewed herself as an average student and did not have a black teacher until she went to an historically black college in the South. By her senior year in college, she was a fraternity pledge queen, had witnessed Martin Luther King's funeral, and was losing high school and college friends to the Vietnam War. Sharon received a degree in music and moved to New York City "to get into show business." She met and fell "madly in love" with an entertainer, but the relationship did not last because he was married and had children. Sharon never married or had children. During the 1970s and 1980s, she devoted most of her time to establishing a career in show business. As a member of several "girl singing groups," she did back-up singing for the studio and on stage. But at some point she reflected: "After you've had so many disappointments you come to grips with the fact that hey, I'm not meant to be a big star." She felt it was time for her "to move onto that other part" of her life; she works professionally with computers, but she still sings "every now and then."

CHAPTER 1

Becoming

Being black in America is first of all being; it is existing. The key, however, is becoming; becoming points toward the future.

The Black Self,
Wyne, White, and Coop

As CHILDREN, the women started their particular journey of becoming cultural and social beings during the 1940s. In this decade, their parents migrated from the South to various parts of the Northeast, Midwest, and Southwest relocating with other family members when they were either young single adults or married couples. Their parents were working men and women of various skills, talents, and education; all were seeking a better way of life.

In seeking that life, the families attempted to lay a foundation that would provide their daughters with the necessary knowledge and skills that would enable them to engage the complexities of their cultural and social worlds. Codes of conduct or rules for family, neighborhood, and community relations were highly valued. Families hoped that the knowledge gained from cultural affirmation would provide a rootedness that their daughters could draw upon to guide them into their future. Sometimes the families were successful in passing on their knowledge of the world to this next generation of daughters; however, at times their knowledge and skills were simply inadequate. Yet fathers and mothers, and often grandparents, aunts, and uncles gave to these girls what they had to give. Their families' dreams stood side-by-side with their disappointments, love with hatred, sacrifices with selfishness, daring with insecurity, and encouragements with resentments.

Also in seeking that better life, the families desired that their great and small challenges to social injustice would stand as personal testament to the possibility that their daughters' lives would be more self-determined and more self-fulfilled than their own. Amidst struggle there was hope. Their daughters were born at the dawn of the modern civil rights movement that would, in the course of their lives, crystallize into a full-fledged struggle for racial justice. Over time, this movement introduced different sociopolitical questions, offered different choices, and posed different challenges for this new generation of daughters. But in the beginning their struggle was simply to become. By drawing upon childhood memories, this chapter introduces the cultural and social environments that lay a foundation for the women's process of becoming and provides a look at their early attempts to claim a sense of being within and against the demands of those environments.

BECOMING A NORTHERNER

With the noted exceptions of Mary, Faith, and Sara, the women represent the first generation of their family to be born and raised outside the South. Their parents moved up North or to other parts of the country during World War II and the early postwar years; they had different reasons for leaving the South. Some parents simply wanted to find a good-paying job, while others were looking to gain access to nontraditional or unrestricted employment opportunities where they could apply their skills and training. Even if some families struggled financially to make "ends meet" all the women's parents worked at some point; what they did to earn a living in their new northern lives would not only have a significant influence on their ability to meet the materials needs of their daughters, but it also had an important influence on the functioning of family life.

Patricia recalls growing up in a working-class two-parent family with her two older brothers, in New York City. Her father moved from the South to New York City in search of a "good job," but Patricia's mother, who had two small sons, relocated because she "wanted something different, better." Patricia's parents met in the city, and "after a couple of years I was born and they got married." Neither of her parents had a high school diploma so they took whatever jobs they could find. Her father was employed as a presser and a tailor at a neighborhood dry cleaners, and her mother earned a living working in garment factories as a piece worker for thirty-five dollars a week. Describing her mother's work in more detail, Patricia said: "A piece worker is an assembly line kind of thing, you get paid so much for how many pieces you sew, like the piece could be a sleeve and you sew that sleeve on, and then you go on to the next piece that needed a sleeve. You got paid by the amount of pieces you sewed on within a certain amount of time. She went from different factories at the time because she didn't have a diploma and that's all the work she could get." Although burdened with the demands of a full-time factory job, her mother made sure that Patricia and her two older brothers were taken care of. Patricia points out:

> She was putting in an eight-hour day in the factory, but she worked an early shift because she wanted to make certain that she was home during a reasonable time after we got out of school to be there to make sure that we were okay, check our homework, to make sure that she got the food together for dinner, to make certain we were ready to go to school the next day. I guess you could say that we were one of the early latchkey children. But obviously we never saw ourselves as that. I do remember wearing the key around my neck inside my dress. At that time the neighborhood that we grew-up in everybody was watching everybody else's child. And we had relatives who lived right under us, and our cousin would keep an eye on us.

In her family, Patricia's mother "took care of the household, lot, stock and barrel." She viewed her family as "poor," but Patricia saw her mother as very resourceful: "knowing how to make things stretch—knowing how to stretch meals, knowing how to hold on to a dollar, knowing that you just don't make bills that you can't pay." Her mother "made ends meet," and "every now and then my father would give her something but it wasn't like it was on an ongoing basis, so the bulk of the responsibility was on her." Although Patricia's family was dependent on both of her parents' income, there were times when her father's contribution to the family was not forthcoming because he was a "functional alcoholic." She said "he drank everyday, from the minute he got up in the morning, until he got home at night. He drank on the job, but he knew when he was working just how much he could drink and still do the job. And he was extremely good at what he did, he was a presser and a tailor, and he could do all of that drunk."

On Saturdays, Patricia's mother would send one of the children to their father's job to "get whatever money he had to give to her before he got off of work." If her mother did not do this, Patricia's father would spend his pay on alcohol and sometimes he would gamble.

> My mother knew that he got paid on Saturdays, and I don't know what kind of arrangements she had with him. She knew that on Saturday, if the money wasn't collected, you weren't going to see any money when he got home. But we always knew to get there before he got off from work, and he would put the money in an envelope, and if it was me I would put it in my shoe and come on home. A lot of times there was nothing to send, sometimes it was next to nothing, but you know we would go anyway. My brother is a whole other story. Sometimes my brother would get the money and he would take some for himself, and then he would give the envelope to my mother and of course she would be furious; or he would tell my father that he lost the money. I didn't go very often, she didn't always send me. I think part of it was because of security. I think that she didn't want people getting in to the habit of knowing which one of her kids were going to the store. Sometimes she would go but mostly she would send us. This is only a supposition on my part, but she didn't want to go around there and he was in one of his moods. The worst thing that you could do to my mother was to start an argument with her in public. You don't do that. That's a sacrilege. She did not take kindly to being humiliated in public. She wouldn't argue with you in the street, but once you got behind closed doors of the house, you would know about it. You just did not embarrass her in the street, that's a no, no.

Patricia's father's unpredictable and unreliable behavior, owing in large part to his alcoholism, and her mother's attempts to negotiate with him on behalf of family needs lead to on-going tensions in the household. More than the other women's childhood experiences, the tensions between Patricia's parents apparently often lead to physical violence, and their fights came to have a lasting affect on her childhood as well as her adult life.

In addition to seeking better work opportunities, the women's parents were also seeking release from the racist cultural and social practices and customs that prevailed in the South during the 1940s. They wanted a chance to explore their human potential in the absence of rigid race restrictions—that is, Jim Crow segregation and racial discrimination. Patricia said, "My mother was determined not to raise my brothers in an atmosphere where they had to 'yes, sir' and 'no, ma'am' to white people. She was not going to raise my brothers where they had to watch every word around white people and had to bow their heads or cross the street if white folks were coming." In whatever ways possible, Patricia's mother, like the other women's parents, sought to protect their children not only from racist violence but also from the violations it could inflict upon their young children developing sense of self.

However, in their search of a new life in the North, the women's parents did not escape or avoid the overt and more often subtle forms of Jim Crow segregation and racial discrimination. Although racism was deeply rooted in the social and cultural fibers of the South, they would find that racism existed outside of the South as well. A commonality among most of these daughters was that they grew up in all-black segregated communities in the North.

With the exception of Sara, who grew up in army housing in different parts of the country and Sharon who was raised in a predominately white town in the Midwest, the other women's childhoods were lived out in black communities. These cultural environments would also have an influence on the functioning of their families. In many instances as their parents left family members behind in the South, they were reunited with other members who had migrated earlier. This connection between past and present was an important part of the women's experiences of growing up. For those living outside the South, especially during summer vacations, they frequently traveled south with other family members, in turn, family members in the South often traveled north for visits. So, as their parents settled with their young families into predominantly black communities many retained close family, friendship, and cultural ties. In this cycle of migration and return, their family experienced both cultural and social continuity and discontinuity in their new environments up North; this cycle was very much a part of Amanda's childhood experience.

Migrating from the South as single people, Amanda's parents also met in New York City and married. She grew up in a large extended family, especially on her mother's side. Amanda said, "My mother came from a large family, originally there were sixteen children, and only two of her siblings were not in New York." She felt close to her many "aunts and uncles, and all of them had children who were all pretty much older than we were, except one sister didn't have children." Initially, upon arriving in the city, Amanda's mother stayed with one of her sisters, where "she met my father through her sister's husband at the Savoy." Amanda's father was thirty years older than her mother, and when he met her, she was wearing "bobby socks and a pleated skirt and had a deep Southern accent."

After they married, Amanda's father continued to work as a porter at the train station, and her mother worked different jobs and later became a noted community activist. Of her large family of aunts, uncles, and cousins Amanda also included all the "dogs, cats, rabbits, birds, and fish," as important members. But in her immediate family Amanda's parents, younger sister, and brother lived in a small tenement apartment. Amanda provided a glimpse of family interactions and living arrangements:

At the time we didn't realize how small the apartment was, but it was really two bedrooms, a living room, a kitchen and a bath. My father used to be a cook, so he didn't mind cooking. My mother made lamps and furniture, and my father cooked. People would come to the house and they would see my father with an apron on cooking and my mother might be making a lamp or something. They would make some comments about it and my father would make a joke and say "my wife doesn't want me to hurt my hands and that's why she doesn't let me use the tools." So I sort of never grew up with the view that men are only suppose to do certain things and women suppose to do other things. I sort of saw them both interchanged traditional roles. We called my mother the holiday cook. She would cook for Easter and Christmas and for people's birthdays. So we tried to eat together on this little table that we had in this little kitchen. When we had Thanksgiving, that table would be moved out into the living room. We had relatives—a lot of aunts and uncles and cousins—that would come to eat in that little tiny apartment. We usually tried to eat together even though sometimes there were very crazy hours based on when my father came home. We lived in a tenement; it was a walk-up fifth floor tenement.

For most of the women, similar to Amanda, their home environments represented more than a sense of place. Their childhood homes represented a sense of connection and belonging to the people who lived there. In a world where they would find their blackness culturally and socially ostracized and denigrated, their homes offered a safe haven and a degree of protection for their developing racial self. This was also true for the neighborhoods in which they lived. Generally, as Amanda remembers, their familiar neighborhoods provided considerable childhood fun. Amanda reminisced about her early childhood experiences:

> At first my sister and I were not allowed to go outside and play beyond the front stoop. The other kids would tease us because we had to stay right there by the stoop. If we went farther, my father would come out and pick us up and bring us back there. The other children said when he did that our feet didn't touch the ground. But eventually we could play with all of the children on the block and that's when I met my best girlfriend, she lived down the block, and we've been friends ever since. The neighborhood was fun and we used to do a lot of things. The parents had a lot of parties for the children. My mother would have elaborate puppet shows, and I remember one time we even had a horror house where we used my mother's bedroom. I don't know how my mother put up with all of that. She would do a lot of stuff and we had big fun.

Their neighborhoods offered not only an early sense of childhood enjoyment, but they also offered places of refuge, especially from the larger white society. Several women, like Amanda expressed being uncomfortable and feeling different when they left the familiarity of their neighborhoods. Amanda explained, "When you went downtown, you always felt like you were in a totally different world. Your clothes and everything always seemed so much shabbier. You would think that you had your best stuff on, and then you would get downtown in the stores, and you would always feel like you were not equal to the other people in terms of your appearance; that you didn't really belong there." Amanda felt a sense of attachment to her neighborhood; even though, while growing up she recognized that living up North did not mean the absence of racial segregation or discrimination. However, she saw some advantages to living in an all-black community: "People are always surprised when I say we lived in a segregated community in New York. You saw white people in the stores or selling you something, or teaching, or the social worker, but you didn't see them just walking down your street causally. The white people were like there; they were part of your world but not part of your world. You didn't have to deal with them on a regular basis."

The women's early childhood relationships were primarily forged in the homes and neighborhoods in which lived. In the home, as Patricia's and Amanda's experiences suggest, both family structure and family interactions for the women varied, and family income affected the economic circumstances under which they grew. Only Faith and Jackie grew up in single-parent households, where they were the only children and dependent on their mother's income. The other women grew up in two parent families often with younger brothers and sisters. Along with their fathers, all of the women's mothers worked even if it was periodically. Their mothers' earning was important to the family household income, and in several instances it was the major source of income, even when their fathers worked. More often, we see a sharing of responsibilities between parents to provide for the material well-being of the daughters.

During the 1940s, given the rigidity and prevalence of racial stratification and discrimination, it is difficult to place or categorize the family household income according to established measures of social class—that is, upper-, middle-, and lower-class standards. Whether their parents worked in white-collar or blue-collar jobs, the women were all raised in working-class families. There was, however, a difference in the economic circumstances under which the women grew up and by which their material well-being was meet. Most of the women lived in two-parent households, where both mother and father worked full-time, and they all discussed instances when their families experienced economic hardships; several of the women grew up under poverty conditions. However, educational achievement and the type of work performed by their parents, more than income, seem to differentiate their families' status, especially in the black community. The influences of education and type of work performed effected their family's position within black society and the level of prestige culturally afforded to them.

Although their initial relationships as children were forged with family members, they ventured beyond the more familiar environments of the home and neighborhood and engaged the broader black community and larger white society as well. For most of the women, interacting with others in the black community proved to be a fairly comfortable extension of their home and neighborhood experiences. Their all-black communities provided a growing sense of familiarity, an important degree of protection, and in some instances a buffer from the racism of the larger white society. But in their growing maturity and awareness, they began to experience different realities created by the differences in their home, neighborhood, community, and the environments of the large society; for it was in those environments that they began to develop a growing sense of self. These differences are reflected in the messages they received about what it means to be girls, Colored girls, and Negro girls in their particular process of becoming human.

BECOMING GIRLS

The women were raised in family environments where their parents generally assumed conventional gender roles. Their fathers, when present, were often seen as the head of the family and usually possessed unquestionable authority in the household. But several of the women came to see their fathers as harboring anger, and this gradually created emotional distance and detachment between fathers and daughters. However, the relationship between mothers and daughters was quite different. An important commonality among these daughters from varying family structures is the centrality of adult women in the shaping of their family life. They saw their mothers and sometimes "other mothers," usually grandmothers, as the glue holding the family together. Most of the women recalled close relationships with their mothers, but these relationships were not unproblematic. Tensions sometimes lead to conflicts between mothers and daughters: for the mothers made household rules, and they were often the ones to punish infractions. Nonetheless, the daughters clearly relied on their mothers and "other mothers" for their immediate emotional and often material support.

The mothers were largely responsible for teaching the daughters gender conformity. In their teaching, these daughters received implicit as well as explicit messages about what it means to be girls, messages that shaped how they viewed themselves. In the household, mothers could assert personal power when it came to the daughters. They were the ones who defined what was appropriate for girls and in their particular understanding imposed accordingly gender constraints on their daughters' behavior. This was certainly the case for Amanda: "My mother was the one who established the rules, and my father said very little." Implicit in the household rules were the mothers' attempts to regulate the daughters' behavior and conduct as girls. In her family, Amanda remembered such rules as:

> You weren't supposed to eat at other people's houses, although people could always eat at our house. You weren't supposed to beg and ask for things. You weren't supposed to take things from people that we didn't know. You weren't supposed to fight, but we would fight anyway. We wouldn't curse. My mother didn't like slang, even things like, "Oh Lordy Miss Claudy." She said "that was stupid," and you weren't supposed to talk like that. We had to talk to people a certain way. We had to call adults Mr. or Mrs. You never called people by their first names. Or, if they were like close family friends but not relatives, you had to call them aunt or uncle. You had to do your homework before you went out to play. You had to change your clothes; you couldn't be going out with your school clothes on. You couldn't go out unless you did your chores first. And don't come back with your hair wild. We used to tussle and play with a lot of the fellas in the block, and if you came back with your hair wild, my mother thought that we were doing things. That was a real sign that something was wrong.

As children, the women's experiences made them acutely aware of the consequences of breaking major household rules, of being disobedient or "bad," because it meant that they would be punished. For most, but not all, of the women corporal punishment—physical beatings or whippings—was the form of punishment they received for breaking major household rules. Amanda said her mother "was like a hell-raiser she was always trying to discipline me. We would always get into things, and she would always be the one that wanted to hit somebody or pick up something and throw it at you. My mother didn't waste too much time with discipline. You got hit." Amanda recalled one such incident among several:

I will never forget the time when my mother beat me with the hair dryer. All of my mother's sisters know how to do hair, so I went to my aunt's shop and I saw how people dried their hair under those big hair dryers. My mother use to wash our hair and put it in what we called screw balls until it dried; then she would take each one out and straightened it. I didn't want to do all that. My mother had just gotten a hair drier but it was one that you hold by hand, so I was drying my hair and it got bigger and bigger. My mother kept saying "Amanda don't do that." I said it's my hair and I want to do it this way. She took that hair dryer and she beat me with it until it broke. But I'm still saying it's my hair and I should be able to do my hair like I want. My sister is telling me to "shut up," and my mother kept beating me.

As Amanda's experiences suggest, the beatings were administered in a variety of ways: "You got beat and by any means necessary. With her hands, and as you got older, I think that my mother would just punch us, and she had belts. I don't remember her using an ironing cord. I remember my mother beating me with my brother's toy rifle one time. But I never fought her back, or I wouldn't be here talking to you."

To varying degrees the daughters were subjected to beatings, and it was usually their mothers who administered them. The old cliché of "spare the rod and spoil the child" could provide a conventional rationale for the mothers to exercise some control over their daughters' obstinacy, willfulness, defiance, and, of course, blatant disobedience. In today's world, there are considerable debates, especially among child welfare advocates, as to whether or not corporal punishment, hitting a child, as a form of parental discipline constitutes child abuse or maltreatment. In the 1940s and 1950s, this was not a topic of debate or even discussion for many black families of the period: children were usually beaten as a form of acceptable parental discipline.

On reflection, no women who got whippings on a regular basis viewed their mothers' actions as a form of abuse or maltreatment, even though they did not like physical punishment. Nor did they see their mothers' behavior as threatening, jeopardizing, or compromising to their sense of self. In other words, they experienced violence, but their mothers' action did not provoke a sense of violation and disrespect.

Such acceptance is possibly explained because the women viewed their mothers, the primary nurturers and caregivers, as protectors who shielded them from injury and harm. Even though they disliked the physical pain associated with whippings, they neither perceived their mothers' actions as intended to inflict serious physical injury or harm, nor did they feel that their mothers wanted to physically hurt them, although to some degree this occurred. Often, in understanding the circumstances that lead to punishment, as children the women could anticipate when they were going to get a beating and gauge the degree of severity of the physical pain that would be inflicted. As such, several women discussed their childhood strategies to lessen the physical pain in anticipation of whippings.

Moreover, their mothers' actions probably did not provoke a sense of violation and disrespect because of their mutual understanding: these beatings did not necessarily mean they were unloved as children; it simply meant that they had violated the rules and their mothers wanted them to "act right."

Finally, as children, the women undoubtedly perceived their mothers' actions as falling within the bounds of community norms, punishments not designed to "break their self-confidence," but rather to make them "act right." As children, corporal punishment was not unique to their experiences. For they recall times when their siblings and neighborhood friends were also beaten by their mothers for being bad or breaking household rules.

Expressing these general sentiments, Amanda said, "I would be the one who got the most beatings. I didn't like them, and there was some anger, but I never felt like I was as abused child, and outcast, and I wasn't loved or anything. I just felt that I was the big-mouthed person who always got into trouble." Similarly, Patricia said: "I never even thought of it in terms of some kind of violent behavior, it was like somewhere inside of me I understood because of the way we were raised." It is important to note that only Sharon expressed strong resentment against her mother for hitting her. As she said, "I got beat with the belt. I got beat with tree limbs. I had to toe the line. I had to be good. If I had kids, I wouldn't do that to them. I would never beat a child." But, for the others, especially those who were beaten on a fairly regular basis as children, there was at least tacit acceptance of corporal punishment. Later as mothers there are occasions when Amanda, Patricia, Jackie, and Mary will also beat their own children as a form of acceptable parental discipline.

Yet in the women's interpretation of what is and what is not a violation, we must not readily conclude that corporal punishment was acceptable and did not provoke a sense of violation or a feeling of disrespect under all circumstances in which it was administered. For instance, in chapter 2, as the women engaged their school environment the meaning that they give to their experiences of violation in the context of corporal punishment change, especially when the corporal and other physical punishment is administered by teachers.

Nevertheless, as children the women unquestionably accepted their mothers' or other mothers' authority over their lives and generally adhered to the household rules. Many of the rules, of course, dealt with household chores and who would be responsible for doing what. Implicit in some household rules were explicit gender considerations—distinctions between boy tasks and girl tasks. Inherent in such distinctions were ideas regarding what were "proper" chores for daughters, and this held implications for how they viewed themselves as girl. Although Amanda grew up with a younger sister and later a brother who was ten years younger, there were no gender tasks distinctions among the children in her household. But for Sara, who had two younger brothers at time, it was a completely different story.

Sara's father became a career army man, and during the early 1950s he was away at war in Korea. While away, Sara's mother decided to "go back to school and she took us to my grandmother to raise us." Living with her grandparents in a midwestern college town, Sara began to see her brothers occupying a more privileged position in her family life. As she said, "the boys were big deals, so there was a thing about me waiting on the boys." Sara explained further:

> Even as a little girl, when my grandmother would have a big dinner, she would give me the stuff to set the table. It was like teaching me how to be a girl, teaching me how to serve people. That was an early part of my training from the time I was a little, little girl: where to put the knives and forks, and to take some kind of pride in the way a table looked and to clean the bathroom. My job was to clean the sink and the bathtub and stuff, whereas my brothers had to sweep up

the porch—a nice kind of outside job; I had to do this little inside nasty job. At the time that's what you did as a girl.

Early on, as Sara's experience suggests, she began to notice that there were important expectations imposed on her simply because she was a girl, and that they differed from those imposed on her brothers. But through her childhood observations, especially of adult behavior, Sara also began to notice the important differences between the role of her mother and that of her father.

When her father returned from the war, Sara had little ambiguity about who was in charge of the family; it was her father, and in many ways family life evolved around him and his military career. Sara hated "moving around a lot," and she saw her mother's "commitment" to her father's career as "very confining." As she said, "when I watched my mother picking up this family and moving every six months and she would bust her ass. I didn't want to emulate her." Even more, the ways Sara's father sometimes treated her mother simply because she was female helped to shape Sara's understanding of what it meant to be a girl. Sara discussed her parents' relationship:

> My father made light of my mother a lot, he teased her a lot. I re-
> member being on a trip, we were moving across country somewhere
> from one place to another. My mother started her period and my fa-
> ther was really mad at her. He told her "this is disgusting, you should
> know this by now, how many years have you been doing this." I re-
> member him belittling her in a way that was supposed to be loving,
> and I could see that it really hurt her. And I didn't want to side with
> her, but I connected to my mother as opposed to connecting with
> my father. I remember that incident. He didn't seem to respect her
> because she was a girl.

What being a girl meant to the women was ever-shifting throughout their childhoods. They struggled with the dilemmas, tensions, contradic-tions that were created by this identity, and often looked to their moth-ers and other adult women in the family for guidance. As a child, Sara wanted to become a writer and a mother when she grew up, but she saw these two aspirations in conflict with each other. She was confused: "At first, I thought that I wanted to have kids and be married. Often I didn't

see a man as much as I saw a kid. But I wanted to write and have a life.
I wanted to travel, too. And if anybody had of asked me how are you
going to do both, being a girl? How's that going to work? I probably
would've turned into a pile of dust. So I had different images that did not
go together." By observing the experiences of her mother and grandmother, Sara attempted to sort through her conflicts, but she came to a
conclusion:

> My mother said she was happy, but that wasn't the message I was get-
> ting. And then my grandmother was married to this guy, and she
> took care of everybody. She was like a big maid to me. She cooked,
> and she seemed to be happy. She was an old farmwoman, and she
> could do everything. She could kill a chicken, and pluck it, and
> cook it, and make soup out of the bone, and take the marrow out of
> the bone. She was like an amazing old lady. But I remembered that I
> didn't want to be either of them.

For Sara as well as for the other women growing up, they did not see
their mothers' life as one that they wanted to emulate. They witnessed
how gender expectations placed constraints on their mothers' everyday
needs, interests, and aspirations. In so doing, they received important
messages about what it means to be girls. In interpreting those messages,
in whatever ways, they all expressed a common sentiment: they wanted
a different life from the ones their mothers led. However, as children it
was difficult for them to imagine what exactly a different life would en-
tail, especially for girls born during the 1940s.

For several of the women, whatever that different life was, they definitely did not see it including physical violence. In the home, even
though adult women could assert personal power over their daughters, as
children the women generally understood that if their fathers were present, he asserted decision-making power over the family. Similar to Sara's
experiences, they learned that males, particularly their fathers, occupied
a privileged position within the family, and his authority was usually un-
contested even by their mothers. For those who grew up in more conventional two-parent households, they began to understand that their
mothers' power was not equivalent to their fathers' power, that the dif-
ferential had something to do with their mothers being female. If their
mothers contested their fathers' authority, then tensions were created in

the family, and sometimes it could lead to physical fights between their parents. Mary and Sharon, but especially Patricia and Barbara, experienced their parents' fights, and on occasions as children they attempted to intervene to stop them.

Patricia grew up in a household where physical violence between her parents was ever-present; in many ways it defined family interactions. Of all the women, Patricia continues to reflect on her parents' violence toward each other and its enduring affects on her life. Patricia blames her father for the violence. She points to her father's attitudes and behaviors, especially toward women and girls, as the major cause of her childhood pain, frustration, and anger. As a young child, Patricia describes her relationship with her father as one of outright fear: "When I was younger, I was afraid of my father. I was very afraid. And my mother even let me know that, yeah, it was necessary to fear him." Patricia's father was an alcoholic, and she believes that his drinking contributed to his unpredictable, volatile, and cruel behavior.

> My father was somebody that you had to learn to gauge his moods. At the outset you have to understand that he was an alcoholic, but he was a functional alcoholic. I didn't realize what an alcoholic meant until I was grown, really. Because I never thought of him as an alcoholic, he just drank. You know, like a lot of the folks in the neighborhood, he just drank, and when he drank he would get stupid. My impression of him is that he was an extremely unhappy human being. He used to threaten to kill everybody in the house big enough to die and the dog too. He used to tell me that "I wasn't his child." He would swear up and down that some other man was my father, and he would go out of his way to make me and my brothers think that my mother was the lowest human being on the face of the earth. From the age of ten, I have been called so many sluts and whores by him. If he had a named me, I guess that would have been on my birth certificate.

Reflecting on her father, Patricia thinks that his alcoholism and bad behavior stemmed from his lack of control over his life as a black man engaging the constraints of white society. In his need for control, Patricia believes that he attempted to fulfill his needs in the only place where he did have privileges as a man—his own household. Although Patricia's mother accommodated and affirmed his male privilege, there were limits to her tolerance; she did not tolerate his physical abuse. Under no circumstances would Patricia's mother allow her father to hit the children. Even though her mother could not control her father's bad behavior, she did not back down from a fight. Patricia said that such fights usually occurred when her father was in a drunken state, and her mother usually had the upper hand in their fights because of his impaired physical condition. For whatever reasons, Patricia believes that her mother did not want to control or hurt her father; she just wanted him to stop his bad behavior. Discussing her parents' complicated relationship, Patricia said:

> A lot of his behavior had to do with control, obviously, I didn't realize it then but I know now. He did not feel in control of his own life, but if he could control somebody else, he felt like he was a man. If he came home late—he would be late quite often maybe 11:00 or 12:00 o'clock—I knew if my mother did not get up and go and fix him something to eat there was going to be a fight; there was no if, and, or but about it. You see there was no talking to him. To be very honest, over the years I have learned that my father really does not like women. In his mind there's a specific purpose that they serve and that's it. I witnessed him miss my mother by a hair breathe with a butcher knife, because he was literally trying to kill her. He told her he "was going to cut her throat because she was fooling around with some man." The ironic thing about it is that he could never do much physical harm to my mother, because he was drunk while he was doing all of this, but he was very deadly. My mother grew up in the South and could handle him. She wasn't a big woman, but she was physically strong, and she could physically handle him. She never wanted to physically hurt him. She just wanted to stop him.

In looking back over her childhood experiences, Patricia said: "Their violence has really played havoc with me. It bent me as a child growing up. It bent me because I looked at it as something that I could never get away from. It's scary because you're always on guard at all times. It seems like I was always around violence. I'm always afraid of the violence that is inside of me that is buried. I don't want it to come out." In Patricia's later experience—and for several of the other women who did not witness or experience their parents fighting—during adulthood, the physical violence "that is buried" came out, sometimes in extremely brutal ways.

Barbara's parents did not fight as frequently as Patricia's, but the violence nevertheless had a lasting affect on her life. During the war years, Barbara's parents moved to the Midwest, where her father "worked in the steel factory" and her mother earned a living as "a day worker, a domestic worker." Through a work-related accident, her father lost his eyesight when she was a young child, and as a consequence Barbara and her five siblings were largely dependent on her mother's meager income to make ends meet and support their needs. Barbara viewed her family as poor. Growing up in poverty, increasingly Barbara witnessed her father's resentment and his anger. She recalls her father as "very bright, but he lost his eyesight, so for a lot of years he was very angry, and I think that kind of messed him up." Barbara recalled what she considered as a "good example" of his anger:

> My dad played the numbers, and my dad hit the number, and the number guy didn't pay him. He's angry. He said Barbara I want you to go with me because I'm going to go down here and talk with this man. Here I am walking down the street with this blind man, taking him down to the number guy. He tells "the number guy this town is too small for both of us and if you don't give me my money one of us is going to have to leave." The man gave him the money and I'm standing there saying hey this man is blind.

Barbara's father's anger was heightened by his frustration of being blind which limited his ability to provide financial support for his family. For Barbara, her father's "fits of anger," especially toward her mother, were deeply disturbing: "He was a strong guy. But he was very, very, very angry. He was a very smart man. I liked the fact that he was really smart, and he was really handsome. I felt loved by my father, and I liked him until he got angry. He would have fits of anger, and there was always a lot of tension. He was extremely jealous of my mother, and I knew that there was going to be a major fight." Due to his blindness, her mother usually had the upper hand in their fights, and often no major physical injuries resulted; this did not, however, diminish affects their fighting had on Barbara. When her parents fought, Barbara said she felt "extremely insecure." Often her insecurity not only provoked a sense of violation but also lead to her to taking action: "What I did, I sort of like put the emphasis on myself, so I would say that I'm going to run away if you don't stop fighting. And I did. If I left, then that meant that they had to stop fighting, and go and look for me, at least my mother. My leaving kind of stopped the fighting. Their fighting really affected me throughout my whole entire life. It kept me jumpy, confused and fearful because I never knew when they would fight. I was really nervous. I was really insecure. But you learn how to deal with it. But as a child I don't think that you never really do."

As children, Patricia and Barbara, as well as the other women who experienced their parents' fights, as witnesses clearly recognized the violent nature of their parents' actions. However, it is important to point out that only through their adult reflections and experiences are the women able to give meaning to and articulate some reasons why they believe their parents fought. From their perceptions they all concluded, in their own ways, that the reasons for the violence rested in their fathers' frustration of living as black men in America. For them, this frustration was directly related to the racial constraints imposed on their fathers, constraints that limited their abilities to assert privileges afforded to males in the larger white society. In the absence of such privileges, they often found segregation and discrimination instead. As a consequence, Patricia and Barbara but also the other women point to their fathers' anger as evidence of this happening. Sharon said, "I don't know why my father was so angry. I never understood it as a child. I guess looking back, maybe being a black man who was very intelligent and never getting anywhere made him angry. I didn't find out until after he died that people would call him nigger at work. I think now, maybe, he took his anger out on us. Maybe that's why he would terrorize us and scream a lot."

However, in offering an explanation for their fathers' bad behavior, the women clearly did not attempt to justify or rationalize such behavior; their mothers most often took the brunt of their fathers' anger. In the absence of equal access to external male privileges, their fathers assumed male prerogative in the home. As children, the women could not avoid noticing the gender differences between their mothers and fathers; nor could they avoid witnessing the often uneven power relations engendered by such differences. They not only noticed, but in some instances actually began to anticipate, what would happen when or if their mothers did not comply with or outwardly contested their fathers' will. Even though all the women expressed the general sentiment that they hated when their parents' fought, the messages they received, particularly from their mothers' actions, were not lost on them.

They did not see their mothers as passive *victims*, who would not or could not defend themselves. Rather, they saw their mothers fighting in defense of self. Expressing this general sentiment, upon reflection, Patricia said: "I never, ever saw my mother as an abused wife. The words, abused wife, and my mother just didn't seem to fit. I never associated it with her, simply because whenever he would physically attack her, she seemed to always be able to handle it. She could always physically put him in his place. And on one level she seemed to psychologically have the upper hand."

For those who vividly recalled witnessing and in some instances actually participating in their parents' fights, the violence they experienced provoked a sense of violation. That violation was expressed in how they felt and how they saw themselves as a result of the disrespect they experienced. Mary, for example, recalls the time she got her father's gun and raised it toward her parents to make them stop fighting, and they did. Her father took the gun away and in return beat Mary with "a wire coat hanger." Mary said she drew the gun on them because she felt "helpless" and "tremendously insecure" when her parents fought. This sense of powerlessness and insecurity was expressed by all the women, and their actions reveal the vulnerability their parents' fighting posed to their sense of self.

The different scope and uneven power between fathers and mothers helped to shape the women's childhood understanding of what it meant to be girls: when compared to boys, girls were different, and that difference offered uneven rewards and punishments. One lesson they learned, especially from their mothers, was that they were not necessarily at a physical disadvantage because they were girls, for they could fight back. And for those whose parents did not fight, they too would learn the significance of fighting during childhood; they would learn its importance through their interactions with other children.

The women were developing their own particular childhood understanding of what it meant to be girls from their relationships with adult family members. However, they were also receiving important messages about the meaning of being girls from the children they played with in their neighborhoods. In many ways play is instrumental to the cultural and social development of children. Child's play reinforces gender roles and gender conformity often through modeling or mimicking of adult behavior. Many of the women's childhood friends were girls, but they played with boys as well. In the process of play, they assert agency, but constraints are imposed, in this instance, largely through childhood codes of conduct, expectations, and rules for interaction.

Playing with other children was at the center of the women's early neighborhood relationships. Recalling the types of games she played as a child, Patricia said: "We played skellies and marbles; we did a lot of running races; and the guys played a lot of stick ball; the girls and the guys played punch ball, which was sort of like baseball; we played handball; red light green light; double Dutch jump rope, and there were always one or two guys who would jump rope with us."

Sometimes as they played, they encountered children who did not immediately accept them into their childhood culture or games. Like Patricia, several women had to go through initiation to become a part of that culture, and fighting was sometimes a part of that rite of passage. Patricia had to fight the "bully and her sister." She discussed her initiation:

> In my neighborhood there was one set of sisters, and the oldest sister was an extreme bully. I think she fought every young girl in my neighborhood. She had this thing where she loved to fight. I fought her almost everyday, she and her sister. It was like this was a ritual, especially if you were new to the block. It didn't matter your age. I will never forget, when I moved to the block, it was the younger sister, she and I were the same age, and she comes and sits on the stoop next to me, and she said, "Oh, I hear that you're from the Bronx. I heard y'all are bad." For some reason this conversation stayed in my mind. Everybody beat the younger sister up. The older sister was very strong, and there were days she would beat my butt, and beat it good, and there were other days, as luck would have it, I would turn around and beat her butt good. I never got like seriously hurt— other than lumps, bumps and bruises—never got a black eye or anything like that. We always fought over some inconsequential nonsensical something.

At some point over the course of their childhood, all the women recalled fights with either siblings or neighborhood children, usually with other girls. And for some, as they grew older, the circumstances surrounding the fights grew increasingly complicated and mean spirited. Fighting was a frequent occurrence for several women throughout their childhood; it was a part of their experiences as girls. Based on those experiences, it was important for them to interpret both the obvious messages and the nuances they received from other children; their failure to do so could lead to another fight. Patricia describes how significance it was for to "read" the different meanings of her interactions, especially with other girls. She recalls:

> I would hate for my mother to send me to the store. Sometimes the females would gather in a group around the store. You knew that you couldn't say, Ma I can't go to the store because the girls are out there. She would say "look you better go to the store and go and get me what I want. I don't want to hear this nonsense." So you had to walk past them. That's truly knowing what aloneness is like. There would be maybe three or four girls gathered in a group, and they would be watching you. You never knew if anything was going to happen. They would be talking about you, and they would wait for you to come close and always one would signify, and there were the followers who would go along with it. It was like walking the last mile. If you got past them and you went into the store, it was like, I've made it this far. But then you had to make the trek back, and you never knew what was going to happen. Most often, I guess, for whatever reason, if you were going to the store for your parents, they pretty much didn't bother you because they knew they were going to have to deal with the parents if that food didn't get back to the house. If they could perceive that you were just going to the store for yourself, all hell could break lose right then and there, and a fight would break out. You had the ripping of the clothes and the tearing out of the hair and the scratching of the face and all that kind of madness and nonsense.

Jackie had little tolerance for "nonsense" when it came to fighting, and as she grew older her fights would become increasingly brutal. Jackie was raised in New York City public housing where there were thirteen different complexes, with more than five thousand residents. Her mother and father were never married, so Jackie lived with her mother and maternal grandmother in the projects, and for eleven years she was an only child. After her mother married, Jackie had two younger brothers and a sister. But in her large public housing development, she was surrounded by aunts and uncles who also lived in the projects. Jackie grew up with cousins, who were mostly boys and similar to her in age. As she said, "I grew up with boys, and I was always fighting." Jackie developed her attitudes about fighting from her uncles and male cousins, and from her sporadic involvement in their street gang.

Unlike Patricia who was often cautious and guarded when it came to fighting, Jackie's attitude toward fighting was emphatic: "If you're going to come after me, let's get this done, and then we'll find out later why this had to happen. My uncles used to say, if you're going to have a fight just go ahead and get it over with. All that arguing and fussing, I'm not going to do that. I'm going to hit you. We are going to hit each other, and get it over with."

Jackie, a fighter, recalls some of the many fights that she had with neighborhood children, but she stressed that she followed a specific code of conduct: "I didn't fight nobody unless I was threatened. That I do know. I never went to pick no fights. But if somebody said that they are going to bodily hurt me, then we're going to have to do this. I had a lot of fights with boys and girls, but more with boys. I won most of them. I don't remember losing a fight really." Although she "never went to pick no fights," Jackie did fight on behalf of her much younger siblings. Vividly recalling two fights she had with boys, who she saw as "picking on" her younger brother, Jackie said:

I had to fight for my brother because they used to smack him on the head because his hair was cut bald when he was little. So when he would walk by somebody they would just smack him on the head. There was this older guy outside, and he would just smack my brother on the head and started laughing, and he smacked him again. So, of course, I had to get a brick and hit him in the head. Did I seriously hurt him? Oh yeah. He needed medical attention. There was another one who I threw into a brick wall in the back of the projects and busted his head wide open. You know, I mean I don't like to fight, but if I'm going to fight, we're going to remember this. You know we're not just wasting energy here.

As Patricia and Jackie's experiences suggest, the circumstances surrounding and the actual fights conveyed messages that were important for the women to learn. Their fights usually occurred as a result of an insult, in retaliation to a transgression, in defense of honor, or for a whole host of reasons where they perceived a violation that resulted in a sense of disrespect. Fighting in defense of self affected how they saw themselves as children. A general sentiment expressed by the women was that they "felt satisfied," especially if they won a fight, and none admitted to ever losing or "getting beat up badly" by another child. Discussing her sense of self-satisfaction for beating up her younger sister, Anne said: "My sister wears this scar over her eye to this day where I threw a toy cash register and hit her. I really remembered that if I could have killed her I would have. I know that I felt satisfied after I did it. She had made me so angry that I looked around for anything that I could pick up and hit her with. I know that I didn't feel upset at the time. She provoked me, and I lit out after her. I intended to do her bodily harm, and I did it, and I didn't have any particular remorse over hurting her either." Of all the women, only Patricia acknowledges that her childhood fights at times affected her self-confidence as a child. This, she believes has contributed to her deep distrust of women, even to this day. Patricia reflected on what she learned as child from fighting especially with other girls:

> Fighting has made me cautious around women who are aggressive, because in my mind there is a very thin line between being aggressive and being violent. From childhood I've seen the violence that women can visit upon other women. When I was growing up, I learned that you had to be cautious around people, male and female. You just don't know what would provoke violence. So it made me watch them more closely and listen even closer to things that they say as compared to what they do, and also to listen to the things that they don't say. It is the things that they leave out, and maybe it is those things that will provoke some kind of violence.

As children, the women came to understand that the power between themselves and other children was not necessarily uneven as in their interactions with adults. With their peers, they could assert their needs, interests, and aspirations. For no matter what constraints were imposed by their childhood culture there was more give and take in their relationships with other children. In fighting, the women generally believed that they "gave as good as they got." And with the exception of Patricia, none of the other women expressed any lasting effects that their childhood fights had on them. But fighting in defense of self was a childhood lesson that would not be lost on several of the women as they moved into adulthood.

Physical violence—whether in the form of corporal punishment, parental fights, or childhood fights—was a part of the women's experiences of growing up, of becoming girls. They engaged this violence in their homes and in the streets upon which they played. The women's childhood experiences of physical violence and the resulting sense of violation or lack thereof in some instances, depended on the given circumstances in which it evolved and how they interpreted the messages they received. In the more gendered context of the home, generally, the women who were beaten as children did not associate the physical violence their mothers' administered through corporal punishment with violation and disrespect. In many ways this violence was not associated with fear of injury or harm to their sense of being. But for several of the women it was a completely different message they received when it came to their parents' physical fights; the nature of this violence often provoked a sense of fear, vulnerability, and insecurity, which would leave emotional scars that would be difficult to heal. And, although they did associate their own physical fights with other children with violation, for a sense of violation was often the motivation for such fights, it appears that their ability to fight back lessens the impact the disrespect had on their developing sense of self.

But no matter how threatening or damaging their experiences of physical violence was, no matter if the women as children did or did not view physical violence as a violation that demeans the integrity of their bodies and sense of self, physical violence represents an important, though only one, dimension of the women's experiences of growing up. It is important to consider another dimension of their experiences, personal violence, and the degree to which it results in a violation—in disrespect for their individual human worth. The resulting injury and harm may not be obvious to our eyes. But the injury and harm that is inflicted is quite real to the women and the effects it has on their sense of human worth would influence how they viewed themselves as children. This is reflected in the women's experiences of becoming Colored girls.

BECOMING COLORED GIRLS

In their homes and neighborhoods, as children the women often found ways to adjust, get around, or even play with many gender rules and restrictions that were imposed on them as girls. However, they did not necessarily escape the subtle but in many ways more blatant cultural messages they received from adults as well as from other children regarding what it means to be girls in the black community. In the black community, they were considered Colored girls. This cultural identity was shaped in part by a color and caste hierarchy that was historically rooted in slavery and systematically reproduced through race relations of the 1940s and 1950s. This hierarchy assumed an important degree of acceptability within the black community where some advantages were afforded to blacks whose physical features appeared more whitelike, while those whose features differed faced disadvantages. In this hierarchy a white standard of beauty was reaffirmed, and the significant markers were skin complexion and hair texture.

All the women as children struggled to different degrees with their perception of self as a result of their physical features. Their perceptions were influenced by their experiences of specific features—for example, left- or right-handedness, height, weight, and stage of physical development. But these particular physical features, in and of themselves, did not determine who was considered attractive or pretty in the cultural environment of the black community. Although their body types varied, their skin complexion and hair texture provided a common understanding for what it meant to be Colored girls. As children, they were aware that girls with lighter skin and straighter hair were considered better looking and more often preferred within black society than darker-skinned and nappy haired girls. Their childhood experiences informed this perception and gave meaning to the messages they received about which girls were the most appealing, desirable, and deserving within black society.

Faith was born in New York City but grew up in the South. As she said: "When I was eight months old my mother left my dad, and she went home." Faith and her mother lived with her maternal grandparents but had separate living quarters in the attic of her grandparents' house. Her mother had a college degree and taught art classes at an all-black high school. Even though she was a teacher in the segregated school system of the South, Faith's mother was also a single parent and had a hard time making financial ends meet. Yet Faith viewed her family as part of the black middle class: "One of the things that I understood about being middle class in the South, is that it has as much to do with education as much as money. One of the biggest things that made us middle class was the fact that my granddaddy had sent all four of his kids to college. But there was a junkyard across the street from us, so I used to always be trying to figure out how it was that I could live across the street from a junkyard, where we never had any money, and yet still I knew that we were considered bourgeois." In addition to education and sometimes money, another important consideration for obtaining black middle-class status was often skin complexion and hair texture. In Faith's understanding of history, she said: "I realized that the first people to go to college were for the most part the slave master's children, and then I begin to understand just that whole dynamic of why light-skinned people were probably the first one to have a college education." As a child, Faith began to realize that her light-skinned complexion could offer certain privileges within the black community.

However, Faith encountered difficulties and struggled with some contradictory messages she received about her looks, especially when she encountered other blacks who did not extend privilege to her skin complexion. She explained that "it bothered me and I used to talk to myself about being insulted because I was yellow." Faith felt disrespected, and this inhibited her from taking advantage of the privileges extended in the color and caste hierarchy. But on reflection, she admits that "if I had it to do all over again, I would play yellow." In taking advantage of the preference and privilege that her skin color offered in the black community, Faith believes that "there were a lot of things that I could have had easily that I got going a much harder route, or I didn't get at all because I just wouldn't press the color card. But if I had to do it again, doors that would have opened just because I was yellow, I would walk through them, I wouldn't take the hard route, and I wouldn't even be concerned."

But Sara rejects the notion that her light-skinned complexion and straight hair afforded certain privileges to her while growing-up. Her perceptions differed from Faith's because she had not grown-up in a pre-dominately black cultural environment; rather, Sara lived in different parts of the country often in integrated army housing due to her father's military career, and this informed her views. So, in discussing her perceptions, Sara said that some black people, "assumed that I was brought up with a certain amount of privilege because I was yellow, but where I grew up once the white folks knew I was black, I don't think that it was an advantage. In the 50s, it wasn't like you're a light-skinned black, it like you're a nigger or you're not a nigger. It was an issue of whether you could go some place or not. So if I had grown up in North Carolina or New Orleans or somewhere in the South with a lot of black folks, maybe it would have made a difference. I would have had a feeling of something special." Unlike Faith and even Sara, Patricia and several of the other darker-skinned women did not have the option to "play yellow." Patricia grew up knowing that she did not fit the image of what a Colored girl was supposed to look like; she was particularly uncomfortable with the darkness of her skin and the nappiness of her hair.

> I guess I did a lot of what black girls did. I never actually wanted to be white, but I was affected by that whole thing of wanting the long hair. I didn't necessarily want to have long silky white hair; I just wanted long hair. I would put a slip over my head and let it hang down over my shoulders and look in the mirror and talk to myself. Of course my mother thought that I was absolutely crazy. I would envision myself beautiful, but not in the sense of with white skin. I did envision myself in the sense of having a lighter complexion. I guess I did what a lot of young females do when they really begin to pay attention to themselves. I would sit in front of the mirror and try to pull my eyes to a slant. I figured that maybe if I had slanted eyes I would look better. Or maybe if I had longer hair I would look better and people would like me.

Patricia's struggle was made even more poignant by the comments and reactions she received, especially from other children: "During the time when I was growing up, I was not considered an attractive female. I was told this one way or another, on a constant basis, from my brothers or from the neighborhood kids. I was considered ugly. After a time I considered myself ugly. You know like when you tell a child they're stupid, and you tell them enough, they begin to internalize it and say, well I'm stupid. I grew up with that. I was self-conscious about myself, extremely so." Patricia's older brothers were particularly "mean" to her. One would call her "moosey or liver lips," and sometimes she could laugh with him, but mostly it was "truly painful":

> Anytime he would see a moose on TV, I would have to leave the room. There he goes, moosey. He told me that when I got older, I was going to have these two tubes of lipstick—one for the top lip and one for the bottom lip. Sometimes I would try to ignore him; other times I would cry. It would hurt, it would sting, and I would cry. Other times I would go and talk to my mother. My mother would say, "Fool, look in the mirror, do you see that?" But when you have somebody telling you this, that's literally what you see when you look in a mirror. You get this out-of-wack image that girls are supposed to have small dainty feet. You are supposed to have small dainty hands. You are supposed to look a certain way, if you're a girl. So I caught hell from all corners. I had the big feet. I was tall for my age at the time. I never looked like anybody on TV because for the most part they were white. I knew that I didn't look like them in the black magazines. So I'm saying, my God what's going to happen to me? My mother was a beautiful woman, and I would say why can't I look like her? Why do I have to look like my father? She always told me, "You walk with your head up, you walk with your shoulders erect, and you walk like you're somebody." But it was hard to do as a child.

As the experiences of Faith, Sara, Patricia, and the other women suggest, their understanding of what it meant to be Colored girls was highly dependent on where they were positioned along the color and caste hierarchy within the black community. Most, but not all, the women remembered childhood incidents that provoked a sense of personal violation stemming from the constraints imposed on them by the color and caste hierarchy in the black community. A commonality—whether light or dark complexioned with straight or nappy hair—was their sense of self-deprecation as a result of their experiences. Ironically, the self-deprecation of some of the lighter-skinned women sometimes evolved in the context of resentment, jealousy, or intolerance by others, where self-doubt was created about the way they looked and the disvalue they felt as Colored girls. For the darker complexioned women, however, sometimes their sense of self-deprecation evolved in the distinct context of rejection, where they felt devalued because their physical features did not comport to idealized images of Colored girls.

Those with lighter skin and straighter hair understood that they were considered attractive by black community standards. But this understanding did not necessarily shape their own perception of how they viewed themselves. Light complexion with straight hair was not enough; Sara said that, as a child, "I wasn't comfortable with the way I looked. I wanted to be either darker or I wanted to be prettier. I figured if I was going to be light, I needed to look more like my mother or be darker and have some character about myself. But if I had my druthers I would be browner, it would be easier, it would be more straight forward, and I think I would be prettier."

Faith's mother, who was dark-skinned, disagreed with the notion that "light makes right." Her mother's attempts to deemphasize the significance of light skin preference had an impact on how Faith viewed herself as a child: "When I looked in the mirror I didn't see myself as pretty. It took me probably a long time to realize that I looked all right. That was because of her. I always wondered if she had any idea that in her attempt not to make me think that I was going to get over in life cause I was yellow that she also made me not realize that I was okay to look at for a long time." The women with darker skin and nappier hair understood as Patricia's experience suggests that they were not considered pretty by the standards imposed on them by the black community. As such, the messages they received became embedded in their own perception of self as Colored girls and resulted in a sense of being physically unattractive and unworthy. Barbara admits that she was "extremely self-conscious" about the way she looked as a child: "I had the idea that I was not an attractive person because I didn't have what was supposed to be attractive for black girls. I was dark, I didn't have hair flowing down my back, and on top of this we were poor. I just didn't represent what was attractive." Patricia, reflecting on her experience of color prejudices, concludes that:

> For a lot of years issues around skin color and hair have been very
> detrimental for me. All black people are not that backwards about

color and hair, but I just didn't happen to run into a lot that wasn't
during my growing up years. Whether it was verbal or otherwise, I
was always reminded that I was too black, I was always made to feel
that I was not desirable. I was always made to feel that because of my
color I was less than. Of course I grew up in a time that being called
black was not a compliment. Being called black was negative. My
brother would always refer to me as "black and ugly with big lips."
So all of those kind of things put you in your place, so to speak, they
cut you down to size. I know this had a lot to do with shaping my
growing up. My mother always said that "skin color has nothing to
do with your brain; you are who you are." But I used to be jealous
and oh how I wished that I were more attractive. I guess growing up
as a black girl meant a lot of struggle to me.

Physical violence does not provide an explanation for the deeply injurious harm that resulted from the women's childhood experiences with
the color and caste hierarchy in the black community. Even though the
focus of attention is on their bodies, the violence was personal and insidious in nature; their sense of violation was rooted in their perceptions
of disrespect for having individual physical features that were both the
same and different from other blacks. In the reproduction of the color
and caste hierarchy in the black community, individual value was assigned meaning and given an importance that both reified and demo-
nized their childhood experiences simply because of skin complexion
and hair texture. In many ways, as attested to by the women's childhood
experiences, their sense of self was threatened, jeopardized, and compromised. In their immaturity as children, often they were unable to offer a
defense of self and ill-equiped to fight the insults, humiliation, and disregard they felt to their human worth because of skin complexion and hair
texture. They were largely rendered powerless in their interactions with
adults as well as other children, as this hierarchy was reproduced in their
lives. For several women, the scars left by their early encounters with the
color and caste hierarchy would deepen as they engaged similar constraints during adulthood.

Moreover, the women encountered another dimension of violence
during childhood that was also insidious, and it too influenced how they
viewed themselves as children: for they engaged the constraints imposed

on them by social violence. This form of violence was also physical and personal in nature, but it is nonetheless demarcated by the systemic devaluing of their individual selves as a reflection of their group experience. The women experienced social violence in their encounters with the restrictions placed on them by the larger white society in their lives as Negro girls.

Becoming Negro Girls

Through their cultural and social interactions, the women engaged the larger white society, and sometimes as children they encountered aspects of the turbulent racial climate of the 1940s and 1950s. In their journeys beyond their more familiar home, neighborhood, and community environments, they experienced racism, which they did not understand, and often an accompanying adult could not adequately explain or protect them from these instances. Generally, this was the situation, especially for the women who visited relatives in the South during summer months. But, in the absence of mature knowledge, their early encounters with the system of racial segregation and discrimination was often experienced as another childhood curiosity, rather than as an absolute constraint on their behavior.

Amanda's early encounters with the system of racism in the South and her unpreparedness in dealing with it, is reflected in several of the women's youthful experiences. As a child, Amanda said, "I didn't know about racism, I didn't know what words and stuff like that meant." However, she did have a growing awareness that "there were white people who didn't particularly care about us and that blacks were treated differently." But as a child, Amanda did not understand the reasoning behind such attitudes and actions. Recalling one of her earliest experience in going south, Amanda said:

> When we were real little, we used to go every summer with my mother to visit our grandparents. We could ride cheap because my father worked at the train station carrying bags. I always remember seeing my father cry. He would stand outside the train car waving and getting sadder and sadder and the tears coming. We would always have matching outfits; my mother would make our outfits. She sewed, my mother made practically all our clothes except for shoes.

She even made hats, these little ugly bonnets. We all three had the same exact outfits. We had to have our outfits to go down South and our box of chicken. The train rides were always fun because we would look out of the windows, although it seems like it took forever. But the fascinating part was when we got off the train and then had to take the ferry. You couldn't go directly by train to my grandparents', you had to take the ferry over. We had to wait in the segregated waiting room. I remember that my sister and I was running in and out of the bathroom, going back and forth, and then we told my mother that it said Colored and white, and the water fountain too. We keep trying to figure out what was going on because they all looked alike to us. We were saying both of the water fountains were white, and we didn't see any colors in the bathroom. The white folks were like giving my mother the eye, and she would just hold her head up, and she would never say anything to us.

As Amanda's experience suggests, the women were curious and perceptive as children, but they did not fully grasp the difficult and complex messages that were conveyed about what it meant to be Negro girls in white society. Several of the women remembered their childhood experiences of going to the back door of stores, drinking at Colored water fountains, riding in the back of city buses, and sitting in the balcony of movie theaters on their summer visits south. And, although, they were aware that these experiences were reserved for Negroes, initially they had no particular significance or impact on how they saw themselves as children.

But they began to learn from their experiences. Racial segregation and discrimination would no longer be a childhood curiosity, rather, it became a painful learning experience as they grew older. In this process of learning, their encounters with racial constraints and racism were not limited to summer vacations in the South. Though their parents tried to protect them in whatever ways they could, they did not provide their daughters with an explanation of the attitudes and actions of white society toward Negroes. The meaning and its implications about the black self continued to be elusive and difficult for several of the women as children, to grasp. Sara, light complexioned with straight hair, struggled in her efforts to understand what it meant to be a Negro girl in white

society. She recalled a childhood incident while living with her family in
a small army-supported town in the Northwest:

> There was this man, who showed movies on an outside wall of a
> building, but he wouldn't start the movie and nobody knew why.
> And then he said he "wasn't going to start the movie until the other
> people left." I was light enough and sometimes they wouldn't know,
> but my brother was very brown skinned. What the man said "was
> when the Colored people left." But I really don't think that I heard
> him say that. And when the movie was over, I looked around for my
> brother because I was supposed to be taking care of him, but he
> wasn't there, and I didn't know where he was. When I got home, I
> got a beating, because they had sent him home because he was black.
> I didn't know, and I had stayed there and watched the movie.

Sara also recalls a similar incident while living on an army base in the
Southwest:

> Once we were going ice-skating with some people from church, and
> they wouldn't let us go ice-skating because this black guy and I were
> there. And the same thing that happened with my brother happened
> again. They didn't know that I was black. The people that I was rid-
> ing back with didn't know, but the minister did. What he said was "if
> they can't go none of us are going to go." So we all piled back into
> the cars and were heading to go have some pizzas or something. And
> I was in this car with this boy who said, "I don't see why we didn't
> let (the black child) go home because he is the only one here." And
> so, I didn't say anything. I remembered telling my mom, and my fa-
> ther yelled at me, and I carried that. How did I know that I was a
> Negro child? It was that kind of stuff, and it came out of the blue,
> and it never would have occurred to me.

Sara came to realize through her experience that if she forgot or did not
pay attention to the notion that she was a Negro girl living with segregation and discrimination while growing up, "parents, peers, and white
folks would reeducate me." And based on her perception, Sara concludes
that "white folks will reeducate you the quickest."

   To understand the nature of racism and how it circulates within cultural and social settings, it was important for the women as children to

grasp its fundamental premise: blacks are mentally and physically inferior, especially to whites; therefore, blacks are subordinate or unequal and must be subservient to the will of whites. Even though they knew that blacks were treated differently than whites, it appears that racism and its implications about the black self were initially difficult concepts for the women to understand as children. For they had no early sense of being inferior owing to race, particularly within their homes, neighborhoods, and broader community, for these all-black environments engendered a general sense of connection and affirmation. However, their growing awareness of black inferiority began to penetrate their more familiar environments. As their experiences suggest, it was not necessarily their direct encounters but rather the more indirect contact with racism that affected how they saw themselves as children. Their increasing understanding of racism and what it said about the black self began to penetrate their more familiar environments; it came about in their living rooms as they watched America's popular culture on television, eavesdropped on adults' conversations, and read or looked at pictures in black magazines.

Amanda remembers her reactions to seeing black people on television for the first time, as she said:

> One of the first times we saw a black person on television, my sister and I sat there crying. We said, what's wrong with those people? And we started crying. I don't remember who they were. They just looked dark, like they had been burnt or something, and their eyes seemed real big and white. And we thought something had happened to them. My mother said "how ugly the lighting was for black people." Everybody else looked normal because everybody else was white. I remembered watching these shows like Howdy Doody and all those other little stupid shows and never saw black people except for these little funny black people. This had to have been in the 50s.

As children, they could not avoid the popular messages and images that were imposed on them, and gradually they began to realize how they were perceived by white society. What they heard and saw evoked an early sense of violation and disrespect. For Jackie, this violation was manifested in her sense of childhood confusion and anger. As a child, Jackie actually appeared in the audience of the popular children's television program, Howdy Doody: Jackie said:

It was in the 50s, and I remember that freckled-face puppet Howdy Doody. We were on his show. I remember coming home and looking at myself on Howdy Doody because I had been in the audience. I was the darkest kid there. Even though there were other black kids, all the others were light-skinned. I realized how much lighter they were from me. I was another color. I asked my grandmother, where am I? My grandmother said, "There. There you are. There's grandma's baby." But I couldn't figure out who the hell I was. But it was me. I was just sitting over there. I never looked at Howdy Doody again. I was mad at Howdy Doody. I didn't like the way he talked to the kids. He was just not the same kind of person I saw on TV. I was just angry and didn't understand.

The grotesque and disfigured images of blacks that they witnessed as children were by no means limited to popular amusement and entertainment, for such images also penetrated the everydayness of black life. An indelible childhood image that remains with all of the women were the photographs that appeared in *Jet* magazine, which covered the 1955 lynching of fourteen-year-old Emmett Till, who was believed by some white Mississippians to have whistled at a twenty-one-year-old white woman while visiting relatives in the South on summer vacation. Amanda saw those pictures and said:

The most poignant memory, that I have never forgotten and probably never will, was the thing with Emmett Till. I remember the *Jet* magazine pictures of him. On one hand I was just fascinated with the pictures. That someone could just be so brutalized and look like that. I mean you couldn't even separate him from the thing that they had attached him to. I remember the picture of his mother and the funeral. I probably didn't have a clear view of all that happened. But I was angry. And I remember knowing that Emmett Till was killed by white people.

Fifty years have passed since the lynching of Emmett Till, but Barbara continues to have vivid memories and reactions to his death:

It really affected me—it really, really affected me. Emmett Till's death frightened me so. I became aware of it because it was on the cover of *Jet* magazine, and we always got *Jet* and *Ebony*. They had a whole picture there, and that was a scary thing. Everybody was talking about it. Then you would hear stories. Like when your family would come over and they would all talk about what was happening in the South. I was afraid to go back there. I was like really frightened. I was just petrified. But the pictures of Emmett Till scared me the most. I had never been as frightened, and at the time he was still a child. I never could understand why blacks were so hated? I just didn't understand that.

By 1955, the year of the Emmett Till murder, as children all the women knew that they were not just girls, or Colored girls, but were considered Negro girls by white society. This gradual understanding was informed by their childhood experiences. Slowly, they began to understand the importance of the distinctions that existed between these identities and the cultural and social expectations associated with each.

During their early years, gender expectations for girls were largely imposed on the women from within their home and neighborhood environments. Through their experiences they began to understand that gender expectations were not absolute, that such expectations were not significant in all circumstances in which they interacted; but when gender expectations were imposed, then they were held accountable for conformity. This allowed the women to assert agency within and against gender constraints and develop their own particular understanding of what it means to be girls. As their childhood experiences suggest, they mostly acquiesced and accepted their gender identity. There were also times when they manipulated or simply rebelled against the imposed gender constraints. Overall, however, their understanding of gender was largely binary: they were girls and not boys, and this distinction at times offered both advantages and disadvantages to them while growing up.

Similarly, they became aware that color and caste within the black community were also not absolute hierarchies that imposed constant constraints; it too was dependent on a particular set of interactions, but by no means all. Their awareness of a Colored girl identity was shaped through their interactions in their family, neighborhood, and particularly the larger black community. In their own ways they assert agency within and against this hierarchy. But generally they succumbed to the frustration and for some the pain that the meaning of a Colored girl identity imposed on their individual reality. The meaning they gave to this identity was also binary: they were either darker with nappy hair or lighter with straighter hair. And depending upon how they were positioned in the color and caste hierarchy, they were more or less valued by the black community.

As children, too, they would gradually learn that the expectations associated with a Negro girl persona were also imposed, but by white society. Their awareness of a Negro girl identity was also binary; they were black, not white. More important, so were their parents, the children they played with, and the people with whom they interacted in their communities. Whether they perceived advantages or disadvantages to being girls, or whether they perceived themselves to be more or less valued as Colored girls, they all began to understand as children that they had no collective worth as Negroes when it came to their interactions with white society.

In their reflections, all the women equated the social dimensions of racism with violence that engendered a violation, which disrespected their developing sense of being. As children, the meaning of racism was difficult to grasp, and their understanding of its significance to their lives was gradual. In that understanding they began to realize that racism could threaten, jeopardize, and compromise their sense of person, whether it was directed toward them or not. In their stories of racism, the social violence they experienced was often revealed in their encounters with systemic processes, procedures, and of course practices that were sometimes carried out by known, but more often by anonymous, unseen, or hidden individuals who participated in maintaining a status quo based on notions of white hegemony and black inferiority. Given the insidious and systemic nature of racism, the women as children initially had difficulty in grasping its meaning and how that meaning applied to them as well as to people who looked like them. Through their childhood experiences as Negro girls, however, they were forced to learn the meaning of racism.

In their growing awareness of racism, the women knew that they were considered Negro girls by white society, and they did not readily reject or embrace this identity; rather, it simply existed and imposed meaning on the reality of their lives. At some point in their childhood they began to realize that to be a Negro, in the eyes of the other, was seen as less than, unequal to, or simply as a "nigger." They learned that "nigger" especially was a word that could pierce their very being. For several of women as children, "nigger" was a fighting word. Patricia explained how she became aware that she was considered a Negro, but did not view herself necessarily as a Negro, and how the term Negro had some association with the word "nigger":

> At that time in my life I just knew that I was considered a Negro. I can't say that something just came to me one day or that I was looking in the mirror and said oh I'm a Negro girl. I just knew simply because of hearing it said, seeing it on the news or reading in the paper the word Negro. But I can't say that I ever thought of myself as a Negro girl. I don't ever remember my mother saying to any of us that "we were Negroes." I find it hard to believe that I don't ever remember thinking of myself as a Negro. And I didn't think of others as Negroes. It's funny, now that I look back on it. I would see my friends and they were just my friends. They were just my girlfriends or my guyfriends. One of the things I do remember was the way— especially at that time—the way to upset someone if you wanted to hurt their feelings, or if you were spoiling for a fight, was to call someone a nigger, or add the word black onto it. Then you could get into some trouble. Obviously at that time being black was not the greatest thing in the world that you wanted to be called. The word nigger for black people in my neighborhood was used on so many different levels. But you knew when the term was used to hurt. It was the term that white people reserved for themselves to throw at us, to hurt us, to make us feel less than. Somehow you knew that when a black person used it in anger, they were using it for the very same reason. And I guess that's why you would get into a fight.

As a child, Patricia gradually began to realize the meaning of a Negro girl identity. She neither rejects nor embraces this identity as part of her own concept of self. This identity exists, and there was nothing she could do about it, for it assumed a degree of ownership over her regardless of how she perceived her childhood self. Patricia's childhood understanding of what it means to be a Negro girl reflects the extent to which she was able to define herself and the degree to which her definition of self was shaped within and against cultural and social constraints. The significance of this understanding is seen in all the women's attempts to give meaning to their early concept of self within and against their identities as girls, Colored girls, and Negro girls.

Different circumstances help to shape different aspects of the women's early self-awareness. The environments that gave rise to their experiences differed in significant ways: accordingly, the expectations that are placed on them differ; their self-perceptions differ; and, their actions differ. In asserting agency, their childhood experiences reveal the unevenness of their interactions, whereby power relations become fundamental to their ability to navigate their childhood lives.

As children, their age and immaturity often rendered them powerless, especially to the cultural and social conditions and practices reproduced by authoritative adults imposing their will. However, this was not necessarily the case in their interactions with other children. They are positioned differently to power relations, and their interactions with other children in their childhood culture reflect this difference. Yet both levels of interactions open up a range of possibilities for their own actions that run the gamut from acquiescence to manipulation to resistance. Their actions reflect not only how they were positioned to their particular environments but also how they saw themselves as children as a result and how they attempted to claim a sense of self within and against those interactions.

In the process of becoming children, the women's experiences of violence and violation emerge in the context of the cultural and social arrangements under which they lived their lives. As such, they recalled vivid memories of physical, personal, and social violence during childhood. In remembering what happened, their sense of violation resulting from interactions in the home, neighborhood, the broader black community, and the larger white society are evident in their experiences. At times they developed a sense of violation as a result of their direct experiences; sometimes their sense of violation evolved from what they witnessed; sometimes their actions resulted in possible violations of others. Yet in their reflective interpretations the physical, personal, and social dimensions of their experiences of violence are not viewed, in all instances, as a violation that breached or infringed upon their sense of personhood, even if that may appear to be the case.

The women's childhood experiences provide a foundation for understanding the complex ways violence and violation developed early on in their lives. Although those experiences are essential to their process of becoming human beings, they do not determine the course of the women's lives. As they continue in their particular process of becoming, the emergence of new knowledge will shape new needs, interests, and aspirations as well as new identities when they engage social and cultural change at various phases of life. But there is continuity in change that is created by recurring patterns of cultural and social constraints. This allows for mapping the women's past while connecting it to the ever-changing realities of their lives. Nowhere is this more evident than in the women's experiences of violence and violation; as they mature, the process of living alters the circumstances of their everyday lives. Their childhood experiences are foundational in establishing a conceptual bridge for understanding: how violence is produced and reproduced; how meaning is interpreted and reinterpreted; and how self-perception is defined and redefined through their sense of violation. But as children, the women still have more lessons to learn, for they must attend school.

CHAPTER 2

Lessons to Learn

We expect because we have learned—learned that
there is something to expect, learned that there are
gifts to be had in this world, that something once
was given and that, accordingly, more just might (on
the basis of experience) be forthcoming. . . . So if
expectation arises from the past, and if the future is
tied up in the past, and if the present, in a way, is the
past being lived out, what hope can we expect to arise
in certain children?

The South Goes North,
Robert Coles

BETWEEN 1957 AND 1966, all the women received
high school diplomas. To appreciate this achievement, it is important to
look at their educational journey. They attended public schools during a
period of political unrest and instability that challenged the very legitimacy of America's cultural and social institutions. Desegregation of public education stood at the forefront of the call for change. On May 17,
1954, the Supreme Court of the United States announced its landmark
decision in the case of *Oliver Brown et al. v. Board of Education of Topeka,*
which rendered racial segregation in public education unconstitutional.
But this legal decision held a broader meaning. As Richard Kluger in
Simple Justice notes, "Black rights had suddenly been redefined; black
bodies had suddenly been reborn under a new law. Blacks' value as
human beings had been changed overnight by the declaration of the na-
tion's highest court. At a stroke, the Justices had severed the remaining
cords of de facto slavery" (Kluger 1975).

In striking down racial segregation in public schools, the justices'
stroke of the pen was indeed a critical legal milestone. However, *Brown v.
Board of Education* was not enough, in and of itself, to sever the deeply

entrenched legacy of racial oppression and injustice that slavery had so thoroughly produced. Blacks recognized that self-directed action was also required. In the South ordinary black women, men, and children were beginning to step up their protest against longstanding racial injustices, inequalities, and indignities, and as a result of their actions the modern civil rights movement began to take its shape during the 1950s. As children, the women were not somehow isolated or detached from the realities of this movement. As witnesses, they were profoundly influenced by the big and small lessons that this period of cultural and social change created. As participants, they experienced many of those lessons as they journeyed through the public educational system in their local communities.

Year after year, as they progressed through school, both change and continuity became salient features of their educational experiences. Moving from childhood to adolescence, change and continuity were essential to how and what they learned. Children learn from their relationships with others, and through their interactions they come to know their own humanity. Like all children, the women learned by listening, watching, and doing, and they could not avoid the messages received; what was communicated was essential to their educational experiences. As they learned, they engaged recurring patterns of interactions that would once again introduce tensions, dilemmas, and contradictions that shaped how they viewed themselves, especially as students. For their school environments conveyed mixed messages: they were expected to excel, and they were also expected to fail. This chapter continues to examine the women's ever-emerging sense of self as they engaged new childhood relationships, expectations, demands, and responsibilities that would shape how and what they learned in the process of living.

YOU MUST GO TO SCHOOL

In 1954, racial segregation was legally abolished under law in public education. As children, some of the women attended segregated public schools throughout the decade of the 1950s and well into the 1960s. Several did, however, attend "integrated" public schools where they were a small minority among the predominantly white student body. Whether they attended segregated or "integrated" schools, the daughters understood early in their lives that they were expected to go to school and obtain at least a high school diploma. Education was seen by their parents as a way of mitigating some of the harsh realities of racial oppression, and once obtained it was thought to be something that could never be taken away from their daughters.

One household rule in common for all the daughters was regular school attendance. This was especially true for Anne, whose father was the first black school principal in the small northeastern town in which she grew up, and her mother, a professional social worker by training, taught on occasions as a substitute. Both of Anne's parents received master of arts degrees from different historically black colleges in the South. In fact, her parents met while attending graduate school and married prior to moving north. Anne was the oldest of four girls, and later she had a brother who was nine years younger. As the oldest girl, she knew that her parents had high educational expectations for her and assumed that she would obtain at least their level of academic achievement. For Anne, "being the oldest meant setting an example for my sisters to follow."

With the start of school, Anne and all the women acquired a new identity: they became students. This meant they had to learn a new role and status; they had to conform to new codes of conduct that emphasized order and obedience; and they had to learn that unchallenged authority was vested in the hands of teachers and school administrators. In their highly structured school environment some of the women eagerly took to learning and adjusted accordingly. For others this environment proved difficult to navigate, and they experienced problems early on in adjusting to the elaborate and often rigid rules of conformity. As a result, some found formal learning difficult and gradually began to lose their initial enthusiasm for required learning as early as elementary school.

Although Anne lived in a black community, her parents fought for her to attend an "integrated" public elementary school, and in the first grade Anne discovered that she virtually constituted the integration, especially in her class: "I went through the whole day being the only black child in class," but "I never felt different because of race." However, Anne did have a strong sense of feeling different: "I felt different because of my left handedness." She talks about how painful it was in her attempts to conform to the established cultural preference for right-handedness. She said, "In the beginning I thought it was bad to be left-handed that it was derogatory and close to evil spirits." Her white first grade teacher confirmed this perception. The school desks did not accommodate Anne's left-handedness, so her teacher would send her to the blackboard to practice her penmanship, whereas "she would put the chalk in my right hand, and I spent all of my time in the penmanship exercises at the black board being the focal point for all the class to see, and as somebody who wanted to evaporate into the woodwork. I didn't want to be on view; I didn't want to be observed. I didn't want to be out there. It was breath taking. It was overwhelming." Anne did not receive "good grades" and was "left back," which resulted in her sister who was a year younger being placed in the same first grade class; they went from elementary through high school together always in the same grade, and often they were the only black girls in the same class. In addition to the jealousy and competition that gradually developed between the sisters, Anne also carried a "heavy" sense of her parents' disappointment, and with maturity these feelings grew more pronounced.

Sharon's experiences were similar to those of Anne. Both of Sharon's parents' also received master of arts degrees from historically black colleges in the South: her father was the valedictorian of his graduate class with a degree in business; her mother graduated from college when she was eighteen years old, and in addition to a bachelor of arts degree she later received a master's in zoology. On reflection, Sharon described her parents: "they were like geniuses with no common sense." But she recognized that "back in 1943, their accomplishments were pretty much unheard of." While both of her parents pursued graduate education they got married and upon graduating from college moved north. They settled in a medium-sized predominately white midwestern town. The oldest of the three children, Sharon grew up with two younger brothers, and recalls that "there was only about 2,000 blacks out of about 75,000 whites" living in her hometown. Sharon said "we were the only black family living in an integrated neighborhood, our neighbors were all white, even with all of things going on in the South there was never a question about going to an integrated school."

Sharon's father worked for the government, and she saw him as the primary provider of the family. Her mother also worked occasionally as a substitute teacher, but essentially she took care of the children and the household. Sharon remembers: "My mother stayed home and doted on me. Even though she had all of this education, she had time to slipcover the sofa and go into the basement and develop pictures, and grow all sorts of plants and know what they all were. I guess I was used to my mother always being there, because when I came home from school she was always home taking care of things." On entering elementary school, Sharon and the other women learned early on that the structural arrangements under which they interacted as students during the schoolday was nonnegotiable. Teachers, in particular, could impose their will on students' academic lives because they possessed a unique authority that is all their own in the confine of the classroom. They could foster a creative learning environment that respects and facilitates the intellectual growth, development, and dignity of children; or they could be mean and cruel, and construct barriers and obstacles for learning where children's confidence in themselves could collapse under the weight. Several of the women's mothers knew this and kept a watchful eye on what was happening at their daughters' school.

Usually the mothers monitored their daughters' educational progress, especially during the early years. And whether the mothers were working or not, all the women said that their mothers took an active interest in their early education and to varying degrees participated in school activities. Sharon's mother was active in the Parent/Teacher Association (PTA); she used this involvement as a way to get to know Sharon's teachers, but it was also her way of keeping an eye on what was going on in the school itself. In her "integrated" but overwhelmingly white public school, Sharon was often the only black child in class. But unlike Anne's recollection, Sharon remembers being treated differently because of her race. Sharon recalled one of many early incidents she experienced: "The week that I should have won the prize for spelling the teacher canceled the prize. I guess she didn't want to give it to a black child. Of course my mother went to my school and caused a big stink about it. I know some of the teachers didn't like having a little black kid in their class in the middle 50s. There were no black teachers in our school. I did feel different. I felt that I wanted to fit in, and maybe white is better than black."

Similar to the mothers whose children attended mostly white public schools, those whose daughters went to all-black public schools also took an active interest in their children's early education. On occasions, they too visited the school, especially if they perceived that their daughter was mistreated in some way. Patricia remembers the precise moment that she began to lose confidence in herself as a student. As a second grader, her black teacher slapped her in the face so hard that she had difficulty in seeing. For Patricia, this experience was "one of my first early lessons" in dealing with authority figures outside of the home. In describing this incident, she said:

> I enjoyed school. I enjoyed the reading, absolutely loved reading. But this brings me to my second grade teacher. I loved reading, and I will never ever forget, we were all supposed to read a certain page. And she said "don't go past that page." She said, "Read it silently, and when everybody is done we will discuss that page and move on to the next one." Well, I read the page, and I was already done, and I just got tired of reading the same page over and over again. So what I did, I turned the page, but I kept my hand on the page where we were supposed to be at, and I'm reading the rest of the book. The teacher was walking around the class to see how we were getting along, and if you were having difficulties she would help you. The next thing I knew she was standing next to me. And at six years old all adults looked like giants, especially when I was sitting down. She was a black woman. She said to me, "Why are you not on that page?" And I said, "I'm keeping the page, I just read it, and I've read it so many times that I just started reading the other pages." Then she said aloud to the class, "Class didn't I tell you to read only this page?" And the next thing I knew that woman slapped me so hard I couldn't see. She slapped me in my face. All I remember was crying. I don't remember anything else other than that.

Following this slapping incident, Patricia said that she developed a rash all over her body and became too ill to attend school. She knew that she "didn't want to go back to school after that. At that point I didn't say anything to my mother because kids got the understanding that all adults were right, and this was a figure of authority, so what chance did I have." Finally, Patricia told her mother about the slap. In defense of her daughter, Patricia's mother went to her school and "let this woman know in no uncertain terms that if she every laid her hands on me again, the principle, police and no one else was going to be able to keep her off of her."

Like Patricia, several women recalled incidents when they were hit by their teachers, especially during their elementary school years. For those who experienced physical punishment at school, intuitively they understood that there was a difference between being hit by their mothers and being hit by teachers. Even though the meaning behind the physical punishment they received both at home and in school may appear similar—to punish unruly behavior—they perceived those incidents in different ways. Not only was there a difference in who administered the punishment and how it was administered, but the circumstances under which it was administered were also different. For some, the punishment they received in school affected not only how they viewed themselves as students but also their school performance.

As Patricia's experience suggest, sometimes their teachers' actions created a deep sense of violation. It is not necessarily the physical pain that resulted from their teachers' violence that provoked this sense of disrespect, rather, the powerlessness that they felt, their perception of cruelty, and the humiliation they experienced by being punished in front of their childhood peers that led to the violation. Barbara describes the beatings she received from teachers as simply "horrible and humiliating." And often, she saw her mother's intervention as making matters worse. Barbara said, "My mother was a curser, and she would come to school and curse out the teachers in front of everybody. The teachers would hate me even more, and I wasn't a great student anyway." Similar to several of the women's reflections, Barbara viewed getting hit by teachers as marking the start of her disillusionment and dissatisfaction with school. As she said, "I started to really hate school, but I really hated what they did to me even more."

Even though their mothers asserted parental authority, and at times some used corporal punishment to discipline their daughters; they did not extend this privilege to their daughters' teachers. However, some mothers were placed in embarrassing situations when it came to school and the disciplining of their daughters. Several of the women's mothers were requested by administrators to come to the school and discuss their daughters' disciplinary problems. Jackie's mother or grandmother received frequent calls with requests that they come to school to discuss her bad behavior. In her all-black public elementary school, Jackie tried to conform, but she said "basically I was a rebel," who had difficulties adjusting to the rules. Describing herself as "basically bad," Jackie said:

> In school I tried to excel, and I wanted to be on the honor roll and things like that. But sometimes I was bad. My mother and grandmother were proud of me until they would get those phone calls. Like the day I tried to burn the school down. We had a lot of fire drills, and my class was on the top floor, like the sixth floor. I was tired of running down the stairs for those fire drills when there really wasn't a fire. So my logic was, if we had a real fire we would not have to keep doing this. So I set the window shades on fire. Everybody at school told on me, but it didn't make no difference because I told too. I don't even know who I got the matches from. I did a lot of little mischievous stuff, and my mother wanted to kill me.

At other times the mothers were requested to come to school because their daughters had been in a fight with another child, usually a girl. Jackie, a fighter, recalled one of several incidents in elementary school. She said "I had a bad temper":

> I realized this when I probably was in elementary school, when I had a fight with a girl in the fifth grade. I remember by the time I finished the kid was bloodied. I had bit her all in her face, punched her all up, and just dogged her. When I looked at her I just saw blood. I had no feelings, none at all. I didn't feel sorry. I was this kid that bit this girl and didn't fight fair. The teacher told my mother. My mother was not a happy camper. The kid had to get stitches in her face. I really went after her. All I remembered is her jumping up into my face. That was it. It was all over. I go for the blood.

During elementary school, several of the women continued to experience physical violence, either at the hands of teachers or with other children. But there was a noted shift in their perceptions, particularly regarding corporal punishment administered by teachers. Unlike the beatings they received from their mothers, several of the women's childhood experiences suggest that their teachers' actions resulted in violating their sense of personhood, which would impact how they viewed themselves as students. There was no discernable difference in their attitudes toward fighting; they expressed no remorse or regret over the incidents and felt justified in their actions. Several of the women like Jackie continued to have fights with other children. Yet by the time they reached junior high and high school, with the noted exception of Jackie and Mary, they no longer participated or engaged in fights. Even though they had largely stopped fighting, as a general principle, none of the women were against fighting; if provoked, they continued to believe that they could give as good as or, in the case of Jackie, usually better than they got.

School Is Not Fair

By the time the women reached junior high school, they all recalled at least one favorite teacher, but generally they did not view their school environments as either nurturing or supportive. They described themselves as either average or good students. On reflection, they acknowledged that they could have been better students. Several admitted that, by junior high, they had lost their enthusiasm for formal learning. As they progressed through school, some grew increasingly aware that they were being sorted, and according to some criteria—stated and unstated— they were assigned specific courses of study and specific roles to play in extracurriculum activities. Their experiences suggest that inherent in the sorting they experienced were gender, race, and class biases. This sorting was induced by the education system, rested on the individual proclivities of teachers, or combined both approaches. During this sorting, there were times when the women as students received uneven rewards and punishments that played a significant role in their enthusiasm for learning.

Several of the women were initially introduced to a process of sorting through a gender specific curriculum that made distinctions between boy classes and girl classes, which formally reproduced gender roles and expectations. They found constraints placed on their educational experiences simply because they were girls. Gradually, as children some of the women developed resentment and anger at being sorted by gender, which affected their school performance. Patricia's attitude toward school started to change as she entered junior high school with mostly black and Latino students. She said "what I viewed as the unfairness of being a girl hit me when I started the seventh grade, in terms of the can-dos and the cant-dos because you're a female." In junior high school, she remembers that girls sat on one side of the classroom while boys sat on the other side; from her perception the boys seemed to receive more attention from the teachers. She also remembers the different class requirements and rules for girls.

> We couldn't understand why there were different rules for girls. We had to take a home making class—the females had to take the millinery class. Millinery is making hats and sewing and all that kind of stuff. It was like a joke, really. I tried to explain to them that you got the wrong female in this class, but all females had to take it. And of course the hat was a disaster, but at least you had to make an attempt to pass the class. Cooking was another thing. While I had no problem with the cooking class, we had problems with a specific teacher. She was an elderly black woman, and the woman was crazy. She could cook like nobody's business, but she was totally out of her mind. I guess she was coming from some good place somewhere within her because she was bound and determined that we had to know how to set a table properly. Being a youngster at the time, you figure that using a fork, a spoon, and a knife, you know; let's sit down and eat. She would go through this whole ritual using all of these different forks and knives. She would also teach you how to cook. She viewed me as defiant. Well, I guess there was some truth to that. I want say that she was totally wrong. I said I've had it. I can't take it anymore. And she told me to get out of her class. I got the largest red D on my report card from her. I also attempted to play basketball with the other girls. But I honestly found the rules stupid. In guys basketball you could dribble all you want, but in girls basketball you had to bounce the ball three times and then you had to pass. It was just a waste of time. So I ended up playing volleyball since there were no boy/girl rules for that.

Patricia also began to realize that within her junior high school students were also sorted according to the complexion of their skin. She noticed that subtle distinctions were made based on skin complexion that were also constraining. These distinctions were often not voiced but rather conveyed through some of her teachers' actions. Because of her dark skin, Patricia said that "you knew that you were not able to do certain things. I did get a sense of prejudice. It manifested itself in school plays, for example. You would try out for the plays, but either a very white looking Spanish girl with long straight hair or a fair-skinned black girl would get chosen for particular parts. The darker kids would get chosen for background kind of stuff, or help with staging. You couldn't actually prove this was happening, but you just knew it."

At her all-black junior high school, Barbara also experienced color prejudice, but she sensed that it was strongly linked to class bias. For her, being dark complexioned and coming from a poor family were inseparable in shaping not only her perceptions but also her experience. Of her junior high school experience, she said:

> At my school they had the meanest teachers in the world; they were mean and cruel. The teachers wouldn't encourage me to excel. They just assumed, especially in my time, that you would get out of school, get married and have kids. Or just have a kid. It was never about career. I had racial stuff from black teachers who were very judgmental, and there were color lines. But they were mainly judgmental because of the fact that I was poor. I always felt that I was different. I always felt less than. I never liked school; it was something that I just hated.

The issue of fairness and the unevenness of rewards and punishment as articulated in the different ways she was sorted grew increasingly complex for Barbara during her preteen years. Because of her father's interest in and love of music, Barbara and her sister attended a private predominantly white music school on weekends. As she said, "I went to the music school in addition to going to regular school. I went from the time I was twelve until I got out of high school. I went for years. It was a part of my life." As a result of this dual educational experience, Barbara found herself in a unique position; she could and did compare her experiences of attending a predominantly black public school to those of attending a predominantly white private music school. She said her music school experience "truly affected my life because I was put around totally different kinds of people that I wouldn't have been around if I would have just stayed in the ghetto area that I lived in." At the private music school, Barbara noticed a difference in her teachers' attitudes toward her, and this difference was important to how she saw herself: "My teachers at the music school were totally different. I guess they were what you call liberals. The white teachers I had were nicer; they were more receptive to me; I was more accepted. I was like in two different worlds. I would go from one extreme to another. I would be around black teachers and I was like not good enough, and I would get around whites, and it was like she's this and she's that. The first time that I was ever told that I was attractive came from a white person at the music school." Barbara perceived her experience at the music school as better than her experience at her all-black public school. Yet her experience at the music school was not unproblematic or uncomplicated; although she did not encounter color or gender prejudices, she did experienced race and class biases that had become familiar to her. Barbara's family could not afford to pay the private tuition of the music school, but because of her father's blindness and her mother's meager income she and her sister received tuition waivers. However, they were expected to work at the school as a way of defraying some of the cost of their studies. In doing her job, Barbara was ever-mindful of the fact that her mother worked as a domestic worker.

> I worked outside the home in a sense that I worked at the music school. I had to clean the toilets, like cleaning all of the bathrooms. That's when I knew I was different. I was treated differently than the other students. My sister didn't have to do that; she was like a receptionist. But all the black students had to do those jobs. I started to notice that all blacks at the school had menial jobs, and of course at that particular time I knew I was black too. I kind of resented that. After you finished your job, the headmistress of the school would give you your carfare, and you would have to go and ask her for it. I didn't want charity. I couldn't ask for it. I just hated it. It represented poverty to me. I couldn't go and ask her for carfare. So I used to walk home. I would say, oh God I got to walk all the way home. But I just couldn't ask, so I walked home.

Similar to Barbara's experience, all the women remembered many school-based incidents in junior high where they perceived unfair and uneven treatment. For some, their perceptions of being treated unfairly took on an added dimension when it came to their interactions with boys, experiences they described as insulting, humiliating, and degrading. Amanda, for instance, vividly remembers her experience of integrating a formerly all-boys junior high school, and the teachers' tolerance of boys' bad behavior toward girls. She describes this three-year educational experience as "horrendous": "we were being felt on and molested every time we walked in the hallway; we told the teachers, but they did absolutely nothing to stop them. That whole three-year experience was awful, truly awful." Anne said that her "more difficult times at school were in trying to establish relationships on a personal level with boys." She talks about the time when a boy "tripped me and I fell down a fight of wooden stairs hurting myself." Patricia vividly recalls one of her most humiliating experiences—"nobody wanted to take me to the junior high school prom." Remembering what happened, Patricia said, "My mother convinced me to go and bought a little tiara that you put on your head. As I'm coming down the steps, a very attractive light-skinned fella was coming by. And I'm coming down the steps and I'm thinking for once my mother is telling me that I'm beautiful and I'm believing it. As I walked down the steps and get ready to turn right this boy looks at me. He looks at me with such disgust and disdain. That just did it. It ruined the whole thing. I didn't tell anybody about this for a long time because I was really, really hurt. I felt ashamed and humiliated."

As in the case of Patricia, all of the women remembered instances where they were shamed and humiliated, as they saw themselves in the eyes of others; and what they saw was their worthlessness as perceived by others. Generally, they interpreted those situations as not "being good enough." They were powerless to control the perceptions and images that others had of them; and those perceptions and images affected how they viewed themselves.

They were also powerless to change the institutional arrangements under which they were educated; the authority teachers had over them; or even the privileges that were assumed by boys. In other words, increasingly as children the women learned that they were powerless to change the circumstances that shaped the unevenness of their experiences. They also learned that if they openly rebelled, resisted, or challenged the lack of fair play in some unacceptable way they faced the possibility of punishment. In junior high school the possibility of receiving physical punishment by teachers had diminished. But several of the women found that other forms of punishment—such as being labeled a troublemaker, placed in detention, or expelled from school—could exacerbate their experiences and deepen the sense of violation they felt as a result.

These forms of punishment, more personal in nature, were experienced as disrespect or disregard to their individual self-worth. As a result, some of the women were beginning to develop a growing sense of personal inadequacy that created self-doubts about their academic ability to achieve and undermined the feeling of what they could accomplish in their lives. Their sense of "not being good enough" was becoming manifested in a growing frustration and anger, which was acted out in many different ways. Several of the women, like Barbara, discussed their developing anger this during period, but they did not identify or connect the cause of that anger to their educational experience or to another similar source. They just knew that they were angry during this period. Barbara was unable to explain her growing anger, but its presence was reflected in her actions: "I must have been about twelve or thirteen years old at the time. I was enraged. I didn't know why. But I would go in the basement, and I would just clean all night long. That was the only way I could get rid of the anger. I would be up all night, and if I didn't clean in the basement, I would go to the attic, and I would clean. I had to get rid of the rage. I just didn't sit there and be angry—I had to do something. But I didn't know where the anger was coming from." Similar to Barbara, several of the women did not necessarily accept the constraints imposed on them during junior high school. But they all acquiesced and complied nevertheless, and as a result several took their simmering anger and sense of violation in stride as they moved into adolescence.

INEQUALITIES

As the women entered high school, several experienced the process of school desegregation, and the racial politics of the period became a focal point for how they interpreted their educational experiences. Increasingly, they were beginning to internalize the connection of their own individual lives with what was happening to other blacks on the broader political landscape. They were beginning to understand that the unevenness of the rewards and punishment they experienced was not simply associated with a lack of fair play. Rather, they were beginning to understand the scope of racial discrimination. And in realizing this, they could see that their educational experiences were not uniquely their own, but extended to other similarly positioned students as well.

Attending a newly desegregated public high school, early on Patricia knew that she and students that looked like her were unwelcome. She said, "The high school I attended was forced to integrate. It had been strictly white. But early on you got the knowledge that you're not wanted and they didn't want black students there. We were in a school in a neighborhood where there was nothing but white folks. And you knew that you came to school, and you got on the bus and went home. That way you wouldn't have too much trouble."

Up until high school, Patricia, like several of the women, had limited contact with whites and viewed them basically as "background people" in their lives. However, this perception changed with more direct contact through school desegregation. Patricia said, "In the beginning I just saw the teachers as teachers, in high school I began to see them as white people, and I began to interact with them differently. They were still sort of like background people to me, but they were white people. I began to realize—something began to become aware in me—that these were white people that were teachers, that they had power over me other than being a teacher because they were white people." Patricia elaborated, "This was rooted in the images I was beginning to see, the demonstrations and marches and news reports. Things began to take on a whole new outlook for me. I saw them as individuals who had authority in terms of being a teacher. But then because of the color of their skin and the texture of their hair, I began to really see them as a part of another that was not connected with me and mine. Because of that, whatever they said or did not say, could, in fact, affect my life on some level."

While attending her desegregated high school, Patricia's sense of "not being good enough" deepened, and gradually she began to think that she was not "college material." This idea crystallized as Patricia interpreted the complicated mixed messages she received from her white teachers: "They gave you the impression that they were caring and wanted to see you succeed, but at the same time, without you realizing it, they were telling you that you were not good enough. It's like no matter how hard you worked, you weren't really good enough, even though they tried not to give that impression. You had to almost be extraordinarily exceptional to get their attention, in order to get, not approval, but a sense of encouragement." Patricia reflected on the powerful dynamics:

There were obviously many black kids in there that this didn't work on, and there were some that it did work on. It worked on me. I'm ashamed to say. But at that point in time it did. When I got to high school, I was doing well in my classes; I had at least a B average. And I kept getting the feeling, the energy, that somehow I just wasn't good enough. Some part of me I guess began to accept it. So then I began to look around at what kind of jobs I could do—I was into reality here; I'm black; I got to deal with this. What kind of a job would I be able to get when I got out of school? When I looked around, I knew that I didn't want to be a nurse. Even at that time they weren't hiring many black receptionists, so even that was out for me. The typical job that black females could get was teaching, and I didn't want to be a teacher. I didn't want to be a nurse. So then there was secretarial left. So I put it in my head, well, if I get the proper training to get secretarial skills, that's a job I can always get. Somebody, somewhere, will always need a secretary. That's how I rationalized it in my head.

Patricia was placed in the "commercial" academic track at her high school, where she focused on developing secretarial skills. Even though Patricia said she made the decision to concentrate on secretarial training, she was sorted and academically tracked by the school system. Her experience was not unique among the other women who went to newly desegregated high schools. Patricia, along with Jackie, Barbara, and Amanda experienced an academic sorting system with its inherent class and racial bias. Based supposedly on academic ability, this tracking system assigned students to a course of study that prepared them for their futures. In this system, they were either steered toward a path that led to college or one that supposedly prepared them for work upon completion of high school. Eventually, all the women who entered this tracking system were placed in either the "general studies" or the "commercial" tracks. They said the "academic" or college preparatory track in their schools was mostly composed of white students.

Amanda was a "pretty good student until I got to high school. But then that's when I got angry." Amanda "got angry" because she felt that black and Latino students were treated differently from the white students. For her, this difference was revealed in the tracking system;

Amanda believed that students were tracked according to race and ethnicity, rather than academic ability.

> At that time they used to track you. And they had an academic track
> for those who were supposed to be going to college, a general stud-
> ies and a commercial track for those who were like going to be sec-
> retaries or go into business. I was supposed to be in the academic
> track, and the general population was divided into these other two
> tracks. And, of course, most of the blacks and Latinos were in the
> general studies and the commercial tracks. There was a general re-
> sentment that those of us who were black should not have been at
> the school, we got this even from this woman who was supposed to
> be our guidance counselor and our English teacher who was black,
> and one of the few black teachers in the school.

Amanda was placed in the college preparatory or honors academic track
during her freshman, sophomore, and part of her junior years of high
school. "Then my grades did not stay up to a 3.0 average. You had to be
in the honor society, so your grade point had to be 3.0. And when I went
into the general studies track I sort of had the attitude that I didn't care.
I just wanted to get out of school. By that time, I'm like, I will just go to
school, and I'm just doing what I have to do. I just sort of lost my enthusiasm." Yet, Amanda still wanted to go to college. But her black guidance counselor, one of the few blacks who worked at her school,
attempted to persuade her against going to college. She told Amanda that
if she insisted on going to college, she should go at night. But she
strongly encouraged Amanda to think about working after graduation for
an insurance company, where she could make "as much as forty dollars a
week."

There was no academic tracking system at Faith's high school. She
attended a private "integrated" high school up North. In 1963, almost
ten years following the Supreme Court ruling on *Brown v. the Board of
Education*, Faith's southern hometown started the process of desegregat-
ing the public school system. As a teacher, Faith's mother had concerns
about how Faith would be treated in this process of desegregation. Faith
discussed her mother's attitude: "My mother didn't want me to go somewhere where people didn't speak to me all day." Her mother decided to
send Faith away to a Quaker school up North because of "their liberal

reputation in terms of race, and she felt that I would be welcome." Faith recalled her arrival at her new high school:

> I remember that they had said that the school was integrated. And I remembered getting there and looking around, and there were four of us, and that just really did not seem like integrated to me. There were four black students—three boys and me—and there were 450 students all together. Three of us were freshmen, and one was a sophomore. One was a day student. He did not live there. He was the one who was sort of wild and his mom worked at the school. I don't think that she was a professional; I think that she may have worked in the cafeteria. There was this other one. He was brown and pretty-boy kind of fine. I think that his family had a little money. And then there was the sophomore. He was a real bookworm, you know, he was bookish, and he looked bookish. And there was me.

Having come from a largely all-black southern cultural environment, at fifteen years of age and an only child, Faith had to adjust both her thinking and behavior to interact in her new high school environment, and at first it proved difficult for her to navigate. She described the situation:

> The first year I had two roommates, and I didn't get along with them my freshman year. One of them had had mononucleosis the summer before, and she wasn't completely well when she came to school. The other one was a really rich kind of farm girl from Texas. But neither one of them was anything at all like me. The first year I had to get used to not being able to use everything that was in my room because it wasn't mine. I had never had any sense of that. I mean anything that was in my house, I could use. It took me awhile to learn that if I was out of something that I needed to ask you if I could use it. That was a big complaint that the farm girl had about me. We didn't argue, which was another thing that I didn't understand. Rather than saying something to me, she would go and talk to the dean. That was a whole new experience for me. So the dean of women and I did not get along at all. She would call me in to talk about it. She was telling me about this girl and saying "I didn't ask to use her things." I don't know why I was so offended by that, but I know that I really was offended. She told me that "I might be better

off if I would be willing to bend over, to extend myself more because so many of these girls had never met any Negroes before and that they were going to form their whole impression of Negroes from me." I remember telling her that that was really stupid because I was not forming my whole impression of white people from her, because if I did I wouldn't like any of them.

By the time Faith and the other women reached adolescence and entered high school there was a noted shift in their perceptions toward authority and conformity and about their sense of themselves. A life stance or a standpoint, was emerging based on their growing awareness of reality as shaped by their own experiences and shared by other black students. Thus, they were beginning to understand that the unevenness of their individual experiences was owing to not simply an issue of a lack of fair play, as they generally thought while in junior high school; rather, they were becoming more aware of structural inequalities, especially those attending newly desegregated high schools. And in that awareness, the differences they experienced were physical, based on their blackness; it was personal, for their individual worth was questioned by others who chose to perceive short-comings or deficiencies in their mental character; and, it was social, for black students like themselves were not valued, their academic ability was not appreciated, and their potential for achievement was never assumed within the educational system.

In their own ways, all the women linked their perceptions of racial discrimination during high school to their understanding of violence. But it was not physical violence that inflicted harm and injury. More important, racial discrimination was often experienced as "not being good enough." However, in the complicated dynamics of their individual as well as their collective educational experiences, two different reactions to their experiences of racial discrimination are evident. As individuals, several of the women believed that "there was nothing you could do about what was happening," as Amanda said. Given their general sense of powerlessness in the face of academic constraints, Patricia said "you just start to feel irrelevant. You feel that you're invisible." Academically, they all accepted the reality that the educational system imposed on their lives.

However, politically they began to realize that they did not have to accept racial discrimination. In their attempts to make themselves "relevant" and "visible," several of the women joined with other black students in protest, as they sought recognition and inclusion into their school culture. This protest occurred mainly over extracurricular activities in their schools, and unlike their personal response to racial discrimination, they learned that collective action could produce change and that they were not completely powerless. Several of the women recalled their attempts to get black girls elected as homecoming queen, placed on the cheerleading squad, or get blacks elected to student government or included on the staff of the student newspaper. These and other collective actions that they remember are not seen by the women as merely the acts of teenage rebellion. Rather, they connected the demands for change in their high schools as forms of protest that was linked to the larger black struggle for social justice and racial equality.

LESSONS OF LIFE

As the women learned the many lessons that formal education offered, simultaneously they were learning lessons outside of school that also shaped their development in the process toward becoming young adults. There was an important interplay between their schools, homes, neighborhoods, communities, and the environments of the larger white society. By their preteen years, as they developed greater independence and maturity, the women actively participated in the process of defining themselves. They had a fluid definition of self; but this fluidity occurred within the changing social and cultural expectations that continued to be imposed upon them as girls, Colored girls, and Negro girls. Increasingly the meaning of their identities grew more complex as they found that independence and maturity carried greater cultural and social responsibility.

As they entered their preteen and teenage years, some of the women continued to rely on their own mothers and other mothers for guidance, and several believed that they could talk to their mothers about anything, except discussions of sex and sexuality. For this, their learning was largely dependent on curiosity, female peers, and experience. In some of the women's experiences, this learning also occurred through what they saw happening to other young females. This was the case for Mary.

Initially Mary and her two younger siblings lived with thirteen aunts and uncles at her maternal grandparents' house in the rural south. Mary saw her relationships with her parents as "sort of estranged": she would see her mother "maybe once or twice a year" because "she was always away working with white families." Her mother was a live-in domestic worker. And Mary saw her father even less because for years he was in the army, and when he was on leave he would usually "go to the town my mother was working in so I didn't see him." Until the age of twelve, Mary was raised by her grandparents.

Mary describes a close relationship with her grandmother, and in fact she called her "mama." She said her grandmother "taught me stuff like ethics, morals, religions and spirituality in terms of my development." But her grandmother also taught Mary "to always tell her if anybody touched my body." Mary heeded this warning when "grandpa would ask me to pull down my panties and I knew I wasn't supposed to," and she told her grandmother. However, Mary's young aunt, who was almost a year older than Mary, was unable to stop her father's sexual advances. Thus, as a child, Mary found out about the meaning of sex and the damaging effects of sexual abuse from her young aunt's experience: her father "molested" his youngest daughter, and she became pregnant as a result. Mary considered her aunt as a sister; they were close not only in age but also in emotion. Her aunt's experience of sexual abuse and her family's response traumatized Mary. Mary's stuttering became more pronounced during this period, and she continues to have strong emotional ties to what happened to her aunt. Mary explained:

> I guess my aunt was thirteen when she got pregnant. She got pregnant by my grandfather. He used to take her down to the basement and molest her. She tried to say that this baby was by this real dark boy from across town that used to like her. But when the baby was born it looked just like my grandfather. So we all knew that it was his then. That's when my grandmother put her out, her youngest daughter. I think she shipped my aunt off to Texas because we had family that had moved there. This placed a tremendous strain on the family because of the exposure and the lies. Mama told grandpa he had to leave. It's hard to talk about even now. I started to stutter more; that's how it affected me. I didn't understand having to ship her away. I started to stutter worse than I did before. We were real close, and she was eleven months older than me. I wasn't aware that my grandfather was bothering her; she never confided in me. The

family in Texas took care of the baby, but he got killed some years back. My aunt was never right after that. And it's hard to talk about now, but my aunt started drinking when she left . . . she just died.

Soon after her grandfather and aunt were forced to leave, Mary's mother returned, and they too moved to another house. Mary's mother continued to work as a live-in domestic worker and was gone for long periods of time. At the age of twelve, Mary also found out what responsibility meant. She found herself in charge of a family and responsible for young children. In addition to her two younger siblings, whom she lived with at her grandparents' house, Mary was eventually responsible for four other siblings because "my mother would have these children and then she would disappear." In talking about this period in her life, Mary said:

> We moved into this house. My mother called herself living there until it was time for her to go on her job. Certain times of the year she would be at home and stay for about three months, and certain times she would have to go other places and stay. That's when my mother would have the kids and then disappear. She would just like have them, deposit them, and off she would go. So it was like a lot of responsibility on me. At twelve is when I moved across town to be in charge of the house. I just thought that the kids had to be taken care of. My favorite uncle on my father's side would be there at night when my mother was away. Only three of us are by my father, and the other four are not by him. So my father had a son and another daughter by my mother, but in between my mother would have other kids.

Mary saw herself as the primary caretaker for her younger siblings and figured out how to provide for their immediate well-being:

> I watched how my grandmother dealt with my sisters and brothers. I would watch how she did things, so that's how I knew what to do. I would be responsible for breakfast, lunch, and dinner. We took our lunch to school and ate our sandwiches there. If the kids weren't school age by that time, which they were not, they would be shoveled off to my grandmother. I was responsible for the cleaning of the house. I would also be responsible for the cooking, and if we didn't have what I needed I would also have to go out and pull some corn

from somebody's garden. And anything I needed I could get right there at my fingertips if I didn't have it in the house. I also did babysitting for the white folks. I was babysitting and ironing their clothes. See you get one set of fees for ironing and another set for babysitting. I got used to taking care of the kids, changing their diaper, and feeding them, and doing whatever had to be done.

In assuming major responsibility for her family, Mary's experience was not that far removed from several of the other women's experiences. With the exception of Faith and Patricia, the other women were also the oldest among their siblings. During their preteen and early teenage years, several of the women's parents had what Barbara called "a second set of children." This "second family" altered the usual sibling relationship. For whatever reasons at times the women found themselves fulfilling a more maternal role. It was not to the extent of Mary's experience, but they had significant responsibilities nevertheless. On reflection and to varying degrees they resented the constraints this care-giving relationship to their sibling imposed on their lives. Mary described her feelings toward her mother, "I always felt that she should take care of her own kids. So I resented her keeping having kids and just dropping them for me to raise. I resented that. But I had an obedient relationship to my mother. I was always taught to do what you are told. So I had to do it, and I just kept my mouth shut. I developed resentment only when I got older. I didn't know that I was supposed to resent it when I was a child."

Similar to Mary's experiences, several of the women lacked complete knowledge to perform the responsibilities they were expected to assume during their preteen and early teenage years. They began to rely more and more on their friends, often girlfriends, to share information about their understandings of life. But this youthful knowledge was incomplete and often inadequate. This was true in the women's attempts to understand the changes occurring, especially what their physical changes meant. Although Barbara's mother had constantly told her "the three Bs don't matched—books, boys and babies—she never told me about the period. That was something that was never discussed. It was like so secretive." Barbara had heard her girlfriends talking about "the period," but from their discussions she was not exactly clear about what it meant. Barbara recalled her first period:

I got my period when I was like ten years old. I knew about periods vaguely. I kind of knew from my girlfriends, but I didn't know what it was. I got my period, and I had such horrible cramps. My mother's friend was over, and my mother was saying, "Barbara is just getting so much better; she's washing her own clothes." But every fifteen minutes I was washing my panties because I didn't know. I said I must be dying. I would go and wash them, and I would hang them up, and then I would go back and wash them again. Finally, I told my mother, and it must have been the next day. I hear people say they were so happy when they got their period. I was very upset when I got mine. I was sick all the time. My mother would say "oh she's in there having her kittens" because I would be sick. It wasn't a joyous experience for me.

Barbara also found out about the meaning of sex from her girlfriends, she said:

I had three friends who had babies before they were like thirteen years old, so they would sit down and talk to me about sex. My mother never just sat down and talked about having babies, and having sex, and you might have a desire. She never discussed that at all. I really got that mainly from my friends who had slept with these guys. In certain ways I was so up on things, and in other ways I was just so totally out of it. I didn't know. But I did know that in Michigan at that time, social status for blacks was very important. They had like different groups. You had the low group, which was my group, then you had the middle class and those were who we called the bourgeois. I was supposed to be in that group that had a bunch of babies and all that stuff, but I was getting out of Michigan.

Even though Barbara's mother never talked to her about "having babies, and having sex, and you might have a desire," she did figure out what all of this could mean for her life. Barbara was twelve years old when her parents started to have their "second set of children," and she was happy when her baby brother came along:

I was very excited about him. He was like my kid, and he was born on my birthday too. I used to take him everywhere I went. He was like my child. My mother had said, this is your birthday present, and

I took it literally, that he was my present. I took him everywhere, and he was so adorable, and everybody loved him. But one day, I was pushing his stroller and these people said, oh isn't it a shame. Look at that little girl with that little baby, and then I stopped taking my brother out. It ended right there. I never took him any place again. I didn't want people to think that he was my kid.

Increasingly, "as a poor black girl from the ghetto," Barbara was becoming aware of the preconceived images that were imposed on her black-and-female existence. She was conscious of not becoming or not presenting herself as a stereotype and succumbing to the expectations that it engendered. Barbara also began to extend this concern to her family. After her brother was born, Barbara's parents had two more children. There were now eight people in her household. Because her family was poor and largely dependent on her mother's income as a domestic worker, given her father's blindness, Barbara resented her mother having additional children and additional mouths to be feed:

I said Ma, you got to stop having these babies. When she had the second one I said, wait a minute you can't afford another child. I said this is too expensive. I told her that. She will say now "Barbara told me not to have these last two." When she had the last girl, she had the baby at home, and my oldest sister and I delivered the baby. That was one of the worst experiences of my life. I was like I know I don't want to have no baby. I couldn't eat for months. I kept telling her, you'd better go to the hospital. I told her this all day long. I said I'm going to have a nervous breakdown. I was like a nervous wreck. I got angry at her because she didn't go to the hospital, and then all of a sudden you heard this loud pop. It was like disgusting. She had the baby, and then after the baby was born, you had to cut the cord and then all of the afterbirth. We dumped the afterbirth in the furnace. My mother relied on us. We took responsibility for the kids.

During this period, Barbara made a conscious decision not to have sex. She knew based on her girlfriends as well as her mother's experience that sex meant the possibility of getting pregnant. For Barbara getting pregnant meant not escaping poverty, which she so desperately wanted to do.

By the time the women had become teenagers, they all knew about sex and what it could mean for their lives, especially if they got pregnant. Several of the women had boyfriends during their teen years, and they all said that intimacy was limited to kissing, foreplay, or petting. This was Mary's experience with her high school boyfriend. She said "we started going out to the movies and different places that were innocent," but as their relationship continued things changed:

> He started to feel on me and I started to get urges. I started to get urges about sex. We would sit on the porch steps and he would just be familiar with me, as I called it. But that is as familiar as it got. Especially after my aunt got pregnant, I knew that if I had intercourse I would probably get pregnant. Nobody talked to you about contraception and stuff like that. I had plans for myself, and I was not going to get pregnant.

Only Patricia said that she lost her virginity while in high school. She dated one boy throughout high school and saw him as her first "true love." Patricia describes him as "sweet, nice, and very attractive. He was medium brown complexion; he had almond shaped eyes with the pretty long eyelashes; he was husky but not fat; and he was bow legged." In love, Patricia said, "I was a virgin, but I lost my virginity to him." After high school Patricia imagined that they would have a life together, but her boyfriend's mother had completely different ideas. Patricia said:

> His mother was quite upset because he hadn't brought home a light-skinned girlfriend. And she let me know in her own way that she was surprise to learn that I was his girlfriend because most of his girlfriends were very pretty and light-skinned, and dark-skinned girls were just his pals. That let me know where I stood with her. His mother assumed that I knew too much and that I could not have been a virgin. She proceeded to call my mother on the phone and told her "well you know if something happens she'll just be left holding the bag." I had never had anything sexually to do with anybody, her son was the first that I had anything to do with. I said well it's done, but now I truly regretted it. I really thought that we were going to stay together—dumb romantic. His mother was a headache, and he became too possessive and too controlling, so it ended.

Patricia's loss of virginity during adolescence is unique among the women's experiences. However, as they moved into adulthood life, they too would experience love, but also color prejudices, assumptions of promiscuity, and regrets with regards to sex and sexuality.

Outside the formal environment of their school, the women's experiences also reflected both change and continuity that embodied essential life lessons. One lesson learned was the meaning of responsibility. As they grew older, several of the women had to assume responsibilities for which they were often ill-prepared and yet still held accountable. Often, through doing, they learned how to meet those responsibilities. In addition to assuming responsibility for others, particularly siblings, they also had to assume greater responsibility for themselves, especially when it came to sex and sexuality.

As they grew older, their experiences were becoming increasingly sexualized. In the face of their mothers' silence, to a large extent, they relied upon female peers or their own understanding to shape the meaning of the changes that were occurring, not only to their physical selves but also to their personal and social selves as a result of the larger role of sex and sexuality in their lives. Absent guidance from or discussions with adults, they were nonetheless expected to know the meaning of sex and sexuality and conform in ways that were culturally and socially appropriate. In becoming aware of their sexualized self and the potential implications that it held for their futures the women assumed responsibility for their own sexuality, and with the noted exception of Patricia, they placed constraints on their own sexual behavior during adolescence.

DECISIONS

As their high school years came to an end, the women had to make important decisions about their lives: what to do next? Except for Patricia and Barbara, all the women had aspirations of attending college following their high school graduation. Some had the guidance of and relied upon the decision making of their parents, while others relied on their own judgment or sought guidance elsewhere.

Sharon graduated from high school in 1966. As she said, "I marched. I wore a cap and gown. My parents felt that my graduation was what was expected of me, and I was told where I was going to college." Following in her parents' footsteps, Sharon was told that she was going to an all–black college in the South. Sharon described how she felt about their decision at the time:

> My parents had determined that with my right upbringing, I was going to a black school, which is the way it ended up. I didn't want to go down south because of all of the stuff that was going on down there. And you would read about it, and you would see it on TV. Here you are a young girl, and you think that's what you're going to be surrounded with, all of this demonstration and everything else. I had never been on a demonstration before, but you would see the fire hoses and the dogs and the churches blowing up on TV. And I really didn't want to go down south. I thought every place you walked down south, this is what happens. I didn't know a soul down there. I cried and cried. A week later after I got there you couldn't have gotten me out of the place.

Amanda graduated from high school in 1963. She said, "I did have a sense of pride and accomplishment. The only thing that sort of stood out was when we sat there and looked at who got the students' awards, they were all white, and that was the only unpleasant part of the ceremony." Amanda's mother wanted her to attend an all-black college in the South. Amanda said, "I didn't want to go. I thought that it was too bourgeois, and I didn't want to go to a black college. I probably was influenced. We all thought that black colleges were not good." Rather than attend a black college, Amanda made a different decision:

> Continue to work and go to college at night. I worked at a city agency. It was a clerical job. And I spent most of my time partying. I didn't really concentrate on school. It was almost like a wasted year. I was frustrated because I didn't get accepted into the schools that I wanted to go to. They all turned me down. They weren't really interested in black students, I think, at the time. I just partied and went to work and school, but I didn't really do too well. So I decided that if I was going to finish school, I'd better go away. I went to the black college my mother wanted me to go to in the South.

Barbara graduated from high school in 1962. She described her resentment: "I graduated. I had this high school diploma and no skills." She was angry but attended her graduation anyway because she played in the band. Barbara was angry because "I didn't get my high school pictures." Because she felt "major anger when they [parents] couldn't afford those pictures," she took a more drastic approach:

> The next day I went and joined the Navy. I was so angry that I walked. And I was walking all around, and I saw this Navy thing, so I said I'm going to join the Navy. I joined the Navy, and on my way back home, I said to myself I'll show them. Then I was like scared, and then I forgot about it, and then the man came to my house. My mother said, "Take her if she wants to go." I didn't go. My mother said, "Look, I have taught you what I know. I've done the best that I can. Now you got to go out there and make you own way." I wanted to start my life. I came to New York when I was seventeen.

Sara graduated from high school in 1965. Her father was stationed at an army base in Germany at the time, and she graduated from high school there. She said, "They tried to make it as easy as possible for American families, so you almost felt as if you were in the United States; it was your basic American high school graduation." Sara's parents wanted her to attend the large predominately white midwestern college that they had attended and where she could also live with her grandmother while going to school: "they had it all planned out." But Sara had plans of her own, applied to an historically black college, and was accepted. Her mother and aunt had attended black colleges for short periods of time, and "they were clear that I could not go to one." But Sara insisted on going, "I don't think that I ever really stood up to them that much, but I was really clear that that was what I was going to do. It was cheap; it was like two hundred dollars a class. My grandfather gave me some money, and I got a thousand-dollar scholarship from some women's organization. But basically they and my grandfather paid for it."

Patricia "wanted to go to college, but I figured that I couldn't cut it." Patricia did not graduate from high school. She said, "I thought that I had taken all of the classes necessary for my diploma, and I found out they wanted me to go to school for another year. That just wasn't going to happen." She decided to go to night school and received her diploma 1966. Expressing her disappointments about not graduating from traditional high school, Patricia said:

I think that my mother was disappointed that I did not graduate from high school. She didn't express it that way, but I know that I had frustrated her to no end. But I did—at least I got a diploma. She felt that even if I didn't go to college, she wanted all of her kids to have a high school diploma. That's because she had never gotten hers at that point. I went on and started working. I was disappointed with myself that I didn't graduate with my class. I just wanted to be able to walk down that aisle, cap and gown, with my diploma. Didn't do it. I was disappointed in myself because I also couldn't let my mother take part in it. I could have gone and walked down the thing, but it would have been a farce. My school picture was not in the yearbook. I have my high school yearbook from the year I was supposed to graduate, but I'm not in it. Not graduating has always been a sore point with me. That I didn't just go ahead when I might have been able to have gone to college. That has always bothered me.

Jackie graduated from high school in 1965, and in rebellion to what she saw happening to other blacks, particularly those in the South, she and her "whole crew didn't stand for the pledging of allegiance [to the flag] during the graduation ceremony." But there was a time when Jackie was not sure if she would graduate. Jackie got caught running what she calls a "small racket" at her high school. Working in the attendance office, she was responsible for giving out late slips to students who were tardy: "What you need? What you want? What you got to offer?" She started charging students "three, two, and one dollars" for the various late slips, which was "a lot of money during that time." Jackie got caught and was suspended from school for her activities, and as a result "I got left back." Describing her feelings, Jackie said that she "felt like such a horrible person, that I had messed up my whole life." But she was determined to get her high school diploma and graduate with her class, so Jackie went to summer school every year and took "nine classes instead of six" during the academic year "to graduate on time." When she graduated, her new "dream was to make money. I didn't know how, but that's what I wanted to do." Jackie enrolled in a community college to try and find out how she could make money.

Anne and her sister graduated from high school in 1961, and both were accepted into college. For the sisters to attend college at the same time, Anne's parents had to divide their limited financial resources, and this division was not equal. Anne's sister was accepted at an Ivy League college, but her parents had to pay for her tuition in addition to living arrangements. Anne was accepted at a college in New York City, and although the tuition was less her parents could not contribute to her room and board, so she came to the city and lived with her grandmother while going to school.

Faith graduated from the Quaker high school in 1967, and said, "Ma was in the audience in a hat. That was really significant Ma in a hat at my graduation. I had never seen my mother so sharp. My mother was just gorgeous. I felt a sense of pride, not just that I had graduated, but I really was aware that I probably knew a whole lot more than my friends back home. And that my mother had managed to accomplish this thing for me with no money." After graduating, Faith was preparing to move to New York City to take acting classes and pursue a career in the theater. But her mother had other ideas; she decided that Faith was going to college, and in the fall of 1967 Faith was attending college in New York City.

Mary went to a small rural segregated school in the South where there were "twenty-six kids in my high school class." She graduated in 1957, with "a sense of pride. I did because it was the first stage of real accomplishment for me in life." Mary was looking forward to going to college, and "I had in mind that I wanted to be a coach: come back home and teach physical education, teach kids about hygiene and all the things that I was really involved in. That was my plan in life. Graduation was the first stage of my goal." Mary received a basketball scholarship from a small historically black college, and during the summer she worked and saved money in preparation of the fall semester. But her mother had different plans, and Mary never attended college.

With their high school diplomas in hand, the women were ready to step into adulthood life. Amanda, Patricia, and Jackie continued to live at home with their parents. But Sharon, Faith, Sara, Barbara, Mary, and Anne were on the move. Regardless of whether they stayed at home or moved away, when they turned eighteen, the women were all on a new journey, and the baggage that accompanied them was filled lessons learned in childhood.

Influenced by family structure, economic status, educational attainment, and geographical location the women's childhood experiences differed significantly from one another. But among these differences, they shared a similar perception. On reflection, they expressed a general sense of accomplishment: They had survived childhood and the experiences engendered as a result of having grown up black-and-female. Their high school diplomas marked that rite of passage. Along the way, some of their childhood experiences were more difficult and transforming than the others. Their survival depended on their ability to create a sense of self within and against cultural and social constraints that at times threatened, jeopardized, and compromised their sense of self. They succeeded in navigating the shifting boundaries and changing expectations of their childhood. In so doing, their different experiences of physical, personal, and social violence that resulted in violations and disrespect would become lasting reminders in their reflections of the important lessons learned in childhood. They carried those lessons into adulthood.

CHAPTER 3

The Worlds of Men

You should go among the menfolk and share with
them our story, so that this knowledge may hasten
their civilization, and so that they may yet be saved
from themselves.

Mules and Men,
Zora Neale Hurston

By the mid-1960s, all the women had left childhood
behind and were embarking upon a new life. By stepping into a new
role—that of an adult—they searched for what this new life and identity
would reveal. Their experiences immediately drew them into the political worlds of men. These worlds reflected the privilege and prominence
of men's thoughts, practices, and behaviors. In these worlds, the women
found that the power between black and white men and the ways it was
culturally and socially reproduced were not equivalent. Yet both worlds
exerted dominance over their lives. It was not an absolute or total dominance, for the women made their own decisions and act accordingly.
But those decisions were made within and against the cultural and social
constraints imposed on them as they engaged the political worlds of men.

Stepping into adulthood, the women's experiences demanded that
they claim a sense of self. For if they did not, they would be subsumed
by men's thoughts, practices, and behaviors in ways contrary to their
needs, interests, and aspirations. This realization was embedded in the
politics of the period. By the mid-1960s, the struggle for black social
justice was taking on a decisively different tone and tenor, in terms of
objectives and in strategies, from what the women had observed and experienced as children. Many young blacks were losing patience with
what they perceived as the gradualism of integrationist ideology and what
they saw as the passivity of nonviolence protest against racial injustices.

They envisioned a "Black liberation" largely based on economic self-sufficiency and a new sense of pride in the beauty of blackness. Voicing the political changes envisioned Stokely Carmichael, chairman of the Student Nonviolent Coordinating Committee (SNCC), popularized the slogan "Black Power" and in asserting leadership he declared that *"Every Negro is a Potential Black Man."*

During this period of political change, the women would find that their experiences defied the notion that *"Every Negro is a Potential Black Man,"* as they confronted the complexities of this political truism in the worlds of both black and white men. In this chapter the women recall their experiences as young women in search of their identity while they engaged the worlds of men. In that search they pursued the more traditional paths to adulthood. For some it was work, for others it was college, and for still others it was work, marriage, and children. As they engaged these paths, the dimensions of their new and complex identity as young adult women are woven within and against men's thoughts, practices, and behaviors.

POLITICAL IDENTITY
Part I

In their search, the women did not have to look too far, for a part of what they were seeking was right before them. With the rise of the Black Power Movement in the mid-1960s, the meaning of race, as defined both externally outside the black community and internally within it, was altered. Borne of political protest and struggle Black, rather than Colored or Negro, embodied a new level of consciousness within the black community. A self-identified "Black" identity conveyed different messages: slogans such as "say it loud, I'm Black and I'm proud," helped to "alter racist stereotypes that had always insisted black was ugly, monstrous, undesirable." Simultaneously, "militant black liberation struggle" provided critiques and challenges that chipped away at the color and caste hierarchy within the black community (hooks 1995). In this new climate of black consciousness, for the first time in their lives, the women self-identified as "Black women." Yet they would find that a name is not the person. Their subjective experiences would give significance to their particular understanding of what it means to be "Black women."

Of the mid-1960s, Patricia said, "This was my time. All of a sudden I'm hearing that black is beautiful, and I'm not even questioning it when I hear it." For most of her childhood, Patricia struggled with her self-perception and self-image, so she welcomed this changing cultural climate that celebrated blackness and readily embraced a new presentation of self that reflected this change. When she decided to wear her hair natural, in an Afro hairstyle, it was indeed a major decision because Patricia had "worn a wig for years." She started wearing a wig when "a girlfriend had put this hair straightener in my hair, and when she rinsed my hair out, all of my hair is coming out in the sink. I'm screaming and hollering, and my mother runs in the bathroom and put this big towel on my head. I take the towel off my head, and my hair is like in the towel; it came out in big patches. I wasn't completely bald, but my hair had come out in such big spots that you couldn't even comb any hair over it. I had to end up wearing a wig." Patricia discussed why she continued to wear a wig even though she no longer needed it:

> It lasted me a good number of years. But I didn't have to wear it for that long. This is how when you got a problem with your self-esteem and your image, how you can get trapped into things. The wig did look nice. It did look human, and I combed it and kept it like it was my hair. I had gotten so accustomed to it like it was a part of me, and I said Lord if I take this thing off my head now a whole other person is going to be showing up, and she no longer is going to be attractive. That was the first thing I thought, and people are going to be saying, oh my God what happened to you? So I just kept it on for a number of years.

This climate where the meaning of blackness was culturally and socially rearticulated enabled Patricia to take her wig off and replace it with a natural hairstyle, an Afro. But, as Patricia said, "Ironically my mother was the first one who questioned it. I remember my mother looking at me and just shaking her head and me telling her I'm going to wear my hair the way I was born with it. She looked at me and said, "Darling, when you were born your hair did not look like that." While dismissing her mother's criticisms, "for a number of reasons," Patricia decided to wear an Afro anyway:

> I looked around and I saw so many of my brothers and my sisters with these Afros, and to me they looked absolutely beautiful. Then developing a consciousness and being made aware of the whole thing about straightening your hair and why many of us did it. I remember Sonya Sanchez stating the absolute insanity of trying to physically look like the other when it is physically impossible. By doing that you were telling yourself that you don't like yourself, and you're denying all that came before you. I said to myself, it's about time that I accept me, and my hair for what it is. I said I got to start going around liking what I was born with, as opposed to detesting it and hiding it all the time. I wore that natural for a long time.

This new cultural climate of black consciousness gave Patricia the personal and social courage she needed to accept, appreciate, and take pleasure in her black physical self. But Patricia's self-defined political and physical transformation is by no means unique. During this period when new cultural and social identities were evolving on the landscape of black America, all the women made conscious decisions to change their perception as well as their presentation of self. In each of their decisions, what it meant to be black-and-female took on different meanings. While Patricia embraced black popular political culture as expressed by the Black Power Movement, Barbara chose to create an identity that allowed her to distance herself from blacks and this movement.

When Barbara left Michigan immediately following high school and moved to New York City, she made two fateful decisions about her life: first, she decided that she would "never date black men again;" second, she decided to live her life totally apart from black people. These decisions were deeply rooted in Barbara's childhood experience and her sense of disvalue based on color and class prejudices. That sense influenced why, how, and in what ways Barbara would recreate herself.

Barbara's first decision was inextricability linked to her first intimate adult relationship with a black man. Barbara said she met her "first love" at a dance where "he held out his hand, and I never wanted to let it go." She recalled what happened:

> I loved him. He was the first person I ever slept with. I just loved him. It was heaven, and he was it. He was going to college. I loved him, but he said "Barbara you're too dark." That's what he said, but

it didn't matter what he said. I didn't care. He was sort of like up-wardly mobile. He wanted this really high yellow girl with straight hair. That's what he wanted. He was in school, and I was a worker. I wasn't in college, and he was, and I didn't represent to him what suc-cess was. He was like this from the very beginning. I knew it when I met him, I knew what he wanted; he wanted the black American dream. Again, I was put into another situation where I had to prove myself, to say that, hey I'm a person and I'm worthy. I knew that at that particular time any black man that I met, I was going to have that same problem. I had enough reality to understand that blacks have a tendency to want to marry up; they don't want to marry down. So I just said I will try everything, everyway possible to keep this man. But things just fell apart. When he was in school, he had other girlfriends.

From the emotional scars left by the affects of color and class prejudices with which she had grown up, Barbara knew that her boyfriend would eventually reject her because she was not perceived as "upwardly mo-bile" and was dark complexioned with nappy hair. Following the "painful breakup" of this relationship, Barbara decided that she would "never see another black man again, never." As she said, "It wasn't as drastic as I thought that it would be because I really wasn't around that many black people by then." So, in her attempt to escape the sense of "always being judged," Barbara decided that not only would she distance herself from black men but that she would also "totally leave the black world."

Given the circumstances of her current life, this second decision ap-peared to be relatively easy for Barbara to make. After moving to New York City, Barbara had not developed any significant relationships with other blacks during this period. She had gotten a clerical job at an ad-vertising firm, which was all white except for her. This job and her in-teractions within it became her immediate world. Of this job, Barbara said, "I think that's when my life started." It was a "whole other life." And as she engaged this new life, Barbara changed herself, and her job at the advertisement agency was instrumental to this change.

Through work, Barbara was meeting "all kinds of people. We would go to Andy Warhol's studio. I would sit in places and say I can't believe that I'm here because I was this poor black girl from Michigan, and here I am in the midst of all these people. I totally erased my early part of life and became a completely new person." Describing who this "new person" was, Barbara said:

> I became a clone. I said, I'm going to walk like this person, I'm going to talk like that person, I'm going to eat like this person, I'm going to dress like that person. I had no identity. I lost my identity. I totally changed who I was. I became a plastic person. I only shopped at Saks. I had to have only this kind of stuff. I was just a real phony person. I became a notorious liar in terms of who I was. I was erasing poverty and adopting class and sophistication. I remember once going out to dinner, and it was like this real posh place and they had so many forks on the table that I didn't even know what to pick up. So I said, you better sit here and watch and when somebody picks up something, do that. When they ordered food, I was like mesmerized. Then I said, you better order the same thing that other person is ordering so when they start eating you will know which fork to pick up. All of that kind of stuff was really important to me. It was just so important.

As this new person in a new life that was far removed from childhood poverty and color prejudices, Barbara said, "I got involved in one relationship after another with only white men." Barbara recalled her first date with a "white guy" and the thoughts she had about dating white men exclusively:

> He was a young guy around my age. He took me to lunch at the Museum of Modern Art, and I was so uncomfortable, really uncomfortable. It was a whole cultural thing. Most of the white people I had dealt with prior to that had been at the music conservatory, but other than that my whole life was just like totally black, and everything I did was black, and I wasn't attracted to white men. I don't think that I saw the guy any more, but what I liked was the fact that this guy was introducing me to things that I had never thought of doing myself. And then from there on as I was more involved in the agency's business, I would meet other white guys, and it was the same kind of thing. It was like I was always being introduced to

things, and I always liked real smart men. It was really funny: it wasn't like I loved them, it was just the fact that they were showing me something that I had never been exposed to, and most of the black guys that I knew had not shown me these kinds of things.

Barbara's new life mainly included dating white men exclusively and "hanging out" with white friends from work. As such, she frequently visited a house in East Hampton, where she would attend big parties and go to Sunday brunches. She said, "I really didn't know who these people were." This experience added to her changing persona. But she started to develop conflicts within herself because no matter how hard she tried, she realized that she could not totally "erase" or deny her past. So Barbara found herself at the parties and at Sunday brunches thinking that "I'm like this little poor black girl; what am I doing here? That whole thing used to always bother me." Barbara found a way to cope with her ambivalence:

> What I started doing was, in order to deal with this, I started drinking. When I drank that's when I had the personality: I could talk and communicate, and I was fun. But I felt myself losing myself because of what I had done. I totally changed my whole life. I turned it upside down, and I just created who I wanted to be. This new person was very insecure. I was a performer, that's exactly what it was. In any given situation, it was sort of like, okay, it's just before it's time to go on stage, now let me get ready, and then I would change into this fun, witty person. The low self-esteem was still there because I would meet people and they would say, "You're so bright, why aren't you doing this and why aren't you doing that?" I couldn't do it because I didn't trust myself, and I was so fearful. The drinking kind of helped because if I didn't drink then I wouldn't have been able to communicate with these people. I wasn't drinking a lot at that time. I knew that I was very uncomfortable, and so I picked up the drink, and then when I picked up the drink, I was very comfortable with myself.

However, in the next chapter we explore the tensions, dilemmas, and contradictions of Barbara's new life, which made her increasingly uncomfortable with the identity she was creating. As a result, Barbara's sense of self gradually became threatened, jeopardized, and eventually compromised by this new identity. She paid a high price for the decision she made to totally distance herself from the "black world" and "pretend that things simply didn't exists by trying to find ways of escaping who I was." Aided by alcohol and later drugs, increasingly Barbara lost her own sense of value. With a growing sense of violation and disrespect, in many ways the decisions Barbara made and the actions she took became self-destructive. But, meanwhile, as she said, "at least I had a lot of fun doing it."

Unlike Barbara, Anne did not distance herself from black life. Nor did she fully embrace black political popular culture as Patricia did. Yet Anne also created a new identity for herself. Her carefully crafted identity only appeared occasionally. And similar to the intent that lay beneath Patricia and Barbara's transformation, her new identity enabled her to mask a sense of personal inadequacy, of "not being good enough."

Following high school graduation, Anne moved to New York City to attend college, where during her first year she "didn't get good grades." By describing this educational experience as "a disaster," she said, "I was really overwhelmed with the subjects that I took. It was a combination of a bad choice, very poor counseling, a very large appetite for someone else's approval, and not meeting my own needs." Added to her frustration were her parents' reactions and disappointments: "My parents were very unhappy; both of my parents had masters and me being the oldest I was expected to continue the family tradition of advanced education and set an example for the rest of the children, and being a college dropout was not acceptable to them. It became a strained relationship; it was horrible." To meet her financial needs, Anne started working full-time as a clerk at the public library, but she was frustrated by her lack of accomplishment up to that point and the low pay that came with the job.

To get away from day-to-day frustrations, Anne became more "outgoing and sociable." During this period, she was "interested in hanging out and having fun with friends. Hanging out meant that on the weekends you entertained yourself." Drinking alcohol was a part of that entertainment. Anne describes herself as a "scotch drinker," who "basically drank maybe five or six drinks a night." On these occasions Anne would "adopt this personality," which aided in masking her sense of personal inadequacy. Anne described this persona:

Ruby was the name I made up. I created this personality for me to be out with these older girlfriends on the weekend. Ruby had red hair and her last name was Brown. I had a whole rap. I had her phone number down; it was my phone number but a digit changed at the end. Ruby was confident, Ruby was very funny, Ruby was very well dressed, and she was educated. But she was also very congenial, and she was principled, and she was out with her girlfriends; she came with her girlfriends and she left with her girlfriends. She didn't go out to be picked-up. She was a full-time employed person. I would turn her on sometime in the course of the evening, probably after we ate. Some stranger would come over and start talking, and I would develop this Ruby persona to facilitate the conversation and make me feel safe without divulging who I really was. The red hair helped me make the fantasy work. So that's how she got created: she was a safety valve; she was a support, it was a big joke with my girlfriends. It wasn't done to hurt anybody, but they knew that if I had turned Ruby on it was mainly because I wasn't interested in doing anything with this guy other than have a conversation and some fun. Basically, I used Ruby as a defense mechanism.

Anne and all the women made conscious decisions to alter their physical appearances in some way. They expressed different reasons for this change. But, fundamentally, they were attempting to alter their own perception of self in ways that expressed their self-defined needs, interests, and aspirations at the time. As Patricia, Barbara, and Anne's experiences suggest, they were attempting to rid themselves of the burden that uneven gender, race, and class relations had imposed on their self-image and how they viewed themselves, especially during childhood. Underlying their attempts to loosen the grip of controlling images, they wanted to distance themselves from the sense of violation that was experienced as a result. In other words they wanted to create a persona, an identity that would enable them to feel good about themselves. The decision to change their self-perception as well as self-image appears to be self-determining. Men's thoughts, practices, and behaviors are not directly responsible for the choices the women made. But as their experiences suggest, to varying degrees, the influences of men's worlds on the decisions the women made were no less effective for being indirect.

Part II

By the mid-1960s, Sharon, Amanda, and Sara were attending historically black colleges in the South, while Faith was enrolled in a predominately white college in New York City. As they engaged academic life, in many direct ways the dominance of men's thoughts, practices, and behavior moved to the forefront of their educational experiences. When they stepped onto their respective campuses, they encountered both conservative and progressive thoughts, practices, and behaviors that often expressed competing, complimentary, and sometimes contradictory political messages in relation to each other. However, where these two seemingly disparate political tendencies appear to have found common ground—particularly on the black political landscape—was in a shared understanding of gender expectations and in the constraints placed on the different interests, aspirations, and needs of black women. In the political climate of the mid-1960s where a sense of social optimism and cultural permissiveness prevailed, black men began to assert their definitions of self. In those definitions, the meaning of black womanhood was assumed in the process. But, as the women's experiences suggest, a sense of one's own personhood is not assumed so easily, especially when the women had ideas of their own.

In 1965, Sara attended a "conservative" all-black college against her parents' wishes. Arriving on campus, to Sara's amazement she quickly discovered that she was enrolled in college that was "so backward." For instance, "you couldn't have boys in your dorm room, you couldn't have company after a certain time, you had to be home at 9:00 p.m., and you had to go to church. It was a very traditional college."

During freshmen orientation, Sara also quickly discovered "many gorgeous men," but all she wanted to do was "just look at them." Sara felt "out of touch" with black cultural life. With her father's military career, she had lived in Germany for the past three years, and prior to that time she had lived on army bases around the country; but she had never lived in a predominately black environment before. So, Sara felt ill at ease and ill-prepared to take on the challenges of black campus life. When she arrived on campus, Sara found that "there were a lot of people from New York and Philly and Chicago and DC that came to college to catch somebody, and they came to party, and they came in Cadillacs, and fur coats, and I didn't have any of that, I didn't come from any of that, I wasn't prepared for all of that. I put my jeans on and never took them off." But Sara soon realized that if she was going to fit into this new black cultural environment she had to "change myself because I was really corny": "I was so corny, and I was told that I was corny. I was so corny that people would stop in the middle of a conversation and say, 'You're a very corny person.' I had watched the Miss America Pageant, and I was talking about it with people, and I realized that I was completely out of touch with what people were talking about. I just didn't have a lot of experience. I had missed the last few years of American culture because I wasn't here. I was just very out of touch." But because of her light skin and straight hair, Sara soon discovered that she could fit in more easily if she "played yellow." Sara was invited to join one of the more elite campus sororities. She was told "you need to stop wearing those jeans because you could be a Delta girl if you get yourself together. I knew that I couldn't compete, and I didn't feel like I wanted to try. So I just didn't deal with it." As a consequence, Sara recalls that people started to make fun of her during her freshman year: "They made fun of the way I looked because I was too light and I was too corny. Yeah, it was about that thing of being too light. It would hurt my feelings, and I would pretend like it didn't matter and laugh. And my hair was long, and I cut my hair off right away. And I started cussing all the time. I started cussing right away because that kind of made it easier, and then I was cool."

Sara did develop friendships with some other female students in her freshmen class, but meeting the cultural and social expectations on campus continued to be a challenge. Sara, like her girlfriends, was a virgin:

> It was a big joke that we were all virgins. All three of us were like virgins. It was completely ridiculous. Everybody was trying to get laid. We were trying to get laid and get it over with because it was clear that we needed to get that out of the way. I was like one of the last ones. I don't think I was afraid of sex, I was afraid of losing respect, I was afraid of the consequences of what the relationship with this man is going to be about. I was afraid of losing power. I don't think that I was afraid of the sex itself. I was ready for that, but I was afraid of the consequences of sex.

A major consequence of having sex was the possibility of getting pregnant. As Sara said, "pregnancy was one of the big fears" for women on campus, and "somehow or another we would all get pregnant." Sara was becoming increasingly resentful of what she called the "bourgeois climate" on campus and how "traditional" the college was in the expectations it placed on students. But she grew especially resentful about the ways female students were treated on campus. "I felt like they treated us like we didn't have good sense and that there was something wrong with us, and they had to make us okay." And in this context, Sara recalls two "horrible" experiences that involved women that she knew getting pregnant. She remembers:

> The dean of women cried about a baby being born in the dorm. She didn't cry because this girl had this baby by herself, which was a frightening idea, but because of the shame of it. The baby and the mother both lived and were sent home, and they were a big joke on campus. They had nicknamed the baby Diploma because the mother came to college to get a diploma but that's what she went home with. It was horrible, horrible, horrible. There was a girl that died my freshman year, a white girl. There were a couple of white people I knew. There were several white people on campus, two that I knew well, and the one that died was one of them. She had an abortion and died. She bled to death. It was very shocking. It was shocking that somebody young could die. It was shocking that she bled to death, and we didn't know. All of her friends felt like I wasn't a good friend. Most of the women who even knew her felt like somehow I should've been able to help. We were all kids, but it seems like she should've said, I need help here.

Sara still thought the men on campus "looked good" but soon realized that many of them were "jive." However, she did meet "this man who was a basketball player, who I eventually became engaged to." Sara describes him as "very straight. He didn't get high. He was kind of conservative." This was Sara's first intimate adult relationship, and Sara recalled this experience:

> He liked me. Pitiful child. If they liked me, I'm like okay, let me see if it will work. He was tall, he had a Volkswagen, and he was a nice

guy, a very nice guy. Actually I slept with him, finally. He got it, and I got pregnant almost immediately, probably the first or second time I think I slept with this fool I got pregnant. I got pregnant, and he wanted to have the baby, and he was pretty conventional, too. I was going to drop out and become this mother, and it was like no way I was going to do that. It was no way that I was going to drop out and be somebody's mother, no way.

So, Sara decided to get an abortion and in her search, because abortions were illegal in the mid-1960s, she ended up going to two doctors. As she said, "I went to this black doctor, who was a horrible person. He gave me this shot, and it was supposed to make me abort, and he told me to go and carry stuff up and down the stairs, and on the way out he kicked me in my stomach. This was a very sophisticated method of abortion that we have here. I threw up, but I didn't lose the baby. After that experience I decided that I would keep the baby." Sara's boyfriend told her "no way, after you had that shot and the fool kicked you in the stomach, and now you're going to have this crooked ass baby. You should've thought of that before you took this drug." Two weeks later, Sara went to another abortionist, and she described this experience:

I went to this old white man with this heavy German accent. There was like a whole room full of tables—this was completely illegal obviously then—and it felt like there were ten or twenty people in there waiting. I wasn't in there by myself. There was a bunch of us in there having an abortion at the same time. It wasn't sterile, but it wasn't like a coat closet; it was a relatively clean place. He was doing the woman before me, and I was like watching and then he got to me. He got to me, and he hurt me, and I told him that he hurt me, and he was like "did it hurt when it went in?" He just kept saying shit like that; "I bet you were smiling then." I already felt like a horrible person. In a way it was kind of a relief because he made it so horrible, and he said all of the things out loud that I was thinking to myself. So it was sort of cathartic, I guess, in a way. I went home in a cab, and my boyfriend was playing basketball some place. So he was gone, and he was mad at me because I was having this abortion. That's when I was going to call my mom that night. I was like, why am I going to call her now and tell her I just killed your grandkid?

I had to forgive myself on some level for that because I do feel like that was a baby.

Sara thought that she was going to die after the abortion because she vividly recalled her girlfriend who had bled to death following her abortion. Sara said, "I didn't know how much blood was too much blood, so I remembered being afraid. I was cramping. The thing was to figure out how much blood is this, and is this enough blood to call somebody and let them know I've had this abortion, or can I wait it out? Because it was illegal, there was just nothing you could do really, but I seem to be okay."

A month following the abortion, Sara's boyfriend left for the Army. "He was on his way to Vietnam, and he drove his Volkswagen to basic training. He came by and I kissed him goodbye and he drove off. I called him the next morning, and he had drowned. That's like maybe a month after I had killed his child, his only child, so that was fucked up." Her boyfriend was given a military burial at Arlington National Cemetery with a twenty-one gun salute, and Sara recalls that there was a funeral immediately before her boyfriend's and one immediately following his. As she said, "It was an amazing time. People were burying boys all over that motherfucker, it was horrible."

Given the emotional trauma of the abortion and shortly thereafter the death of her fiancé Sara said, "I felt like I was going crazy." She remembers thinking that "being helpless had a certain charm and certain kind of good, but it also meant having no power at all and I couldn't stand being powerless." To deal with her growing sense of powerlessness Sara said "drugs became much more a part of my life." Sara used drugs as a way to "self-medicate" herself. It worked, but she gradually began to lose herself in the process of getting high. Recalling one of too many instances during this period where she was impaired by drugs and betraying her own sense of well being, Sara said:

> Once this guy gave me a big purple pill, and I just dropped it. I never asked what the shit was, and I hallucinated the whole day. It was great. I was a head then; I really wasn't a head before that. I just started hanging out with a whole different crowd of people, and we had a good ole time. I remember I went to a party and ended upstairs on the coats in the bedroom with this guy. I don't know what people thought, here I was supposed to be grieving over this loss of this

man, and I'm screwing this man on the coats at a party. That's how I dealt with pain and his death to a certain extent. I think what I did were a lot of sex, a lot of drugs, a lot of rock and roll, and politics.

In creating an identity that would allow her to fit in and be part of black campus life, Sara defied many cultural and social constraints that were imposed on her. In so doing, she made conscious decisions within and against those constraints that held important implications for how she viewed herself. Sara defied the color and caste hierarchy at her school, which was embedded in Greek cultural life on campus, by refusing to join a sorority. She rejected gender codes of conduct that prohibited female students especially from engaging in premarital sex. As a result of having unprotected sex, she became pregnant but refused to have a baby. She challenged legal restrictions that denied women the right to an abortion, by having an illegal abortion. And, in experiencing the grief and pain of her fiancé's death, Sara engaged in sex with a man on top of coats at a party. In her search for an identity that would accommodate her needs, interests, and aspirations she chose not to adhere to the cultural and social expectations imposed on her, which extracted a tremendous toll on Sara's sense of self. Her sense of physical, personal, and social violation as a result of these and other experiences eventually led to self-abuse. Increasingly, Sara began to "self-medicate" as a means of coping with not only her pain and frustration but also a growing sense of inadequacy and a lack of self-worth. In chapter 4, I discuss Sara, who aided by drugs and alcohol, gradually began to lose important bits and pieces of herself until she became in her own eyes a disvalued person.

Amanda shared experiences similar to those of Sara. Leaving New York City, Amanda found herself in the rural South, where she discovered that "the Klan were still marching down the main street," and "colored and white only" signs were still hanging in store windows around town. Arriving on campus, Amanda also quickly realized that her historically black college was "conservative" with strict codes of conduct for student behavior, especially that of females. Her first impression of the college was that of a "black finishing school," which required female students to bring "a black dress, pearls, and little white gloves" as part of their campus attire.

At Amanda's "conservative" black college, "there was a lot of party-ing where there was a lot of drinking, but if there were people who were like really into drugs, I wasn't a part of that." Campus life for Amanda was focused around the activities of Greek sororities and fraternities. Amanda joined the Alpha Kappa Alpha (AKA) sorority and "went over in the spring of my sophomore year." With some of her sisters, years ear-lier Amanda had gone to a ball game at the college Sara eventually at-tended, where she met up with her sorority counterparts. Amanda found a "big class" difference between the two, although they were a part of the same sorority. "Their main thing was to have green suede skirts and expensive silk blouses, and they were all daughters of doctors and lawyers." On this trip Amanda started to have ambivalent feelings toward her sorority, and said, "I liked the clothes and all that stuff, but I really didn't come from the same class background that a lot of the sisters came from."

In addition to class distinctions, another thing that Amanda grew in-creasingly uncomfortable with was the color and caste hierarchy that ex-isted in the Greek culture on campus. Amanda described this hierarchy:

> It was clear in the sororities that color was a big thing. Like the Deltas, for the most part, were all very light-skinned. The AKAs were brown. And the Zetas were very dark and supposedly very stu-dious looking, or I guess they would call them nerd now. The Kap-pas were sort of mixed, light and brown. The Alphas were mainly brown to dark, and the Omegas were all light, and their queens, if you look at a picture of the queens, they were all light. It was a color thing in terms of how men chose women; it wasn't that big a thing between the sisters themselves. There was only one person I remem-ber who made a tremendous issue out of it. She was very fair and had straight hair, and she thought that she was better than everybody else. I don't remember that tension because I had a mixture of friends, brown, black, whatever. As a matter of fact, I remember one sister that they used to call black beauty, she was very, very pretty. She was black, and very beautiful. But there was this historical thing about who would be a queen, they wouldn't even think of picking a brown-skinned queen. These were like homecoming queens, and the different fraternities would pick queens to represent their fraternity.

It really stood out in terms of how men would pick and choose women and who they thought were attractive.

In addition to Greek culture dominating campus life, Amanda found that sex played a major role as well. She said her college administration "pretended" that there was no sex occurring on campus. "It was like one of these typical hypocritical situations where you could trip over sex, but everybody pretended that it was not happening. It was going on everywhere all the time with everybody. It was like rampant." During her freshman year, Amanda vaguely recalls a young woman getting pregnant, but "toward the end of my senior year, it was almost like a fetish. Women were getting pregnant to get married." Amanda considered many of the men on campus "dogs: they would start reputations about women if they just walked past you. The next day it was like a bulletin. They were awful. And if you did sleep with them forget about it, everybody and his mother knew about it. You had to really be very careful." Amanda did become involved in a relationship with this "brother who was an Omega man," and at the end of the semester, when she returned to New York City to work a summer job, Amanda discovered that she was pregnant.

> I was using foam, which did not work, and I got pregnant. I went to the family doctor who didn't tell me that I was pregnant. Of course abortions were illegal then. He told me that I had some kind of blood clot, and he was going to help me bring it down. He gave me some injection. I bled and bled and bled, practically that whole summer. I went back to him. He keeps on giving me shots, and they weren't working, and eventually he did a D&C. I didn't realize that I was pregnant. I bought into his story. I felt that I had used protection, and maybe there was something wrong.

In one of her frequent visits to the family doctor, during an examination Amanda was sexually abused by the family doctor:

> He tried to sexually abuse me, and then I found out later from some other people how he used to do women. I remember one time that I went there, and he was supposed to be examining me, and then he kept on making comments about my breasts. Then he started fondling them, and then he bent down and actually started sucking. And I was like what are you doing? And I pushed him away. But I

didn't know any better then. He was a black doctor, and as a matter
of fact, my mother used to go to him. I didn't get sick or anything
other than the bleeding. I just took it in stride.

During this particular period, unlike the other women, Amanda did
not consciously make a decision to alter her identity in response to her
perception of self; such a decision and change would occur later. For
now, her presentation of self was a reflection of the dynamics that were
occurring in black popular political culture of the period. As such,
Amanda's experiences brought her face-to-face with the dominance of
men's thoughts, behaviors, and practices that would hold implications for
how she viewed herself. Although she was becoming increasingly aware
of and was beginning to question the significance of the cultural and
social constraints that were imposed, particularly on black women,
Amanda's experiences suggest that at times she actively participated in
and surrendered her judgment to the dominance of those constraints.

Her acquiescence was seen in Amanda's participation in Greek culture, where she recognized the unevenness of class and color relations
that structured not only campus life but also the relationship between
male and female students. Additionally, her acceptance was evident in
her experience of being pregnant: she relied on the authoritative opin-
ion of the family doctor that resulted in an illegal abortion, which was
medically coerced, and she acquiesced to his accompanying lies and succumbed to his sexual abuse. As a result of her sense of physical, personal,
and social violation, Amanda would learn. Gradually, as Amanda continued to engage cultural and social constraints, she began to determine
the meaning of her participation and relied more upon her own judgment for guidance. Later, this self-reliance would become essential to
her life as a political activist and in the shaping of her unwavering commitment to social justice.

POLITICAL WARS
Part I

During the mid-1960s, America was in the throws of an undeclared
war. On the homefront the battles were fought in cities and town across
the country. Essentially, the divergent thoughts, practices, and behaviors
of men and the uneven power that exists between them created this and

all wars. Of this war, the battles lines were drawn over economic fairness, equal opportunity, and social justice. And this war, like all wars, was violent. As a result of the calculated and uncalculated brutality that evolves in war, many lives were destroyed, for the struggles were bloody and left deep physical, personal, and social scars on the social and cultural landscape. The women found themselves in the midst of the battles and could not escape the direct as well as indirect impact the violence had on their particular lives.

Arriving at her historically all-black college, Sharon had left behind her predominately white midwestern hometown along with her parents' "strict" household rules. As she said, "I had finally gained my freedom." Initially hesitant about entering the tumultuous racial climate of the South, Sharon immediately took to her new all-black campus environment. She found objectionable, however, the rigid academic and campus rules imposed on students by the college administration. With other students Sharon joined in protest: "There were a lot of protest rallies on campus," and the first rally Sharon attended "was to get rid of rule that you had to go to chapel every morning." The students also "wanted black history classes and a change in the curriculum." Under pressure and begrudgingly, the administration conceded to the students' demands.

But the sense of hope and optimism that followed the student protests was dramatically altered during Sharon's second year at college. In her reflections, she said "the biggest thing that happened at college was when Martin Luther King was killed." Her college was located in Martin Luther King's hometown, and she recalls hearing someone "screaming and hollering King has been shot. Everybody was very upset. It was a Thursday. By Friday we had heard that his body was going to lie in state on the campus where he went to school." Sharon described her experience surrounding this event:

> The dean said that anybody who can go home, go home. So that meant that we weren't going anywhere. On Saturday afternoon they brought his body on campus, but I wouldn't go in there. I never went in there. I never saw his body. I had never been to a funeral before; I was a little sheltered child. I have seen pictures of it. There was glass over the top of the casket to keep people from touching him.

By early Sunday afternoon, the reviewing lines were snaked all around every building on campus. His funeral was on Monday, and we got out there early and got a good spot in front of the church. We saw everybody there was to see. They said that there were 200,000 people out there that day. I had never been in the presence of so many people at one time. We saw the wagon coming through the gate. Mrs. King, Bobby Kennedy was there, Jackie Kennedy was, and every politician. The crowd was very orderly, very quiet. And when Mahalia Jackson sang "Precious Lord Take My Hand," the crowd went wild. People started bursting into tears and passing out, the whole routine, Mahalia was just so fabulous. At the end of his funeral we sang "We Shall Overcome." I can't stand to sing it to this day because it reminds me; it was such an emotional moment for me when King was killed.

Like Sharon, Amanda also became a witness to Dr. Martin Luther King's brutal assassination. Prior to his death, Amanda joined with other students at her school to protest rigid academic and campus rules governing students' conduct and activities. Initially, Amanda "really liked school" but started to develop doubts when "they got rid of my favorite history professor during my freshman year." He was a young white professor who taught American history, and he talked about "what black folks were doing in that history. I was never taught that before, and they had an excellent library on black history and culture where you could read about what he was saying." But the college administration wanted to get rid of this particular teacher, and the students reacted to show their disagreement with that decision.

What happened was that he was trying to form an NAACP chapter on campus. They used some trumped-up bullshit to get rid of him, so we took over the administration building. I was more on the periphery, but I participated in the takeover. But some people got thrown out because of that. The fellow who led it got thrown out. My mother heard about it and immediately called and told me that "I wasn't sent down there to land-in, sit-in, jump-in, crawl-in, or any other kind of in. I better just pay attention to my studies." She called me, and she sent messages. Well, I listened to her, but I knew I was still going to participate in some way.

Amanda recalls several student protests on campus and viewed them as a struggle to "reject the plantation kind of mentality" that she thought the administration was imposing on campus life. The students' activism produced changes on campus, as Amanda said:

> We got the hours changed, we got the library opened later, and restrictions dropped about where we could go in town. We also changed things around: we made them get rid of the policy that we were supposed to sit in the back when white folks had cultural functions on campus. The college was the only cultural center in that whole area; there was no civic center or opera house, so the college would bring ballets, plays and all kinds of entertainment, all different cultures events to the school. And when white folks would come to the school, we were told that we were supposed to sit in the back. Of course we did not do that; we did not listen. The administration would get mad at us.

Amanda was a college senior when "Martin Luther King got killed." She remembers that "everybody was very sad," but there was no particular response by the administration to his assassination. As she said, "I don't remember anything particular that happened on campus. There was no major disruption or anything." But Amanda found out from her mother that a major disruption was occurring in Harlem. She said, "shortly after the rebellion broke out up in Harlem, I remembered thinking that black folks had run down to Wall Street to rebel; I simply couldn't imagine that black folks had just stayed in Harlem burning stuff down."

Like Sharon and Amanda, Sara recalls the change in the political atmosphere on her campus following the assassination of Dr. King. And she too remembers the collective sense of violation that was felt as a result of his death. The students at Sara's college wanted change, not only on their campus but also in the city in which it was located and the country as a whole. Although it was a "conservative black college," the political climate at Sara's college was different from the schools of Sharon and Amanda. SNCC had an active chapter on campus, and she went to meetings "a couple of times, but I felt uncomfortable." But while working at the school newspaper she got a chance to meet notable black political figures and do interviews. "So that was one way that I got to know people and got to know a little bit about the city."

Even though Sara did not actively attend political meetings on campus, she did embrace the black political climate on campus and became quite active. She recalls a "national black university conference" that was held at her college. One organizer asked Sara to be in charge of security for the conference. Sara described this experience:

> I was in charge of security, if you can imagine me. So what I did, because I knew that I couldn't do it, was asked a friend to help me. I got these guys who came back from Vietnam who were kung-fu and karate people. It was really a big deal because we were supposed to be protecting Mulani Ron Karenga, because everybody wanted to kill him, including me. These guys from the Revolutionary Action Movement were ready to kill him. They had already said they were going to kill him; they had already sold wolf tickets to people. In some cases they had shot at each other. Somebody called Ron Karenga a squeaky-voiced faggot, and so his boys were going to shoot this one and shoot that one. And I was in charge of security. It was crazy. But it was a really good conference; black students from all over the United States came. The Panthers were there, SNCC was there, the Revolutionary Action Movement, and West Us, Karenga's people. Somebody got shot, but I never did find out who shot him.

Sara also recalls when Martin Luther King got shot and how the city where she lived "blew up." She said, "James Brown was on TV telling people to stay in their houses, and so I watched James for a while, and then I went out into the streets. Somebody was having a march, and the march turned into a riot. "The National Guard was rolling through the streets in trucks and tanks, and they fired tear gas at us. I got gassed, and I got separated from the people I was with. There was a lot going on, stuff happening, and you could like just put yourself into it." Of this incident, Sara said, "I didn't feel the violence coming back at me personally from those guys in the tanks as much as I felt it was the violence of the system against me. You know, that it wasn't personal with those white guys even though they may in fact have been racist and have been more than willing to just shoot us. But I really did feel like it was the society, the institutions, the broader society that was coming at us, that was committing violence against us."

In contrast to Sharon, Amanda, and Sara's college experiences, Faith was enrolled at a predominately white "liberal" college in New York City. When she arrived on campus in 1966, Faith did not find the rigid student codes of conduct that the other women encountered upon their entry into black college life. However, Faith did find student protest. In her first semester at college, the school administration fired a black dean because he had "written articles that were very critical of Jews in the New York City public education system." The black students protested this firing by forming a daily picket line around the administration building. For Faith, these protest rallies were an opportunity to meet other black students, particularly the "brothers." As she said, "For me, who had been at the Quaker school that was primarily white just to find all of these brothers on the picket line, that's what it was for me. The rest of the girls were falling out there looking rough on the picket line, and I was there in full make-up and false eyelashes. I hadn't seen any brothers to speak of for four years, except in the summertime." And following the protest, Faith "knew everybody on campus, because the protest was such an icebreaker."

Faith also remembers that she was getting ready to take the subway train from Harlem when she heard Martin Luther King was assassinated. She said, "I had been uptown on my way downtown and people went nuts. I had never seen masses of black people out of control. They were throwing and breaking things." Once on the subway, Faith recalls that "the energy on the train was just so volatile to the point that I really wanted to get home. I really wanted to get back in the dorm because I didn't feel safe. You could just feel it. It was like a balloon getting ready to burst—the tension. The open hostility was immediately apparent to me after his death between blacks and whites." Having grown up in the South and closely followed the Civil Rights Movement, even while attending the Quaker school, Faith felt a profound disappointment over Martin Luther King's death:

I don't remember feeling angry when King got killed, as much as disappointment. I was really disappointed with white people. This was the best chance at moderation that they had. If you will kill somebody who is a man of God, I don't know how to explain it any better than that. King's politics was his politics, and he was absolutely right about the fact that you have to include all of your citizens in the growth of your country or you don't survive. I think that America was finding out that once again you just can't decide that there's a whole group of people that you're just not going to deal with, you're not going to include them in this world. Folks aren't just going to lie down and die: they're going to survive; they're going to live; they're going to take care of their children. And if you don't find a way for them to be included, then they will put upon you. King was really trying to make America understand how it was that it could function better as a whole society. He was trying to see that this country became integrated without any serious conflict. Nonviolent resistance is one thing, but now it seems that it was going to be about a much more physical kind of fight.

In the mid-1960s, student protest and the calls for cultural and social change was commonplace on college campuses across America. Initially, on many black campuses this call centered on administrative changes that would eliminate traditional student codes of conduct and restructure the academic curriculum to reflect the intellectual history, world views, and struggles of blacks on the continent of Africa and in the Diaspora. There was a similar call by black students at predominately white college campuses. But these particular calls were neither isolated nor separated from the broader calls for racial and social justice that was made beyond college campuses.

The women participated in such calls for change. They were largely drawn to protest by the desire to seek practical changes to the constraints that were affecting their immediate lives as students. As individuals they played no major or significant role in the changes that occurred on their campuses during the period. Yet as individuals who were a part of a group, their protest in unity with their fellow students was essential for forging a collective commitment to action, which could foster cultural and social change. Different circumstances influence different aspects of self-awareness in different ways. In this instance, the women's involvement in protest gave meaning to their collective sense of being; the self as individual was expressed though the self as community of people. The constraints imposed on their lives as students and the disrespect that they felt were experienced as neither a purely individual encounter nor an individual violation; rather, they understood that such constraints created a shared sense of violation for those who were similarly positioned.

Nowhere was this collective sense of violation felt more than in the political assassination of the Reverend Dr. Martin Luther King. The effects it had on a black sense of being and worth was palpable; it resonated especially throughout black society. It was manifested in frustration, disappointment, and anger that would create a deep schism in black political life. The assassination of Dr. King, as well as what was happening to other blacks during this period of violence, was a part of the women's experiences of violence and violation. Similar to childhood, the meaning engendered by racist violence whether embodied in a black female or male existence not only affected but also gave meaning to how the women viewed themselves as part of the black community.

Part II

Engaged in war at home, America was also embroiled in an undeclared war abroad. In 1963, President Kennedy stepped up America's military involvement in the war against Vietnam. In 1964, following the assassination of Kennedy, President Johnson launched a full-scale undeclared war against North Vietnam. With the 1968 election, President Nixon expanded this war by invading Cambodia and bombing Laos. By the late 1960s, antiwar protest dominated the mainstream political landscape as the destruction of Vietnamese lives was paraded on the evening television news and the count of body bags of dead American soldiers increased in the nightly news. Men were in armed conflict. During this period some of the women engaged the conflicts of this war through the experiences of male relatives and friends. Others were beginning to engage a different kind of conflict as they attempted to settle into married life. Yet both experiences produced conflicts of interests.

All the women were aware of the Vietnam War, but some were more focused on this conflict than others. At the time, Sara's father, an army officer, was stationed in Vietnam. They wrote to each other. She characterizes his letters as factual, the style "like he writes his military reports." And Sara explained to him how she felt about what he was doing in that war. Sara discussed their correspondence:

He was riding around in helicopters, and he didn't need to, he could sit in Saigon at a desk at that point. He was an artillery officer, so he would get in helicopters and fly around. My mother was hysterical. So I remember writing him a letter and telling him he could play like a little boy if he wanted too but not to tell my mother because it was unfair. He had five children, and he needed to sit his black ass down at the desk like he had good sense. I also sent him a card with a picture of a rifle with a daisy in it, and I sent him all this antiwar stuff. Jumping forward, when he died, he never really understood that my brothers and I, who were against the war, were not against him. He left all his medals to someone else, all his medals. He said that we were never interested in what he did, that we were always ashamed of him. It really hurt that he didn't know that we were proud of him, but we were very much against the war.

Echoing Sara's position, several of the other women were also against the war. They had relatives or friends who were fighting. They, too, faced the conflict of being against the war while supporting the warriors. Patricia's oldest brother went to Vietnam. He was too young to be drafted; instead, he enlisted with the Marines. Prior to his enlistment, Patricia's father had accused her mother of having an "affair with my oldest brother." Patricia "thought that was the most lowest, degrading, disgusting thing a man could say to his wife." As a result, her brother decided that he had to get away or he might end up hurting his stepfather, so he attempted to join the Marines. But he was under age at the time and needed his mother to sign his enlistment papers. Patricia described his argument to convince his mother to sign:

> My oldest brother told my mother "if you don't sign the papers, in a couple of months I will be of age, and I'm going anyway because if I stay here I'm going to kill your husband: it's as simple as that"? He said, "I can't see him abuse you anymore." Ironically, the night my brother had come in to talk to my mother about signing the papers, my father got upset because my brother did not come and talk to him about going into the service. He wanted to know why my brother didn't talk to him. He got into words with my brother and wanted to attack him, but my mother got into the middle of it.

That's when my brother said, "Ma, I got to get out of this house."
My mother realized that she might as well sign the papers.

Patricia's brother was in the Marines for four years, and he was twenty-
one years old when he returned home. She thought that he had changed
a lot as a result of his experiences. As she said, "He was always quiet. He
seemed to be even more quieter, but he needed to be around a lot of
laughter, and he was drinking. When he came back he was drinking and
drinking heavily":

> He was more intense when he came back. I used to write him a lot,
> and I would tell him about how some people felt about the war in
> Vietnam and especially about black men being over in Vietnam and
> on the front line. We lost a lot of people we knew personally to that
> war. I did try to talk to my brother about his experiences in Vietnam.
> He just explained one incident to me, and I guess because he saw the
> expression on my face he never talked about it again. I don't know if
> his drinking was tied to Vietnam or whether living under my father
> had anything to do with it. When he came back, he stayed at home
> for a while and then he got married and moved out. There was no
> way that he was going to stay in that house with my father still there.

All the women recalled men that they had known who had fought in
Vietnam. But what they remembered most was the dramatic physical and
personal changes that had occurred in the men upon their return home.
Unlike Sara and Patricia, Jackie did not have a relative who went to war.
Rather, she was engaged to a guy who fought in Vietnam. Jackie had met
him at church and shortly after their engagement he was drafted. For reasons she did not explain, Jackie never wrote to him while he was in Vietnam, but "he would write me a letter a day." Her fiancé was injured in
combat, and Jackie remembered how she found out:

> I heard that he had gotten injured from the television. He was in this
> battalion, and they said it was blown up, and there were only two
> survivors. My girlfriend and I waited until it came out in the news-
> paper. And there it was. I had called his mom, and she would not talk
> to me. She just thought that it was my fault that he went into the ser-
> vice. She was buggy like that. She was stupid. But nobody knew

nothing. We didn't hear anything for a long time. I'm like oh God he's dead, and we just lost another one.

Jackie's fiancé was not killed; he was one of the two men who had survived the battle, but he did not have his "tags and stuff because they had lost all of that, and it took a long time to identify him and let his family know what had happened." When her fiancé finally returned to the States, he was sent to a veteran's hospital in New York City for rehabilitation. Jackie said that he had been seriously injured in the attack and was not found for days. In the meantime he developed malaria:

> He had malaria so bad, it would be almost equivalent to a seizure. He would snap just like that and go into convulsions. There was no cure for it; the doctor said there was nothing they could do about that. I was there one time when he kind of flipped out. I said okay, it was nothing you could control. He stayed in the hospital a year. I would go out to the hospital every day, except for when he would come home for visits. He was glad to see me all the time. I got to know the other people while he was there. But our relationship started to dissolve before he got out of the hospital. I already knew that I was not going to marry him. That was because of his injuries. He didn't even want to get married at that point. I agreed with him. He didn't know what was going to happen to him. His seizures were uncontrollable. We hung out for a while, but then I started dating my children's father.

In fact, Jackie would marry her "children's father." Of the nine women, four were married during the 1960s. In their own ways, they all expressed the general sentiment that they "got married because it was what they were supposed to do." This is the reason why Jackie said she married a childhood friend in 1968.

In a matter-of-fact way, Jackie said, "We just went downtown to City Hall and did it." She had decided to get married "because that was a part of the American dream. I felt obligated, and I was getting old—I was nineteen or twenty." Jackie was not sure as to whether or not she "was in love." But she was sure that he was "a friend, and we got along well together. But love, I don't know if I would categorize it that way." Jackie and her husband settled into their own apartment in the public housing project in which she had grown up. In January 1969, she had her first daughter; she explained, "I don't know if I was pregnant when I got married. I don't think so; it must have been a couple of weeks in between." She describes a "fairly easy labor" and said her "husband was ecstatic; he was very happy about this." But Jackie looked upon the birth of her daughter as simply "something that you were supposed to do when you're married." Her best girlfriend at the time told her "she didn't know why I ever became a mother because I just wasn't the mother type of person."

Similar to Jackie's reason for getting married, the other women who got married during the 1960s also viewed marriage as an obligation that had to be fulfilled as part of their identity as women. This was the case for Anne who was twenty seven years old—"I guess that it was just time to get married." As the oldest girl, Anne felt "pressure from her family to get married: my mother and different relatives would hammer home, when are you going to get married"?

Anne believed that her husband "possessed an interesting balance for her life." She said "this was a guy who had a job, who was nice, he dressed well, he had a college degree which I didn't have, and he was going to graduate school to become a hospital administrator. So I thought, okay." Anne had a traditional church wedding. She "spent a whole year organizing, reading, and working this whole thing out," and her "parents were very happy that I was getting married." Soon after she got married, she quit her job at the public library. Anne elaborated on her decision:

> It was too much to juggle a six-day work week. I literally had one day to myself, and then I would have to do the housework and all that. My husband came from one of those squeaky clean southern grandmother oriented matriarchal home. His mother had a lot of personal principles, and I was a northerner. They were very concerned about appearances, presentation, and status. They had more money than my family did, but they didn't have the education. They didn't have what might be considered middle-class values. I think that was a struggle for me. The struggle became more intense as the relationship began to be problematic. I stopped working, and that changed the economics of the house: there was less money; there

had been two salaries. I felt financially dependent on him at the time, and I hated it.

Anne's marriage gradually started to unravel during the first year. After quitting her job, her life started to change in ways that she had not anticipated:

> When I decided to quit my job, I think that he was appreciative of the fact that I did leave because that meant I would have more time to be the wife. That was the first time I remembered reacting to the label of wife as a thing. It became an issue in our relationship because he had expectations of his wife ironing his shirts and cooking the meals. I used to get a report card for dust left on he dresser top or a ring around a glass. If I just dusted around the edges and he would pick up this bud vase and see this ring, he would come back and say, Anne look at this and there would be my F. I tried to do those things that were expected of me, I seriously tried during the first year, and I finally said this is not me.

This was the beginning of an unraveling that eventually lead to divorce. But the conflicts leading to divorce are not based solely on the gender expectations that her husband imposed and Anne assumed in her new role as wife. The conflicts also evolved from Anne's perceptions of who she thought her husband to be and who she saw him as, in actuality. This conflict between perceptions and reality was not unique to Anne's marriage. Both Mary and Patricia had similar conflicts, and early on their marriages also began to show signs of unraveling.

Mary's parents moved from the South and relocated in New York City. When they moved, she had decided to finish her last year of high school and accept a basketball scholarship that would allow her to attend a small all-black college in the South that coming fall. But her plans quickly changed. Mary's family became "sick with the Hong Kung Flu," and her mother demanded that she come to New York immediately following her high school graduation to take care of the children. She resented having to abandon her college plans, but even more she resented having to assume once again a caretaker role for her younger brothers and sisters. Mary said, "I never wanted to come to New York because I knew that there would be problems."

To escape this expected maternal role, Mary decided to marry her "childhood sweetheart because I wanted to get away from my parents. I was tired of taking care of everything, you know." Mary, twenty years old when she married, felt that "if I didn't make the move then, I would probably get stuck in this rut, and never do anything with my life, so I decided to get marry." She "always knew from the time that I was eight that I was going to get married; who I was going to marry; and how many kids I was going to have; and, they were going to be two boys." Mary knew the course of her life because she "had a revelation in church and I could see all of this stuff happening to me." With this foresight and knowledge in hand, Mary said her boyfriend "followed me to New York, and he was waiting for me to tell him yes. I said, well let me think about it because I knew that I had to have money for a wedding, and I was working in the cleaners by then. I decided to get married. We were both working. My parents weren't unhappy with me getting married." But the night before the wedding ceremony, the night before they were to be married, Mary overheard her fiancé talking on the phone: "I heard him talking to his girlfriend. He was apologizing for not being able to get away because we were upstairs doing wedding plans. I confronted him with it, and I went home, and I told my mother that I wasn't getting married after we had invested all of that money. I said, my mind tells me this is not the right thing to do. I said, I can just wait, I said, because I have somebody else that I like in the South better anyway. I was very matter of fact about things. My mother and my father listened, and then they finally decided that I would go ahead with the wedding."

Once the commitment was made, Mary was determined to make the marriage work. She became even more determined after the birth of her two sons, who were born a year a part. Mary attempted to fulfill her responsibilities and obligations as wife and mother, but, similar to her childhood revelation about whom she would marry, Mary knew from the night prior to the wedding that her marriage would be fraught with conflict, and so it was.

Unlike the other women, Patricia said she married for "love." Even though, on reflection, she expressed serious doubts as to whether this was really true at the time. Similar to Mary, Patricia said that there were signs that she should have really paid attention to before she got married.

But Patricia wanted to get married; she wanted to be a wife; and she wanted to be a mother.

Patricia was working a clerical job at a bank when she met the man whom she would ask to marry her in 1969. Her first impressions of him were unflattering: "he was arrogant, boisterous, and he just knew that every woman in the universe, not the job, but the universe, was madly in love with him." He was from the South, and "he just broke down all of my barriers." Patricia said, "I just knew that I was in love." Given her ongoing struggles with a lack of self-confidence and her sense of "not being good enough," Patricia was drawn to "his arrogance. He had this air of I know who I am, and I don't care if you don't like who I am, I like me, and I'm important. I was attracted to that I'm-sure-of-myself kind of attitude and I'm not afraid of the world."

Patricia soon discovered that they had some important experiences in common. Namely, "his father tried to flush his mother's head down the toilet, and when he came in to stop him, his father ran into the back room and got the shotgun and was going to kill him. But his mother prevented that from happening." Given this and other similar experiences and what she thought were common views on life, Patricia asked him to marry her. She clarified her specific reasons for asking: "I have to be honest. I think a part of me got married because I didn't think that anyone would want to marry me. I got to be honest here. I asked him what he thought about getting married, and he said, sure. I wanted to be married, but I had this whole fairy tale idea of what my marriage would be like, as opposed to what my mother's was like. I was bound and determined to make it happen, but I didn't think that anybody would ever want to marry me. So when he was receptive, I hopped to it." Patricia had a traditional church wedding and her father "gave me away and I didn't want that to happen, but he was there dragging me down the aisle like he was in a hurry to get rid of me." She said that at the ceremony there were real "signs" that she did not pay attention to. "The groom was late for the wedding, and the preacher couldn't even remember my name. But, of course, I was determined to go on and do this thing."

When Patricia settled down to married life, one of the first things the newlyweds did was make a pact. This agreement outlined the kind of marriage they wanted for themselves: "We wanted a marriage that was not violent because we both grew up under that. We were going to sit down and talk over our problems. We knew that there might be a little screaming and hollering, but there would be no hitting. We agreed that we would not think about having any children until we were married at least three years." The first part of their agreement—no violence—was broken three months into the marriage:

> Three months after I was married, we had this huge fight. I mean a physical fight, not an argument. People tickle me when they say we had a fight, and I'm thinking physical and they're talking words: two totally different things to me. It started because I was standing outside talking to some friends. It was hot. It was August. Our apartment was so tiny it was like you couldn't breathe. It was just one room. My husband had come out of the building and just looked. I waved and kept on talking. They said he came out again and he looked again. And he came out again and said very loudly, "I think that you better get in the house." Now that was the worst thing that he could have ever done, the absolute worst thing. So I deliberately stayed there ten more minutes. I'm not a child. I go into the apartment, and he's just carrying on like a crazy man. I'm giving as good as I'm getting. The bed was one of those metal frames with sharp edges. When he pushed me, my mouth hit the edge of the bed, and it broke my tooth. Of course there's blood everywhere. This is a full out war now. I'm grabbing butcher knives. I'm trying to cut his heart out and all of this kind of nonsense. We ended up out in the streets. Either he was chasing me, or I was chasing him. I forget at this point. The people outside were trying to split us up because neither one of us was willing to give any ground. I was embarrassed and outraged over the nonsense he was talking, and I guess he was on some kind of macho trip. I called my brother to come and help me remove my belongings to go to his house. I said, oh God, I've married my father. I always swore that I would never marry a man like my father, and first try, bingo. I married my father.

Like Patricia, several women discussed their particular experiences of physical violence in the context of physical "fights" with male partners and for some their "fights" with other women. During this "honeymoon" period, only Patricia talks about her particular experience. In recalling the first fight she had with her husband, on reflection, Patricia does not conclude that she was an "abused woman" in that situation, notwithstanding the fact that she was left bloodied by her husband's actions. She did not see herself as a victim because she asserted agency, because she "gave as good as she got." Her conclusion does not rest on the fact that the blows she administered or the chasing of her husband with a butcher knife was more compelling than her husband's action toward her, for this was not the case. Important to Patricia was the fact that she fought back in defense of her own self-worth.

In fighting back, it cannot be assumed that Patricia was unaffected by this altercation, for she felt a profound sense of violation and disrespect. She was angered by what she was supposed to be angry about, her "husband had the audacity to hit me." Her husband's actions represented a blatant breach of the promises they had made to each other. His actions also disrespected the integrity of her body. But it appears that her sense of violation was heightened by the decision that she made. On reflection, it was important for Patricia to acknowledge "the error in choosing someone who had ways, who was physically abusive like my father." Patricia said, "I thought that I was choosing someone totally different from my father." By acknowledging her self-responsibility to herself, Patricia was not attempting to deny, shift, or misplace blame; she knew that her husband was to blame for this fundamental breach of trust that had occurred in their marriage.

However, it was important for Patricia to acknowledge her sense of self-betrayal and all that she knew to be true based on her experience with her father's abusive behavior toward her mother. Of her husband, she said, "I wasn't afraid of him, I was just disgusted with him." And herself, she said, "I was more disgusted." But betrayal of her own needs, interests, and aspirations become a consistent part of Patricia's experience over time as her sense of violation in relation to her husband's actions grew. After their first fight, Patricia "loved" and "still wanted to create a life" with her husband; their relationship continued along with conflicts, physical violence, and her ever-growing sense of violation and disrespect.

War is not only large armed conflicts that occur through structured military engagements between nation-states, as was seen in Vietnam; there is no debate or doubt that this is a fundamental aspect of war. However, war and the theaters of conflict are not limited to armed combat between governments. Arguably, political conflicts created within and against uneven power relations are also a fundamental aspects of war. The physical, personal, and social destruction of human lives that can result link both forms of conflicts. Marriage is by no means a form of war; for women and men alike often engage in marriage through feelings of love and affection. But as a male-centered cultural and social institution, marriage exists on a political landscape. As such, marital responsibilities and obligations can become contested terrains between women and men as they negotiate the unevenness of gender constraint in the intimacies of their relationships. The women's experiences suggest that the unevenness of the responsibilities and obligations to which they were expected to adhere can and do create a theater of conflict within marriage, where the outcomes can be similar to armed conflict.

Likewise, the women who were married during the 1960s embraced mostly traditional views about what marriage was supposed to be. In accepting tradition, their ideas about the roles and expectations of wives and husbands reflect those standards. Early in their marriages, as Anne, Mary, Jackie, and Patricia's experiences suggest, they were unable to accommodate or reconcile their individual needs, interests, and aspirations within the traditional identity of wife. The women found that the traditional roles and expectations of wife imposed constraints on their sense of personhood. Immediately, conflicts arose that resulted in a sense of violation that affected not only how they viewed themselves as wives but also as human beings. They endured violations to their physical, personal, and social selves in their attempts to fulfill their marital responsibilities and obligations. Over the course of their marriages, they drew many lines between acceptable and unacceptable behavior while they attempted to negotiate their relationships. There came a point, however, when the cost of trying to maintain their marriage as weighted against their own sense of value became too high a price to pay. And they drew a final line between themselves and what they saw as their responsibilities and obligations to their husbands.

CHAPTER 4

The Worlds of Women

My anger has meant pain to me but it has also meant
survival, and before I give it up I'm going to be sure
that there is something at least as powerful to replace
it on the road to clarity.

"Sister Outsider," Audré Lorde

As THE 1970s approached, the women were no longer
in search of an adult identity. However, as they settled into particular patterns of life, they were still searching: some were seeking to fulfill dreams;
others were pursuing hopes; but all were looking to develop their human
potential. The decade of the 1970s held possibilities. Women with diverse
and sometimes divergent political agendas were stepping up organized
efforts in their campaigns for social and cultural equality. Through their
actions, women decided that the 1970s would be the "decade of the
woman."

The critical question moving to the forefront of mainstream political debate in America was: What do women want? Women gave different
answers to this question, depending on their cultural and social position
in society, depending on the nature of their lives, and depending on the
interpretation of their needs, interests, and aspirations at the time.

The "women's liberation movement," as it was popularly known,
was composed of broad-based national campaigns that included efforts to
get three-fourths of the states to ratify the Equal Rights Amendment
(ERA), legalize abortion, stop violence against women, and end pay discrimination and other forms of gender inequities in the workplace. Simultaneously, there were important women-led efforts during this period
that were not necessarily associated with the broader women's movement.
These campaigns were more local or grass-roots based, but they too had
national implications for women's lives. The local campaigns included

efforts to reform state welfare systems, gain community control over local school districts, and press demands for more and better child care services for working women.

Both nationally focused and more locally based campaigns for gender equality influenced some of the decisions and actions the women would make about their lives. But during this "decade of the woman," the women's own interactions with other women became notable. This chapter follows the lives of the women as mature adults who negotiate and renegotiate various relationships, especially those with other women. In their attempts to realize their human potential, their stories are by no means limited to or only defined by their interactions with other women, for they actively engaged all the dimensions of life that shape their worlds as women.

Mothers and Daughters

For most of the women, their mothers continued to be important influences in their adult lives. But this relationship was constantly undergoing change. Now, as adult children, they had to negotiate a different understanding for their mother/daughter relationship, and sometimes this created tensions, dilemmas, and contradictions that shaped the interactions. Central to this relationship were their mothers' continuing expectations of them as they struggled to achieve the expectations they had for themselves. And those expectations were not necessarily the same.

Anne describes her mother as "a brilliant and manipulative and a talented woman." She felt that her mother wanted her "to be something that she wanted me to be, not necessarily the person that I wanted to be." But Anne did not view her mother's life as a model that she could follow in meeting her own needs, interests, and aspirations. Of their conversations, Anne said:

> I began to hear her. I begin to listen to some of the things that she had to say to me. I realized that she was not a happy woman. She was unhappy living a life of repression as a wife and as a mother. I, of course, was stunned. I tried to listen, and I also tried to be honest. She would ask me did I understand what she was talking about. And I told her no, I don't know. I'm trying to, but I don't understand. Your choices would not be the choices that I would be making for

myself. I was making changes in my life, getting rid of the negative driftwood, and building a new foundation whatever it may be. I felt that it was important for me to keep this identity that I had worked so hard at sharpening and feeling good about. I didn't want to say that I understood something that I didn't understand. And I said so. But I still haven't figured it out yet.

Like Anne, in making decisions about their lives, several of the women struggled in their attempts to understand the choices their mothers had made in life, even when they shared similar experiences as adult women.

This was the case for Patricia, who had difficulty in understanding why her mother continued to stay with her abusive father. After she married and moved out of her parents' apartment, Patricia only visited her mother when her father was not around. On those occasions when she would visit and her father was home things were "just always hectic in my mother's house because he would still try to fight her." Patricia recalled an incident when she was forced to intervene in one of her parents' fights during a visit:

> My mother would call the police on him. Yeah, they would come and take him around the block and tell him to calm down, and then they would send him back home. They never arrested him. I remember at one point he attacked her, and I had called the police, and they didn't even bother to come. That's the time when I jumped in the fight, and he literally almost killed me. Later my mother said to me "that's why I didn't want you children getting involved because I'm used to him, and I know what he will do, you don't, and you're not used to fighting with a man." All I know is that he was trying to do some damage to my mother.

Patricia resigned herself to the possibility that her mother was never going to leave her father. She tried to explain:

> Obviously she stayed with the man because she loved him. I think now, as a woman, she just loved him. She knew him before he got this crazy, so there was something that she was holding onto, and there's that whole abuse syndrome. It's ironic because I never, ever saw my mother as an abused wife. The words, abused wife, and my

mother just didn't seem to fit. I never associated it with her, simply because whenever he would physically attack her, she seemed to always be able to handle it. She could always put him in his place. And on one level she seemed to psychologically have the upper hand.

In her reflections, Patricia tries to make sense of her mother's decision to stay with her father "for all those years." In recounting her mother's experiences and what she thought to be important, Patricia could only speculate about why her mother stayed. It appears that one of the main reasons her mother stayed was because of the value she placed on preserving the integrity of the family. Patricia believes that her mother took her commitments as wife and mother seriously and may have felt a deep sense of responsibility and obligation for holding the family together. Her husband was a part of the family, and she "definitely did not want to see her children growing up fatherless or raised by another man." Also, Patricia thought that her mother understood the role that racism played in making her father "crazy" and contributing to his alcoholism. As such, her mother may have not wanted to abandon him. Another reason may have been that her mother did not see herself as a "victim" of her husband's violence because she not only participated but also drew on her own physical and psychological strengths to prevent him from doing serious injury and harm. Finally, her mother may have stayed because she had important stakes in the marriage. Patricia speculates that her mother had invested time and effort into building the relationship and a life with this man, and it had not been all bad. For whatever reasons, perhaps her mother may have simply valued her love and did not want to give up on either her husband or her marriage.

Leaving her husband may not have been seen by Patricia's mother as a viable option or an appropriate response for her experience of violence, given her decision to stay in the relationship. As a black woman, with a high school diploma and a young child's interest to consider, Patricia confronted similar tensions, dilemmas, and contradictions as those of her mother. As she said, "it's interesting because certain parts of my life parallel my mother's life." Patricia also confronted the same question of whether to stay or leave her own marriage. In weighing the options and alternatives available to her, eventually Patricia made different decisions and came to different conclusions from those of her mother. But the cultural and social constraints imposed on the choices Patricia was forced to make exacerbated the struggle to leave her marriage.

Some of the women questioned the decisions their mothers made, while others accepted their mothers and the life they had established for themselves as they were. Jackie described pragmatically her overall relationship with her mother: "My mother is my mother. She will always be my mother. I will never know more than my mother, and pretty much what my mother says goes." Although Jackie lived in the same public housing complex as her mother, after she got married, she too did not visit her mother on a regular basis because she did not particularly care for her stepfather. Similar to Patricia's experience, there were occasions when she went to her mother's house and had to intervene when her mother and stepfather were fighting. Jackie remembered one such incident:

> Him and my mom must have gotten into an argument, and folks were calling around for me to come home. I didn't live there. I am already married and had kids. This was about 1974. He was acting up, and they said come home, your stepfather is acting up. I think about it now and say, this is what they really must've thought of me. I was the only one who could control this man that was in the house. And so I go home, and my grandmother hands me a machete, and in my mind I'm like oh it's like that. So, when I confronted him he pulls out his gun on me, and I pull out my gun on him. I knew he wasn't going to shoot me, and he pulled the gun out because he had one. He didn't know that I had one, too. If he would've shot me, I would've shot him too. I was like you got a gun, so. Big shit, I do too—plus a machete and a couple of switchblades.

As in childhood, Jackie continues to be protective of her family, especially of her mother and grandmother. But she could not prevent violence from occurring; she could only engage it. When it comes to physical violence, Jackie continues to take a matter-of-fact or a no-nonsense approach. In those situations, Jackie does not believe that she is at a disadvantage or that there is an imbalance in power. Beyond those situations where physical violence meets physical violence, as the nature and the circumstances of Jackie's life change and her experiences of personal and social violence become more pronounced through her political involvement, the meaning that she gives to violence and her sense of violation also begins to change.

Similar to Jackie's experiences, most of the women knew what to expect from their mother and what their mothers expected of them. However, at times some of the women were unexpectedly surprised by the decisions and actions their mothers made in a life that appeared to be settled. This was the case for Sharon. Her mother had a master's degree in zoology, and while growing up on occasion she would substitute teach but mostly she stayed at home to take care of the children and household. After Sharon and her two younger brothers left home, her mother decided to work full-time as a junior high school teacher. Sharon learned from her brother that her father "was having a fit because she went out and got a job. He was mad about that, and the arguments increased." But Sharon learned that there was more going on than just verbal arguments. Her parents had started to have physical fights. Sharon discussed their relationship during this period:

> Once she got the teaching job she got independent, and their relationship became more explosive. She had pulled a knife on him or he had pulled a knife on her, and my brother was home and he jumped in the middle to stop it. In another fight my parents had, my father broke her arm. All of this happened with me in New York, my brothers going off to college, her getting a teaching job. She was like only in her early forties, and saying "I'm not putting up with this anymore." I think getting her arm broken is what made her leave. She moved out and rented a house across town. And my mother died; she just dropped dead. She just sat down and died of a heart attack. At the time she was divorcing my father, and I know why because I have all of the divorce papers. But they were still married at the point of her death.

All the women discussed the importance of their relationship with their mothers. They expressed deep affection for their mothers and appreciated their struggles, but none of the women viewed their mothers' life as a model by which to pattern their own. To the contrary, they wanted a completely different life from the ones their mother had led. This was especially true for those who experienced their mother's experiences of violence. Five of the women—Sharon, Patricia, Mary, Barbara, and

Jackie—discussed their mother's fights with their fathers, during this period. Of the women, only Patricia said that she tried to talk with her mother about the fights; their discussions, however, usually focused on Patricia's efforts to encourage her mother to "divorce him." But generally, it appears that the adult daughters did not engage their mothers or avoided the more difficult conversations with them. Underneath such conversations lies a difficult question: What happened to their mother's sense of being when love, responsibility, and obligation become deformed, defiled, and disfigured by violence?

Clearly, this was not a question the women may have even thought about, or, if they did, they were unprepared to ask their mothers. In their own ways and within their own lives, they were struggling to find answers, not in their mothers' experiences, but in their own. The women experienced the violence that happened to their mothers as a violation to their own sense of self, and for some their growing anger turned into hatred for their fathers. But largely they experienced their mothers' violence in silence. It appears that their mothers also experienced their own violence in the same way. Their mothers often attempted to defend themselves by fighting back and their daughters took important note of their action. One cannot assume that this freed the mothers from a sense of violation or disrespect, but this is unknown. From the women's discussions it seems as if their mothers were not prepared to open up the decisions they had made about their lives to their daughters' scrutiny. And in return, the daughters seem to have respected the boundaries of the parents' marital relationship with their silence. Even though some may have intervened in their parents' fights, as Sharon said of her mother "there were just certain things that we could never talk about when she was alive."

SISTER, FRIEND, AND OTHER FEMALE RELATIONSHIPS

With the exception of Sharon and Faith, all the other women have sisters. None of the women viewed their sisters as close friends, but they all saw themselves as extremely supportive of their sisters. Generally, their sisters were younger, and several of the women viewed these relationships as more maternal in nature. This was the case for Sara, whose only sister was fourteen years younger. She recalled when her sister got married and what happened to her as a result.

My sister was living with me, met this black guy in the army, he was horrible, I hated him, and she married him. I planned the wedding. They moved to Germany, and he started beating her up. He was a drunk, and that's essentially what his problem was. Our relationship was all long distance because she was in Germany. She would call me, but she was really secretive about it. When she finally left him, I picked her up a JFK (airport), and she was sitting on top of her little green army bag and her eyes were black. I started crying when I saw her, and she said "child you should see him, we fought like men." She was funny, she would tell me stories. She would say something like "my family is going to kick your ass." He would say "your little punk brothers can't kick nobody's ass." She would say "my brothers nothing, my sister can kick your ass." That's one of my favorite lines of all times.

Given the distance and her sister's silence about the violence that was occurring in her marriage, Sara did not have the opportunity to intervene or a chance to try and protect her sister from injury and harm.

But Mary did have the opportunity and the chance to try to intervene, yet she was unsuccessful in preventing or protecting her sisters from her father's sexual advances. Mary had four younger sisters and a brother, whom she had helped to raise when they all lived in the rural south. As an adult she continued to be very protective of them. However, after following her family to New York City, getting married shortly thereafter, and moving out of her parents' home, Mary did not visit often and was not able to keep an eye on what her much younger siblings were doing. One day Mary returned to her parents' home unannounced and discovered her "father molesting my sister." Mary described this incident:

My sister wasn't my father's child, so I guess he felt that it was all right to molest her. I asked him why? I asked him how long had he been doing that to her? He said, "Nothing happened." But when I walked in I could see the covers moving, I don't know if he actually penetrated her because I came in the middle of it. So I made her get out of the bed and get dressed. She was frightened; I could look at her eyes and tell that she was frightened. She was probably frightened of me because she knew that I would beat her butt. So I made her get out of bed, and I told him that I was going to tell my mother.

I told him that he could go to jail for this, although I didn't know, I figured that had to be an option if he didn't stop. I told my mother. I think her response was, "Well, you got to keep her away from him." She put the responsibility on me. I know that she had a talk with him because I heard them screaming and fighting about the situation. But all of this made me think, what is he doing to my other sisters?

This was the second time that Mary had experienced incest in her family. The first had occurred between her grandfather and his youngest daughter. Other than confronting her father, sister, and her mother about what happened Mary was lost as to how to respond in this situation. Her mother "didn't report it to the police"; rather, she responded by throwing her husband out of the house. This took some of the pressure off of Mary in this situation, but she felt a deep sense of responsibility for her younger siblings anyway. However, given the demands of her marriage, motherhood, and working life Mary was unable to closely monitor what was happening at her parent's house; a lot was happening, and Mary generally found herself in the position of constantly reacting to family crises. But she was unable to prevent or protect her younger siblings from the harm and injury that would occur.

Of all the women with sisters, only Anne discussed the contentious relationship that she had with her sister, who was a year younger. The competitiveness of their relationship evolved in childhood but continued to occur throughout adulthood. After having graduated from high school together the sisters went off to college. Anne was forced to drop out because of "bad grades," while her sister not only graduated from an Ivy League college but received a scholarship for graduate study in England. Eventually, both worked in the predominately white fashion industry in New York City; her sister was a top model in the industry, and Anne worked her way up to becoming an associate fashion editor. Physically, they were different: "My sister was attractive, thinner, and always smaller than I was. I looked liked a well-rounded size fourteen." Although they continue to interact the sisters are not close. Anne did develop sisterly relationships, but with girlfriends. Of her friendships with women, Anne said, "It like growing flowers, it takes a lot of hard work, but it is worth the effort."

All the women talked about the importance of having friendships with other women. And during the 1970s, the significance of their relationships with other women increased as they became more rooted in their adult lives. The women not only sought but also depended on the guidance, companionship, support, and above all else the trusted ear to share their experiences with. Their relationships with other women encompassed a range of interactions. Yet they readily admitted that tensions, dilemmas, and conflicts developed in all of their close friendships and to maintain, especially those relationships that were deemed important, they had to constantly renegotiate their interactions, or walk away if they were deemed not in their interests to maintain.

In discussing their personal friendships with women, Amanda expressed the general sentiments of the other women. Amanda identified what she expects from her women friends:

> I like women who basically like women and don't incorporate a lot of negativity about women. I look for honesty, but I know that I'm not always honest when I think I'm going to hurt their feelings. But if you think a problem is serious enough, then I think that you have to overcome that. I like friends who I feel comfortable being able to say something to them even though they might not be ready to hear it at that time. And because I love them I'm not going to try and tell them in a way that's going to add hurt to their feelings. I like women who are supportive in my time of need, and I know that I'm going to be the same to them. I like women who are sisters; women who are thinkers and doers; who are doing things to make the world a better place. They don't have to walk around holding in a lot of pain and anger but can say I feel bad or I'm having a problem now, but I don't want any advice. I just want you to listen.

Particular to Amanda's experience, she said, "Most of my girlfriends have always tended to be fighters. They don't take any shit from anybody—men, women, family, or white folks. They are thinkers, someone who stands up for what they believe. We have a bond, we have a space where we can talk to each other, we can get advice from each other, and we know where we are coming from." However, beyond friendships and familial relationships, Amanda and the other women readily admitted there were occasions when they have had particularly difficult times in their interactions with other women. Several of the women recalled incidents where they have actually had physical fights with other women. Amanda remembers an incident that occurred late one night at her apartment building when a white woman she did not know started a "ruckus because her boyfriend would not let her into his apartment." Amanda detailed this incident:

> I was in my bed trying to sleep after a long night. I came in late. This white woman was trying to get entrance into to building, and she was making all of this noise. Her boyfriend wouldn't let her in, and so she started yelling and screaming and calling him all kind of names. She was banging on the door and going on, on, on. At first I looked out of the window; then I said, "This noise is right underneath my bedroom so would you please stop; there are people who got to get up and go to work, you can't just be acting like this." The next thing I knew he (boyfriend) took a big rubber maid trash can fill with water and poured it on her. And she still wouldn't leave. Somebody must've called the police. But I got dressed, and I went outside and said enough of this. She's standing there, and the next thing I knew she said, "you black nigger bitch." It was like I had taken four or five steps at a time to reach her, I was so enraged. I took my hand and wrapped it in her hair. I was beating her, and I yanked her body down to the ground. My foot was over her face when the police got there.

In addition to actions, words also have important meaning. For Amanda to be called a "black nigger bitch" was fighting words that embodied the ultimate insult or disrespect to her sense of personhood. This insult was given added weight because it was a white woman doing the name calling. Amanda's anger and sense of violation gave her permission to act in defense of self. Several women acknowledged that they could do violence when provoked; Amanda said "it is within me." In some instances, their anger as a result of a perceived violation appears to be a strong motivation for instigating physical violence. Amanda also recalls the time she sublet her apartment completely furnished to a young black couple, "who were trying to get their lives in order." Later, she found out "they weren't paying any of the bills and that I was going to be evicted." Amanda returned to her apartment to discover that they had already moved and "they had stole all my stuff." Amanda described what happened next:

> I was so angry. I had been so violated by them. Here I am bending over backwards to try and help them, and I didn't even know them. I called the woman and asked what happened, and she got real arrogant and nasty on the phone and called me a bitch. I was so mad, I hung up the phone, I got in my car, and I drove over to her mother's house; my brother went with me. I was ready to kick her ass. I went to her mother's house, someone else answered the door, and she was standing at the top of the stairs. And she said, "Bitch, what do you want?" She made me snap. I went up the steps, and I took my hands, and I put them in her hair, and I dragged her down the steps. My brother had to stop me because I was getting ready to stomp her.

Similar to Amanda's experience, Faith and Patricia also attacked women. They too talked about their anger as created by a sense of violation and disrespect. Unclear in their accounts of the incidents they recall is whether their anger evolved like Amanda's, which appears to have occurred in the moment as a result of definable insult, or whether their anger was attached to a larger sense of violation that had been festering and revealed in the circumstances that were created.

Faith also acknowledged that she could do violence and remembers when she beat a woman. But this was more than a fight with another woman. Out of a sense of anger for which she has difficulty in explaining, Faith attacked an elderly friend of her mother. Faith drove the woman home from a visit with her mother, who was in the hospital at the time. She tried to explain:

> I don't know what she said to me when I pulled up to her house. Earlier she had said something off the wall to me while we were driving, and I just pulled over to the side and said get out of the car because you're not going to talk to me like that. She didn't get out, so I took her home. I don't know what she said to me as she was getting out of the car, but I lost it. I got out of the car and I jumped on this old woman back, and I just started beating her—physically. I had knocked her down into the flowerbed, and I was just picking up this rock to hit her in the head when this neighbor came behind me and

picked me up and pulled me away from her. I'm screaming and saying let me go. It was just a big mess.

While living in New York City, Faith had gone home to visit her mother,
who was in the hospital, and no one in her family, not even her mother's
closest friends, had told her "my mother is at death's door. I realized that
my mother was dying when I got to the hospital, she was a lot thinner,
her color wasn't good, and as much as she tried she couldn't get the
sparkle back in her eyes. I was really concerned that my mother wasn't
going to make it out of this." In this context, Faith believes that her
mother's elderly friend thought I should have intuitively known that
something was seriously wrong with my mother. It is unclear what trig-
gered her reaction: the silence surrounding her mother's illness, the fact
that her mother was dying, or the total helplessness she felt in the situation. As a result of that confusion Faith's anger and sense of violation produced this attack. Faith did not give a single reason that provoked this
attack; she simply said, "I just snapped."

Also out of a sense of anger and violation, Patricia admits that once
she actually tried to kill a woman. She recalls an incident where she
ended up in a "physical confrontation with this woman." Patricia recalls:

I was hanging out with some friends, and for whatever reasons we
stopped by a woman's house and I fell asleep in the chair because it
was very early in the morning. I was talking to this woman who was
sitting across from me, and the next thing I knew my eyes were
closed. This woman jumped up and was attacking me. God only
knows why she did it. Yet we had all been drinking but not to the
point where anybody should've been stupid. When she did this, I
yelled because I didn't know what was wrong with her and I got up,
and I grabbed her, and I commenced to beat her. I did kind of lose
it. I got stupid. I don't drink and drive, but I had my car that night,
and I got in the car getting ready to leave, and this guy came out and
said something about me attacking this woman. And then she comes
out again with foolishness coming out of her mouth. And God only
knows why I did this, but before I knew it, I don't know how it happened, the next thing I knew my car was up on the sidewalk. I was
trying to run her over. Everybody was saying, "She's crazy." I honestly don't know why I did that. I was literally trying to kill this

woman, and I had never done anything like that in my life. They kept saying I'm crazy. At that point I was out of the car, and I lost my temper again. But out of nowhere I saw some white cops show up, and they kind of calmed me down. I scared myself because I had never tried to take anyone's life before.

Patricia acknowledges that she was angry, felt that she had been violated, and for her this was the impetus for the fight. However, following the fight that occurred inside the woman's house, Patricia struggled to find answers that explain why later, when she was intending to go home, she instead tries to run this woman over with her car. As she said, "I honestly don't know why I did that." And more important, Patricia said, "I don't know where any or all of that anger came from."

What is becoming more apparent in Patricia's experience during this period is that she started to drink heavily. Patricia does not acknowledge that her abuse of alcohol may have impaired her decision making or sparked her anger when she attempted to kill the woman. However, in her reflections she does acknowledge that one of her "major regret was the heavy drinking I did." She said, "If I had a clearer or sharper head, I would have done a lot of things differently, but then again on some level I never thought that I was that smart. I regret not treating myself better, and all of that drinking was a part of that." Patricia realizes that drinking was a way of masking her sense of inadequacy and her continuous feelings of "not being good enough." This sense would continue to influence the decisions and actions that she may have otherwise not taken, especially if she had had a "clearer head."

The women's interactions with other women were physical and personal as well as social in nature. For some of the women, race provided an added dimension to the difficulties they had in their interactions with other women. Several of the women acknowledged that some of their more difficult relationships had been with white women, both generally as a group and specifically as individuals. The tensions, dilemmas, and contradictions that developed usually occurred in an organized setting, for none of the women discussed a personal friendship with a white woman. This was the case for Amanda in her work with white women in political organizations. In joining a "progressive white organization," composed of both men and women, Amanda said:

I felt that I had found a political home in terms of being involved with this organization. It was mostly white, and right away there were contradictions. There were some white women, and one in particular, who had appropriated the position of being the black/white woman. She supposedly came from a working-class background, but it turned out that she came from a real lumpen background. And what she did was intimidate the other white women who came from more like petty bourgeois/working-class backgrounds. In other words, she was more working class than everybody else, she was more black than them because she had a black child and she had been in relationships with black men. So, then, I came on the scene. There were a couple of other black women, but they were very intimidated by her. I had connections with people in the black movement—there weren't that many black people in the movement anymore, only remnants. I became like a black commission, I had to go to all of these black organizations, and she resented that immensely. She thought that she should be doing it. She began to get very angry with me, and she started challenging different things that I would say. So, then, she and I got into a whole big mess. The whole issue of internal racism on the left came to the floor. She was totally surprised because I took her on because she was pretending to be a black woman.

Amanda resented the white woman's attempt to appropriate and gain political currency from the identity that she claimed for herself. She viewed the woman's actions as "racist" and was "appalled." For Amanda, the woman's attempt to usurp a black identity was an unacceptable insult, and she refused to surrender her judgment or active participation in the group to the will of this woman because of this. In her refusal to give deference—by not allowing herself to be intimidated, ostracized, or silenced—animosity, competition, and anger was created within the organization.

For Amanda, the center of this conflict evolved around issues of race that were rooted in the privileged status that the white women assumed over black women in the group. But, for her, conflicts were also rooted in issues of gender, and the privileges that males assumed in the hierarchy of power in this "progressive white organization." The internal political power struggle revealed both the unevenness of power relations between black and white women as well as those between males and females.

The intragender conflicts over racism created divisiveness between black and white women that inhibited their ability to establish an alliance to address common concerns about sexism in the organization. In discussing how race and gender intersected to shape her experience, Amanda said that she and two white women found out that they were pregnant around the same time. The male leadership "talked about how irresponsible we were when we have all of this work to do. How did we think we were going to get all of this work done and you're pregnant and have to take care of a child"? For Amanda "the only conclusion from what they said was that you had to end the pregnancy." But she later realized that this was not the only conclusion to be drawn, for "the white women had their babies. But I had another abortion." Although Amanda said that she felt pressured by the white male leadership to have the abortion, she acknowledged that the ultimate decision to terminate her pregnancy was hers.

Both racism and sexism were parts of Amanda's experience of working in this political organization. But Amanda's commitment to issues of social justice would not allow her, at that point, to walk away from the internal struggles that she thought inevitable. She continued her work and simply concluded that "progressive politics is quite complicated."

In a different political context, Jackie also worked with "progressive white political organizations" and concluded that her involvement was complicated. She recalls her experience of working with a white women's group that was attempting to organize "community women" to become active around issues in their own neighborhoods. Jackie said:

> During this time I began looking at the living conditions in public housing. So I joined this organization. I'm trying to learn as much as possible about public housing. But I'm also trying to learn the front and back of this organization, and who's really running the show. I figured it out real quick, to the point of what would stop them dead in their tracks. It was black women controlling their money. Well what about diversity? So the women of color pulled a little coup. We got a majority of the board to be women of color. It was supposed

to be about community women running a national organization. But it was an illusion, something that is never what it appears to be. I was an officer because the white women never wanted it to appear that they were really running the show, and they wanted to show the diversity of the organization. When we tried to make decisions, they said that we were racist. I said, yes, at least we know it and will admit it. But I liked the work that we did, and I told them I could separate the two. I just don't let their racism get to me. I did get to meet a lot of people, learn a lot of things, some good, and some bad. I learned that white women are rough; they really are. It's like they can be very scary. I can almost see lynch mobs and seeing the kkk, and their women having a party at the lynching.

Bluntly, Jackie admits that "white women get on my goddamn nerves." For Jackie this was more of a political critique than a purely personal assessment. Working with several white women's organizations, this critique was rooted in her experiences of racism, which resulted from the uneven power dynamics that often evolve when she along with other black women decided to become fully active instead of mere tokens in such political organizations. Jackie rejected the "patronizing attitude" that she found. For her, the largely middle-class white women with whom she worked were interested in black women's participation. But Jackie believes that they were not interested in sharing the power to make decisions over allocating resources or defining strategies. In the struggle over decision making, Jackie often found herself in conflict with white women.

Based on her political involvement with white women, Jackie said that "there's no such thing as hidden racism"; for she viewed the racism of white women with whom she had worked "as blatant." As such, she concludes, "You always know that they think that they are really better than black women, and you get this no matter what you do with them." But Jackie also realizes that white women's organizations had greater access to resources that she viewed to be important for her community. So, admittedly, Jackie attempted to "tolerate their racism." To get what she wanted, Jackie said, "I just tried not to let their racism get to me, I was clear as to why I stayed." Yet their racism would get to her: "The internal political battles over racism and power became to emotionally draining for me." The longest period of time that Jackie would work with any "progressive white organization" was about four years on average, and even though she continues to attend meetings here and there she decided not to be fully involved. Rather, Jackie began to refocus her political activities on her own public housing community.

During the 1970s, the women's relationships with other women become a prominent feature of their day-to-day experiences. In some of those interactions, they experienced violence and a sense of violation—in their relationships with mothers and sisters or friends and political acquaintances. Depending upon the context of those relationships, the women experienced violence and a sense of violation in different ways. What appears to resonate in their experiences is that they often found themselves reacting to the immediate situation at hand, and by no means did their actions provide a buttress for preventing or protecting themselves or others from physical, personal, and social violence.

For those who experienced secondhand their mothers' and sisters' experiences of violence, the women's actions were a complicated mixture of direct action and silence. In those instances where it was possible to intervene, several of the women did so in their attempts to stop the violence. But they were powerless in their ability to prevent violence from occurring or recurring, even if they did not necessarily see themselves as powerless in their reactions. Their actions offer a clear statement of their concern, support, and desire to protect female family members from harm and injury. Yet in their silence no such statement was offered. Presumably, their silence and those of other female family members spoke to their feelings of shame, humiliation, and the profound attenuation to their sense of value. In other words, their silences spoke to their sense of violation and the powerlessness that resulted from the violence they had experienced.

But the women were not powerless in all circumstances where they could prevent violence from happening. There are instances when several of the women instigated and perpetrated physical violence against other women. Their experiences suggest that they could do violence, and they empowered themselves to act in such a way. Their anger, as an expression of their sense of violation, provides motivation and permissiveness, but not necessarily a rationale or justification for their actions. Their anger responds to conditions and practices that they view as disrespectful and unacceptable. The ways that their anger is expressed, in this case through physical violence, reflect their judgment as to what they will and will not tolerate. For them a line has been crossed, the demarcation of which centers on their sense of being and the perception that their personhood is threatened, jeopardized, or compromised in some way.

Even as the women established boundaries with regards to what they will and will not tolerate, the lines are ever shifting. The varying boundaries depend on the situation at hand and the nature of their interactions. Their actions also vary in the process. In discussing their relationships with white women in political organizations, several of the women reflected on their anger as a result of their perceptions of racism and the unevenness of power relations that are produced. In those instances, Amanda and Jackie's experiences suggest that their anger was rooted in a sense of violation and that a line had been crossed, but they did not resort to physical violence as a response. Their actions destabilized the dynamic of those relationships in ways that did not allow white women to dictate the terms of the interactions. Yet in their attempts to assert their needs, interests, and aspirations they made conscious decisions to tolerate the insidiousness of racism—and for Amanda also sexism—in order to get what they wanted. Even though they were aware that racism could threaten, jeopardize, and compromise their sense of personhood. But eventually, they knew that the cost of tolerating racism would become too high a price to pay for their continuing involvement. Before it reached a point where it would infringe on or breach their sense of personhood, they moved on and focused their political involvement elsewhere.

The women's relationships with other women were important features of their experiences during the 1970s. But their interactions with other women by no means formed their only relationships to their cultural and social worlds. For several of the women, their relationships as mothers to their children also played significant roles in shaping their experiences.

MOTHERS

Four of the nine women in this study have children. Although three were married when their children were born, all eventually raised their children as single mothers.

Mary was excited at the birth of her first child. It was a boy, and she named him after his father; "he was a junior." She had taken maternity leave from her job, and after the birth of her son she "only wanted to work part-time" so that she could be at home with him. But soon after she returned to part-time work, Mary "got pregnant again with her second son." Following his birth, she returned to work sooner than she had anticipated because her "oldest son needed some shoes, and I didn't have money to buy them, so I said to my husband, I'm going to get a job today, and when I came back home that evening I had a job." In order to work, Mary and her husband had to share childcare responsibilities for their young children: "I worked from 6:00 p.m. to 2:00 a.m. My husband worked from 8:00 a.m. to 4:00 p.m. He would get home around a quarter to five. He worked for transit in the maintenance department. When he would come in I would leave, so we didn't have to pay a baby sitter. But I missed my kids, especially the baby, when I went to work. I couldn't breastfeed either one because of work."

Over time, Mary gradually began to notice a change in her youngest son's behavior, but she did not know to what to attribute this change. Something had happened, but Mary did not find out what until her son had reached adolescence. Her oldest son told her that their father, her husband, had "abused my youngest son." Mary explained the circumstances:

> I left him with his father very early because I was working nights. My husband would tell him that he wasn't his father because he didn't look like his brother. He was more verbally than physically abusive. They would have told me if their father had of hit them. My youngest son began to develop a complex; he was introverted, he was extremely introverted, like a hermit. He internalized a lot of stuff his father told him. At the time I wasn't aware of the damage that was being created to him.

Mary began to experience problems with her sons.

> They started to experiment with drugs when they got to junior high school. I moved from the area we were living in thinking that I was taking them out of whatever environment they were getting involved in. But by then drugs were in the schools also. They were

close as brothers; close enough to keep secrets. By the time they reached high school, my oldest son was on track to become a lawyer, but he stopped going to class. I got him re-instated three times. Then after that, he said he was going to just get his GED. He was courting this girl quite actively; they were into sex and everything. I saw a letter that this girl had written to him that said "if you don't give me a baby I will find somebody that will." I was shocked, so I called the girl's mother to tell her, but the girl was already pregnant. So they got married when he was seventeen. Her mother signed off on something, and they had a civil ceremony. I wasn't even aware that they were married; he sort of did it without my consent. I was hoping that he was going to college. My youngest son followed in his brother's footsteps. He was devastated when his brother left. He started hanging out with, I guess it was a gang, and he would not go to school. I would ask him why he did drugs. He said, "Why do you care? My daddy didn't want me, and you don't want me either." I tried to get help, taking him to counselors, trying every avenue to circumvent what was happening. I felt guilty about the early damage, that I wasn't aware, that I didn't detect it. I dealt with this pain by getting a severe stomach ulcer.

Mary said that one of her major disappointments in life was her inability to prevent and protect her youngest son from harm and injury. She was unable to "circumvent what was happening" to her son, and his drug abuse deepened with age and would posed an even greater challenge for Mary. For not only his life but also Mary's would be seriously threatened, jeopardized, and compromised by her son's addiction.

Jackie, like Mary, had two children who were close in age. She had her first child almost nine months after she was married. Jackie worked the whole time she was pregnant and returned to work soon after the baby was born. But she did not work for long. Jackie quit her job because she thought that she was on the "verge of having a nervous break down." She said, "I mentally couldn't take it, and maybe it was cause I had the responsibility now of another person." So she stayed home to care for the baby, and her husband took financial responsibility for the family. But within a year of her daughter's birth, Jackie was "pregnant again." Shortly after she gave birth to her son, Jackie decided to go back to work because "now I needed to buy a washing machine and dryer and all that other stuff the baby needed."

Jackie's oldest child was two years old when she decided to look for another job, but before she could go back to work she had to "look for daycare" for both of her young children. This is when Jackie said she became active with daycare issues:

> That's when I got politically involved. My husband's aunt told me that they were fighting for daycare and for parent-controlled daycare. Since I didn't know what daycare was anyway, parent controlled daycare was something totally different. So when I got involved with them, I realized that they were fighting for parents to have some say over what children were doing in their schools, and the fact that they could be there if they chose to or not; that parents could hire teachers and all that kind of stuff. I said, yeah that's good. That's when I got involved in daycare and the sit-ins that they did at ACD (Agency for Child Development), to make sure that the kids had food and the books were there. And they didn't want to fund us. We made sure that the school stayed opened, coordinated parents cooking and bringing in food, and just making sure that things ran as smoothly as possible. I didn't play a leadership role; I was in a learning role. I was trying to learn what was going on; what the politics were; why certain things were a certain way. So I just wanted to learn, and then try and find where my place was going to be. I knew that I was going to stay in that kind of work.

Similar to her general approach to life, Jackie was pragmatic about the raising of her children. She describes her relationship with her first two children as close, but Jackie was clear about who was in control of her household, as she said:

> My relationship with my children was, they were children, and I was the mother. They had to just really understand that there was no equal stuff in the house. I would punish them, and if their behavior got really out of hand they got a beating. Basically when my kids got older, I couldn't give them beatings. I had to give them a beat-down, so that they could remember the difference. The difference is a beating is like you can't do that no more. A beat-down is like you

are trying to kill them. Look, I'm going to kill you. And you take anything—a pipe, broom, fist, anything. My thing would be like, don't make your mother act crazy, meaning don't make your mother act up, even say yes, if you mean no.

Jackie viewed herself as "very family orientated." But she admits that she could not think of herself "as being a good mother." She said, "I was writing the script as I went along. I didn't pay that much attention to anybody raising me or what they were doing, so I couldn't remember what was supposed to be going on." But Jackie did draw upon an old script when it came to disciplining her children. She remembered that children must be disciplined, and that mothers are culturally and socially responsible for controlling their children's behavior. Similar to her own childhood experience, now as a mother she did not question her use of corporal punishment as a form of acceptable parental discipline. Nor did she view it as a form of violence that would evoke a sense of violation or disrespect for her children. Jackie had no second thoughts regarding her use of corporal punishment. She beat her children as a way of making them conform to her will. But in looking back on her experience as a parent, Jackie said, "I think a lot of times a lot of the decisions I made, I didn't think that they were anybody else's decisions, or take into consideration anybody else's feelings but my own. So I basically raised my kids in ways that were right for me."

Reflecting on her mothering style, Amanda expressed a similar sentiment:

> I think that from the time my daughter was born, part of me recognized the fact that priority had to be given to her. I think from all practical standpoints, taking care of her basic nurturing, I did that. But I think another part of me always tried to fit her into what I was doing. I did not want to relinquish basically who I was and what I wanted to do. I felt that she had to adjust to my life style. I don't know if that was correct or fair to her. But I recognized that that's sort of what happened. I wouldn't neglect her, although some people might say emotionally I might have not always been there for her.

At the time Amanda was working full-time at a Model Cities program, where she directed a program to provide safe and affordable daycare to inner-city mothers. But her political commitments also led her to take a part-time job on the weekends at a local hospital, so she could help unionize the workers there. And she continued her active involvement in political organizations and attended meetings at night. At a "police brutality meeting" Amanda met her baby's father, and they "became friends." He was interested in having a long-term relationship with her, but Amanda said, "I wasn't interested in him in that way." He gave her "an ultimatum" that if they were not going to get together as a couple, then he was going to marry another woman he was seeing. And so he did, but that marriage did not last, and Amanda renewed an intimate relationship with him. She got pregnant, but decided not to tell him because she knew that their relationship was over. Amanda discussed this period in her life:

> A friend of mine who was very supportive during that period said that I had a responsibility to allow him the opportunity to be a man, so that he had the opportunity to either do what he is supposed to do, or show that he's not going to do anything; but if he doesn't know, then I'm not affording him a choice. Initially, I wasn't going to have the child and actually went to the abortion clinic with the full intention of getting an abortion. I had already made up my mind that with my lifestyle, I didn't want to be a single parent. I couldn't fit that in to my life, and I didn't want to be with him because he was a lunatic. So I go to the clinic—I will never forget it—and the woman confirmed what I already knew. I was really going to make an appointment for an abortion, and when she said, okay when do you want to come in? Something made me hesitate. I said well let me think about it. I went outside and instead of me being sad and depressed and everything, I really felt kind of good. It was a sunny day. I talked to a very good friend who I worked with in the hospital, a Trinidadian sister who was a nurse. She was a single parent, and her whole thing was, "You don't want to grow old and not have anybody. You can make it; you're a strong woman. Look at me, and there are other single mothers."

Amanda decided to have the baby, and she also decided to tell the father that she was pregnant. In so doing, she said, "He was kind of cool, surprisingly so." But a few days after she had told him, he called her on the telephone and "started ranting and raving about how I was ruining his life and he was going on like a crazy person, so I hung up on him": "I can't remember exactly all that he said, but it was so humiliating and it was insulting. He was basically putting me down and criticizing me. I felt so bad. I decided I was going to struggle and have this baby. I said, maybe this will make me a better person. I won't be so self-consumed, and I will have somebody else to be responsible to, and even though this isn't the way I wanted it, I'll make it. I have a job, and I have a place to live." To meet the needs of her daughter, Amanda knew that changes in her political lifestyle had to be made. But she continued, "I still tried to do what I was doing before, and still tried to be a good mother." Amanda described how she attempted to balance her own needs with those of her daughter:

> I felt very close to my daughter, and I never felt that she was a burden. At points I sort of took it in stride that I had responsibility for her. The only time that it would really come to the forefront in my mind is when we were having a struggle inside of this political group and people started talking about the differences between the women in the group. Some women who were married and had husbands who were making decent money, verses the women in the group who were single parents. Separate and apart from this, I didn't belabor the fact that I'm a single mother. I just sort of went about doing what I had to do. I wasn't that much in contact with her father. For the most part he was very antagonistic to what I was doing politically and even threatened at different points that he would take legal action to get her from me because I was being irresponsible. But he never moved on that. To compensate for her being a single child, I always tried to put her in group-settings. I believed in daycare, and I put her in a family daycare home. She was always in a family or group setting. I had friends who would always help out. To me I thought that that was a good thing; it wasn't like I was abandoning her or that I was too involved in my political work and not paying attention to her. When she started school I became active in that too. I didn't feel—probably some other people did—that I was not being a good mother.

Amanda saw her daughter as a "model child up until about the age of fourteen." She "did exactly what she was supposed to do. She had a key

to the house. She would come home from school or she would go to my
mother's house, and she would check in with everybody." Then, things
started to change with her daughter. Amanda said, "She started being a
lunatic. She was hanging out—I found out that she was going out with
somebody who was twenty-four. And she was just a wild child." Amanda
described this as one of the worst period in their mother/daughter
relationship:

> I was outraged in terms of this older man abusing my child. The fact
> that he was involved in drugs, who knows where that would have
> led? I was furious with her disrespecting the advice that she had been
> given. I can't remember the exact breaking point. But all of this sort
> of came to a boiling point, and one day I found out that she had
> been with him. I came home, and I was ready to murder her. Her at-
> titude was just so arrogant too. So I literally dressed as we used to
> dress when we were ready to go to a fight. I put on my street clothes,
> like jeans and stuff, and I tied my hair back, and the only thing I
> didn't do was put Vaseline on my face. I was ready to beat her up.
> And something stopped me. I called a friend who used to be the di-
> rector of a foster care program. I wanted to know what kind of pro-
> gram I could get her in. I said I'm going to kill her if she and I stay
> in the same space, and if she continues to behave like this. She's re-
> ally out of control.

For Amanda, her daughter's behavior had crossed the line. "Out-
rage" by her perception of child abuse and angered by her daughter's apparent "disrespect," Amanda was well aware that she could do violence in
response to her own sense of violation: that she could fight; that she
could beat up her daughter. But in this moment of crisis, Amanda also
realized that violence was an ineffective way to address the situation at
hand or control her daughter's behavior. She realized that something
more was needed. After all, she was not responding to another adult or
to broader cultural and social insults; instead, she was reacting to her
daughter's behavior. This made a difference. In that moment, Amanda
was forced to consider her daughter's needs, interests, and aspirations and
what physical violence could mean for her daughter's sense of being.

Consequently, Amanda got her daughter enrolled in a program that
had a reputation for working with troubled youth. But her daughter did

not want to participate in the program because she said that "the other children were juvenile delinquents." She then placed her daughter into a small private school that had a "progressive reputation," where she "seemed to calm down and get more focused." Also, in an attempt to establish a better mother/daughter relationship, Amanda decided that they would both go into family counseling. She said, "I was feeling guilty because all my political involvements weren't leaving too much space for her at an age when, even though she was getting older and could be independent, it was an age where there was a lot of confusion and craziness. We started going to counseling. I felt like I needed something so I wouldn't go off the deep-end in terms of all the changes that were going on in my life, and she went with me." Amanda's daughter graduated from high school and went on to college.

Like Amanda, Patricia also had only one child, a son. Although there were major tensions in her marriage, Patricia "intentionally got pregnant" because she loved her husband and wanted his child. She said when her husband found out that she was pregnant "he made all of these promises to me. I should have known better than to listen to him. Part of me didn't believe him, but part of me wanted to believe him." Based on his promises to take care of her, Patricia decided to quit her job: "I stopped working early on during my pregnancy." Soon after, her husband broke his promises.. He did not pay the bills, and he was "hanging out, partying, and seeing women." During this period her husband also started to sell drugs. This was something that Patricia said "I was not going to allow." When she told him to leave, the situation disintegrated:

> He went absolutely off, so I had to go and get the butcher knife. He was screaming and hollering all up in my face. He was too big for me to allow him to put his hands on me. I was pregnant. Obviously I knew I couldn't beat a man, but I knew that if I didn't jump and act like I was crazier than he was, he might very well have hurt me. He actually had to leave the house because I was acting like I had totally lost my mind and that I was going to kill him that very night. So he left. He had to go. On top of him running around with whoever he was running around with, then having the nerve to think that he was going to come home and sleep with me, knowing that that was not

going to happen, and then he wanted to bring drugs into my house. No, that's not going to happen.

Finally, Patricia had drawn a line by deciding that she would no longer tolerate her husband's behavior.

But her husband returned to the house, and "he made the pronouncement that he wasn't going anywhere, and there was nothing I could do about it." Patricia decided that there was something she could do and was determined that he had to go. She acted with a sense of desperation:

> I had packed up all of his clothes in big garbage bags and had them sitting in the hallway of the apartment for him to take out. He said he wasn't going anywhere. I said I tell you what I will do, I will run smack into this wall and knock my fool self out, and when I do come around, I will call the police and swear to God that you did it. And when they find out that I'm pregnant, you're going to have a problem. At that point I saw it as self-preservation. I saw it as if I didn't do something drastic, I was going to be in the position of a truly abused woman, and there was no way I could live my life that way. I had just gotten myself so worked up that I probably would have done just what I told him I was going to do.

Not knowing how her husband would respond, in that moment, Patricia could only decide how she would react. And she decided to risk it all. Her husband's actions placed Patricia in jeopardy of harm and injury. But in her attempt at "self-preservation," Patricia placed her entire sense of being on the line. For her it was all or nothing; she would either have control over her physical, personal, social self and deal with the consequences or surrender to her husband's will. Unlike her mother, Patricia was willing to risk it all to get out of the intolerable situation she found herself in. In her struggle to sustain a sense of self, she faced the consequences of her actions. Following the threat, Patricia's husband did leave, and she found that there was a high price to pay for the value she placed on her own life.

Pregnant, angry, and depressed, Patricia was not working and "didn't know what I was going to do, so I just sat for months." The rental office of her apartment building "kept sending eviction notices," and Patricia's mother tried to help out with the rent, but Patricia was falling further behind in her bills. She said, "I finally realized that nothing was going to get done with me just sitting in the house." Six months pregnant, Patricia decided to go to the Department of Social Services, to welfare for help. She describes this experience as "pure hell":

> I'm feeling horrendous. I'm in there with a lot of screaming babies, people demanding all sorts of things, and you're waiting forever. You're scared to get up and go pee for fear somebody will call your name and you won't hear them and when you come back you have to go to the end of the line again. And people being talked to as if they are lower than dirt. They make you feel as if you are begging for the money personally out of their pockets. I said to myself that I was not going to succumb to this. I said I have worked all of my life since the age of fourteen. I paid taxes. I'm in a bind right now; I need help. This is what I'm here for. My rent was like $342 a month, and this woman tells me that I have to move because "they are not going to pay my rent." I told her if I could move, why would I be here in your office asking for assistance? Obviously I need help. You go in there and you tell the truth and you catch hell. If you go in and you lie, and can make that lie sound convincing, you seem to get help quicker. I realize now why they have guards in welfare centers, simply because of the way the workers talk to the people who need help. They talk to you as if you are the scum of the earth: how dare you need help. You used to work and now you're here, and now you got to beg me for assistance.

Patricia experienced the systematic degradation and humiliation imposed on those seeking needed assistance from the welfare system. For her, receiving welfare was not an option she wanted to pursue, but it was one of a very few options available to her, and out of necessity she resorted to applying for welfare. This was a low point in Patricia's life, and her struggle to sustain a sense of value waned. With poverty, grief, and despair Patricia seriously considered suicide, the details of which she refused to discuss. But she also considered that she was carrying new life, which outweighed any attempts at self-destruction. Patricia did experience joy during this difficult period in her life. Her son was born in 1974, and she describes his birth as "the most beautiful experience that I have ever had in my life."

Patricia stayed on welfare for three years following the birth of her son. She faced a dilemma: she had wanted to go back to work right after her son was born, but her caseworker told her that "we're not going to help you find a job until he is at least six years old." So she waited until her son was three years old, and then she "pounded the pavement looking for a job." Her mother helped with childcare. Patricia said that she "didn't have any major disappointments with her son when he was young." But as her son got older he did not perform well in school. And one of Patricia's biggest disappointments was that her son, like herself, "never graduated from high school," but he too would eventually get his high school diploma.

As women and as mothers Jackie, Mary, Amanda, and Patricia had to constantly negotiate their own needs, interests, and aspirations with the responsibilities of child rearing and parenting. Whether they were married, semi-married, or single they were all primary caregivers responsible for their children's physical, emotional, and material well-being. Similar to their mothers, they were the ones who established the household rules and the ones who punished the infractions. All the women used corporal punishment to varying degrees as a form of discipline and did not view their actions as reproducing violence. Similar to their own childhood perceptions, they did not see the beatings they administered as a form of abuse or maltreatment of their children, nor did they consider the implications their actions could have on their children's sense of being. Yet, beyond this obvious similarity to their childhood experiences, the women followed their own particular course to mothering.

They did not necessarily conform to the more established cultural and social expectations for mothering. As such, in their reflections they expressed different degrees of guilt for not doing so. For Jackie and Amanda their sense of guilt was rooted in their perceptions of being "selfish"; for they knew that mothers are expected to sacrifice everything for their children. They recalled instances when they placed a priority on their own needs, interests, and aspirations as women, over those of their children. Contrary to expectations, in many ways they expected if not demanded that their children conform to the life they had established for themselves: Jackie told her children, "if you don't like my parenting style, then you can go and live somewhere else." Also their sense of responsibility required that compromises be made, that what was best for their children be seriously considered, and in those circumstances where this was needed they did so.

Another area where both Amanda and Mary harbored a degree of guilt was in their inability to protect their children from harm and injury when their being was threatened, jeopardized, and compromised. They were not only aware of their responsibility but also the cultural and social stigma attached to a mother's "failure to protect" their children. This was seen when Mary was unable to prevent the "psychological abuse" her youngest son experienced as a result of either his father's action or the "physical abuse" he experienced as part of his drug addiction. Consequently, Mary developed "a bleeding ulcer." And, it was also seen when Amanda could not prevent the "child abuse" of her daughter, which lead to a major crisis that threatened to break her family unit a part.

None of the women viewed mothering as their primary role or identity. And in comparison to what was fundamentally expected of them as mothers—self-sacrifice and child protection—they did not generally see themselves as "good mothers" in the more established or conventional sense of mothering. Instead, they raised their children to the best of their abilities. The tensions, dilemmas, and contradictions of simultaneously being women and mothers shaped the nature of the relationships they had with their children. Similar tensions, dilemmas, and contradictions shaped their lives as women with the expectation of being "good wives" and "good lovers."

HUSBANDS AND MEN

Six of the women were married; five of them got divorced in the 1970s, and one continues to have a long-term separation. But all the women, at some point, in their lives would have relatively long-term intimate relationships with men.

Mary said that she "learned from her grandma that you're supposed to get to know a person, become their friend, and then you're supposed to get married and have babies." Mary seemingly followed her grandmother's advice and married her childhood boyfriend. Although married to her husband for twelve years, she describes it as a "rocky relationship because he was always with other women and because he would also try and keep track on my every move." Amidst on-going conflicts in their relationship, Mary tried to keep the marriage together primarily for the sake of the children. She wanted "to work it out because of the boys and because I came from a semi-broken home myself. I wanted to keep the family intact." But Mary realized early on that she would eventually have to make a decision about her marriage:

> I knew mentally that I had to make a change because I could see that it was going downhill. He began to bring card games and reefer into the house around the boys. I didn't like that, so we began to fight over stuff like that. I don't like fighting, and I don't like arguing, and I don't like liquor. It got so bad that when we started fighting my sons would come in the room with bats, and I knew that they would kill him. They were young, but they wouldn't let him touch me. They didn't know that I could defend myself; they would just hear the arguing. One time I found some rollers under my pillow that didn't belong to me. We were living in the projects then, and he had contracted some kind of disease, but he was trying to make me make love to him. I put my feet up and pushed them in the air, and I knocked him through the television set. That woke up my sons, so they came in with the bats, and they were getting ready to beat him, and I just took them and left the apartment.

From the beginning of their marriage, Mary said that she did not trust her husband; based on his infidelity and what happened the night prior to their wedding, she believed that she had good reasons for mistrust. But the mistrust deepened as the conflicts between them grew. For the sake of the children, Mary stayed in the marriage where she both tolerated and resisted her husband's attempts at dominance. Her husband's controlling and coercive behavior was an attempt to place constraints on Mary's autonomy by insisting that she prioritize his wants over her own. His attempts to exercise male privileges are revealed in his possessiveness, in his monitoring and surveillance of Mary's activities and whereabouts, in his demands to have access to her body, in sex, in his infidelity and sexual transgression, and in his insistence that his income belong to him rather than the household. All of these were exacerbated by his drug abuse and alcoholism.

Mary said her husband was an "alcoholic," and she didn't know whether he "drank" a lot before they got married. But after they were married "he drank, and then he started with reefer, and then he started experimenting with other drugs which made his behavior impulsive and unpredictable." Toward the end of the marriage fighting between them escalated. But Mary was adamant and confident in the fact that she could defend and protect herself, especially because the fights occurred while he was usually in a drunken state. And by the time Mary decided to end the marriage, she said, "I knew by then I would kill him, so I threw away the guns in the house. Because of my temper I would have shot him dead."

Mary had gotten tired of the "bickering and fighting" and her husband's constant attempts to monitor her every move. She could see that their relationship was taking a toll on her sons. So she decided that "it didn't make sense to try and struggle and stay in a marriage after that." Following the divorce, Mary met a man who she "really loved during that time." He became for her the kind of father she wanted her sons to have. Mary recalled this relationship:

> At that time love meant that I would get excited when I would see him coming. I would smile inwardly and outwardly, and just to hear his voice made me feel good because I knew that we had a mutual situation, and he was just the opposite of my husband. He didn't drink to excess. He was a church man. He was not the best looking man but he had beautiful eyes. We could talk about everything. I met him because he was a principal of one of the schools, and he was looking for someone. We went together for about thirteen years. But the only thing was he would confuse me with his teachers or students in terms of trying to control me. He was dogmatic and controlling. He would like to know where I was every minute. I said who set up these rules? I made him look at himself and see why it's not practical to expect somebody to go along with your agenda all the time. He was a good lover, a good provider, and a good friend, and that's what I loved about him. But I wouldn't marry him because of his dogmatic and controlling personality.

In this relationship, Mary was not willing to place herself in another situation where she could foresee the conflicts that would be engendered as a result of his "dogmatic and controlling personality." In other words, she refused to place herself once again in a situation that would threaten, jeopardize, and compromise her sense of personhood, particularly her autonomy as a woman even though he was "a good lover, a good provider, and a good friend."

Anne found herself in a marriage where her husband expected her to conform to the cultural and social expectations of a "good wife." As such, her husband also expected that she would prioritize his wants over her own. With pressure from her family, at twenty-seven years of age, Anne had gotten married in 1969, but by 1974 she was separated from her husband. Although she had quit her job at the library to become a full-time housewife, she attempted to fulfill what she thought to be her marital commitment and obligation, and in many ways she embodied the identity of a "good wife." Anne describes the first year of marriage as "easy because I knew who the person was that I had married. I figured that a sense of love was something that I was going to learn."

During the second year of marriage, Anne's husband decided to go to graduate school in another state, and she "encouraged him to do it." By mutual agreement, "he would come home at least once a month, and hopefully I would go down there once a month. So twice a month we would see each other." But the distance put a strain on their relationship. Anne thought "the marriage was disintegrating because of distance, because of incompatibility, and separate interests. And I also think that I was more mature than he was." But she also thought that the "marriage was fixable," so when her husband completed his two years of study and moved back to New York City, they decided to go to marriage counseling. During one of the therapy sessions, Anne found out that her husband was "gay":

> When I realized that he was gay I was shocked and surprised. I was shocked and surprised that I didn't know it, that I couldn't see it, that I didn't understand it, that I wasn't able to define it. I wasn't angry. I was more concerned about wasting time being with the wrong person. That's what I was upset about. I recognized that I had spent time trying to make something work. I was upset over the fact that I could never get that time back. I can't say that I felt deceived because I was pretty clear in my own mind that he didn't know who he was as a person. I couldn't be angry; it would have been unfair for me to be angry at him for something that he was not aware of, at least aware enough to be honest about it. In retrospect as we move

along with out lives, I think he knew something, but I think he was
not comfortable with addressing it.

After having invested time and energy in her marriage, where she both
conformed to and resisted the established expectations for being a "good
wife," Anne was not exactly sure who she was anymore. Following the
divorce, she was struggling to figure out the value of her life. She no
longer thought of herself as a wife, but as an ex-wife. But she did not
know exactly what this identity meant. Anne said, "I knew that I wanted
to be somebody. What that somebody was, I didn't know in particular.
Personally I was on very shaky territory. I saw myself as somebody who
was struggling. I was trying to figure out what kind of female I was that
had been in an unsuccessful marriage and what kind of female I was beyond marriage." In her attempts to sort this out (see chapter 5), Anne
began to create another identity for herself, but this time through work.

Having made the conscious decision to never a date black man again
and to distance herself from black people in general, Barbara was struggling with the "plastic person" she had become. An identity largely created through work, she was now unemployed. Barbara "was out of a job"
and "miserable," when a friend told her, "I have a perfect person I want
to introduce you to. You're going to love him. He's a tennis pro, and he's
fabulous." Barbara met him. He was an African from Nigeria. She said,
"I was thinking survival; it was a crucial period in my life: I didn't have
a job and was wondering what am I going to do, and how am I going to
make it?" And when she met the tennis pro, Barbara said, "This is for me.
This is a black man. He's really black because he is African. He was cul-
tured, and I liked the way he looked in tennis shorts. That was one of the
key things." Barbara described what happened in this relationship:

> He kept pressuring me. He wanted to get married. I had dated him
> for about a year, but I was a little leery about marrying him. At the
> time, I was still drinking, and I was taking Valiums. I was very de-
> pressed, and I said, well you know, I might as well marry him. I guess
> I decided to marry him because I felt like I had to marry because I
> needed a job, and at that time I was twenty-nine years old. I figured
> at twenty-nine, you know this might be my last chance, and this was
> a black man that was a successful black man, and that kind of stuff
> was important to me. I wasn't in love with him at all. He was just

pressuring me. So I was at my girlfriend's house, and I said to her, are you doing something tomorrow? And she said no, and I said well can you come with me because I'm going to get married? She went to the window and said I don't believe this. You didn't tell a soul? I didn't tell anyone else.

Their wedding was held at a country club, and Barbara said, "The whole time I was getting married was the worst experience of my life." As she was walking down the aisle, she kept remembering the movie *The Graduate* and "thinking you can't say no right now. I said, you can't say no; look at all of these white people here. But you didn't tell your parents, so you can still get out of it." Barbara said, "I do." Needless to say, the marriage didn't work. "I was only married to him for a week. I really sabotaged it." The night before her wedding Barbara had picked up a stranger at a bar and took him home with her. Immediately after the marriage, Barbara told her husband what she had done:

> I told him that I was out with another guy before we got married. He went berserk, he went totally berserk, and at the time I didn't understand why he was going berserk. I think he was destroyed after that. I don't think that he loved me; I really thought that he wanted his citizenship. I do know that he was very nice to me. I couldn't really think straight because I was taking Valiums and drinking, and I had no touch with emotions or feelings or anything like that at the time. My justification for that was this is what you get when you're trying to marry somebody for citizenship. Right after that, I said, I'm going to have this annulled. So I gave this big annulment party, and everybody came with all kinds of booze and was saying congratulations for this whole thing. Of course he had all of the power because he was a tennis pro, and he said he wasn't going to annul the marriage. It turned into this huge mess. So I said, well I'll fix him: I'm not going to get a divorce. It was logical to me at the time to stay married because I might make the mistake again of marrying someone else because of some crazy thing. I stayed married for seven years, but we never lived together.

Barbara's experience suggests that she had no intentions of adhering to marital conformity, of complying with the established cultural and social norms for a "good wife." But ironically conformity was a major part of the reason why she got married. At twenty-nine years of age, she thought that it was time to assume the social mandate for marriage and the normative identity of wife; with the opportunity to marry an "authentic" black man she could adhere to cultural demands as well; and, given his profession, she would marry up in social status. For Barbara, all of this had little to do with marital commitment and responsibility. Getting married would meet a fundamental need that Barbara had; it would provide a means for her material survival. However, her survival instincts did not totally erase her doubts, for Barbara did not want to be dependent on a loveless marriage. She was not willing to risk her sense of independence to marriage, so Barbara created an easy out for herself through sabotage. Barbara knew that her new husband would end the marriage after learning from her that she had had sexual relations with another man the night before their wedding. Barbara wanted the privileges of marriage in the absence of commitment and responsibility, and she got what she wanted by staying separated and married for seven years.

Jackie found herself in a loveless marriage. She explained, "After I have grown older, I understood that there is a real difference between loving somebody and liking somebody." Early in her marriage, Jackie began to resent her husband's lying. She said, "My husband used to lie so much. Lying really used to get on my nerves. It's just something that I can't tolerate. I think that my relationship with my husband had fallen off a long time ago because of it." Around the middle 1970s, Jackie decided to separate from her husband, but during this period unexpectedly she found out that she was pregnant with her third child:

> I just thought that I was tired because I was whipped, just dog tired from the stuff I was doing. I said let me go to the doctor and see what's going on here, maybe I have high blood pressure. So I go to the doctor and take all of these tests: everything's fine. He said let me take a pregnancy test. I was still having my period, so pregnancy was the furthest thing from my mind. He said the test came back and I was pregnant. I passed out. I probably was on the table for about twenty minutes unconscious. I couldn't move from the shock of him

saying, "baby." I said I was going to have an abortion, later, for a baby, I'm not having no more kids.

Jackie decided to have the baby, and during this period she also decided that her husband had to go. "Besides the lying, he had gotten tangled up with this guy and started taking cocaine. So when he decided he wasn't going to pay any bills, he didn't need to be there. I could pay my own bills anyway." Jackie allowed her husband to have visitation with the children. She said, "I was not the type of person that said you can't come over. Take them whenever you want to; you can come and hang out with them. We just don't have nothing going on, period. He was probably the best father that he could probably be, and the children were crazy about him, so this is how it's been every since then." Primarily because of the children, Jackie decided not to get a divorce and has continued a long-term separation with her husband.

There were a lot of "adjustments" that Jackie had to make in her life with a newborn baby and with raising her family as a single mother. She said that her youngest child was not an "unwanted baby, but the fact that I just wasn't prepared to have any more children threw me off." Even though she received support from her mother, grandmother, and girlfriend, Jackie had problems coping with the stress, and she became depressed. She said, "During this period I literally went to bed. It was real hard to just get up out of bed at the time. I could hear the baby crying, and if my girlfriend wasn't there, I don't know if I could have gotten up to see about her. It went on for a little while, and then I got it together, and I got up out of the bed and went to work."

Patricia like Jackie, separated from her husband during the same period, but she eventually divorced him in 1977. Unlike the other women who married, love was one of the main reasons Patricia married her husband. Over the course of their marriage, however, they lived more apart than together as husband and wife. There were many reasons for conflicts in their relationships. Although Patricia points to her husband's behavior as the source of much of the conflict in their marriage, she also points to her own behavior as creating conflict as well. She said, "I take some of the blame for our failed marriage. I do have to admit that there was a time when I begin to be extremely possessive, and an extremely jealous individual. I don't know what came over me. I began to become what I didn't like in others."

> I just made his life miserable in terms of arguing. He would get angry. Of course if someone is constantly screaming at you that you're fooling around, you get tired of it, and you walk out. I carried on like that until like something within me took hold and said you know you're being an absolute fool. The best way to chase anybody away is to constantly be accusing them. Maybe something in me just got tired. I figured if he was fooling around there was nothing that I could do about it. The more I let up, I could see the more relaxed he became, which meant that our marriage got better.

But Patricia and her husband started having "serious money problems," and "after a while he just wasn't bringing any money home. He would go to work, and there were times that I wouldn't see him from Friday morning until Sunday night." Patricia reacted to her husband's behavior: "I did something which was stupid. All of a sudden, I was going to be defiant, and I said well if he can go out and party, I can go out and party too." She elaborated: "You know that two wrongs don't make it right. I was going to make it right by doing just what he was doing. So I went out partying, and I would stay out for weekends. I was involved with other men. Not like a lot of other men, but there would be one or two guys that I knew and I would just go and hang out and party with them. Then my husband and I would get into a lot arguing, a lot of accusing, a lot of name calling. There was no physical violence, but we separated for a while."

During this particular separation, Patricia stayed with another man until she discovered that she was pregnant by her husband. She said, "I ended up not having the baby; I ended up aborting it. I did not feel emotionally ready to bring another child into world, especially in the kind of relationship I was in." Patricia told her husband that she was pregnant, but she "lied to him, and I did it deliberately. It wasn't nice, but I was under a lot of stress": "I told him that, because of everything that he took me through, that I had lost the baby. I know that it was wrong, but I was striking back. I was striking out. I went to the hospital and had an abortion. I went by myself. After I did it, I kept telling myself this is the right thing to do. I didn't talk about it to anybody. But I have dealt with that everyday since then." Patricia also admits that "alcohol was a part of our relationship." She would drink a lot of beer, but she would not drink "during the week because I knew that I had to get up and go to work, and I had certain responsibilities." In addition, Patricia started to gain weight, and her husband told her "jokingly, but apparently he meant it, that if I gained weight, I was going to be in trouble because he would end up leaving. He did leave in his own way, he didn't physically leave." However, Patricia describes this period of marriage as a "fun and intimate" time in their relationship, as she said:

> Sometimes on the weekends we would just drink and pig out. Oh, this sounds so disgusting to me now. We would get one of those pounds of slab bacon and fry it up, and we would make all of this toast, and we would get big bowls of popcorn and potato chips, put it all in the bed, and we'd be sitting there either listening to music or looking at TV and talking and laughing. Me, not realizing what this was doing to me physically. Those were some really fun and intimate times because we were really close. We could sit and easily laugh and talk about anything, any subject, and I really felt close to him. I went up to about 182 pounds. I didn't see myself in a negative way until I had on a pair of pants one day, and somebody thought that I was pregnant. But I would still drink and eat, drink my beer and eat up all the junk.

By the end of her marriage, Patricia realized that "I had just let myself go. When I looked in the mirror, I said what's wrong with this picture? My mind and my mouth said everything." The fighting, infidelity, alcohol abuse, lack of money, and all of the bad decisions had taken an enormous toll on Patricia's sense of self. In many ways Patricia found herself repeating what she had most wanted to avoid in her own life—the destructive dynamics of her parent's relationship. In her reflection, Patricia understands what happens to a sense of self when love, responsibility, and obligation becomes deformed, defiled, and disfigured by violence. She realizes that she lost important pieces of herself and did it for reasons of love: "I knew, even with all the anger and pain, I still felt that I loved my husband."

But now, Patricia said, "I don't know if it was really love or that I felt that I got this husband and I'm determined to make it work":

I learned how you're suppose to just hang in there, no matter what, you're gotten married and you're made your vows, and you know young people now a days jump up and get married at the drop of a hat, and tomorrow they get divorced. I don't know if I was trying to prove something to myself, to other people, or to my mother. I just don't know what I was trying to prove. But I was trying to prove a point to somebody, like I was going to make something in my life work. And I almost ended up losing my life trying to prove something, to somebody.

Sara was also trying to prove something, and she, too, was trying to make something work in her personal life. Before getting married, Sara spent a lot of time with her future husband "trying to figure out if we were going to be a couple and if we were going to get married or something." They moved in together, and in 1973 got married shortly thereafter. But within months of her marriage, Sara's mother died. This was a critical period in Sara's life. Unsure of herself, she started to drink heavily. Sara describes this period as an "emotional bottom":

> Some of the stuff that happened with my husband was a bottom. I wrecked my car when I was drunk. I rode down the highway and hit the back of a car with some kids in it. Actually I was lucky nothing happened to them. I hit my head on the steering wheel, and knocked my teeth out, and bit my lip off, and it had to be sewn back on. What I did, two days later, I was all sewn up, and I went to the bar and drank my martini through a straw cause I couldn't drink it the regular way. I really was unhappy with my husband. I thought that something was wrong with me, clearly, and I would be found out, and the drinking helped that.

Sara realized that she did not love her husband "the way that I needed to love him." She also realized that she could not "make a commitment" to him, and so she made the decision to separate from her husband. Her husband "filed for a divorce" on the grounds that she had abandoned him, and she did not contest his claim. But, more important, during this period, Sara thought that she "was going crazy." Sara was sinking further and further into the quagmire of alcohol and drug abuse, and her addiction would come to influence herself-destructive decisions and behavior.

Amanda has never married, but prior to the birth of her daughter, she lived with a boyfriend during 1970s, while attending graduate school. Discussing the dynamics of this relationship, Amanda said:

> As it turned out he was like a real womanizer. But when he was with you he made you think that you were the only person in the entire world. At one point, he started going out and staying out overnight. I wouldn't know where he was or anything like that, and we got into a whole confrontation around that. Also the more I became more politically involved, the more I felt more confident to argue on my point of view about things. Before I was like enamored of him; he wrote for this paper, he was involved in all this political stuff, he knew everything, and I knew nothing. And then as I got more confident, I would challenge him around things, and he didn't like that.

In challenging his opinions, Amanda realized there were consequences that she did not anticipate. She recalled an incident: "One time we were talking—I remember we were sitting on the floor—and he told me to shut up, and I was like, oh, no you don't tell me to shut up. The next thing I knew he backhanded me. I was hysterical. I was like furious. That was the first time that any man had ever hit me. I was screaming. He was so apologetic. He went and got ice. He was coddling me. I guess I was hurt cause I just couldn't believe that someone who cared about me would hit me like that. My face and mouth and everything were swollen and stuff."

While she was growing up, Amanda did not experience physical violence between her parents, and up to this point she had never considered the fact that some men hit women as a way of imposing authority, exerting control, and showing women who is the unquestionable "boss" in the house. So, until he hit her, it had not dawned on Amanda that she had committed a transgression against his privilege. Experiencing for the first time a sense of violation as a result of being hit by a man for arguing and disagreeing, Amanda was determined that he would not do it again, regardless of his apologies. But just in case he tried, Amanda was on guard, and another incident did arise. Amanda described what happened this time and how she reacted:

He had this whole thing about how his eggs had to be prepared. You had to fry them with butter, and you had to move the pan back and forth. It couldn't be like any crust on the bottom, he wanted his eggs to be perfect. I tried to do the eggs like that, and something happened, and they didn't turn out exactly the way he wanted. So I just put them on his plate. He started getting real crazy about his eggs. I said, "Oh, I'm very sorry," and I took the plate and I turned it upside down so like the eggs were on his head. He was so angry. He was furious, so he acted like he was going to hit me again. He used to be into hunting, and in the kitchen he had this big Bowie knife there and all this other stuff. So I grab the Bowie knife cause I was like, after he had hit me the first time it was both anger and fear, I had made up my mind that he would never ever hit me again. I don't know what I thought I was going to do with this knife, cause I had never held a knife before with any sense of trying to attack anybody. He thought that I had totally lost my mind. I decided that after that I didn't want to be in the house with him anymore. So then I decided I was going to leave, and I packed my stuff, and I had no place to go. I put all of my belongings in my Volkswagon, and then I slept in the car. I was embarrassed. I slept in the car just overnight, and then I went to my girlfriend's house.

Similar to Mary's and Patricia's experiences, Amanda too came to the conclusion that she would not tolerate being hit. But no matter what they did, no matter how they tried to negotiate a nonviolent relationship, their actions did not prevent or stop the violence from occurring. They all eventually decided to leave those relationships and accept the consequences of the decisions they were forced to make.

Notably six of the women—Sharon, Sara, Barbara, Anne, Faith, and Jackie—did not discuss experiences of physical violence in their intimate relationships with men. This noted difference does not suggest that they did not experience violence in those relationships; it only means that physical fights were not a part of their experiences. They did experience violence, and there are distinctions to be made between the ways physical, personal, and social violence affected their individual lives. However, it is not necessarily the violence, regardless of the different form it takes, that links their different experiences. Rather, it is the meaning given to their experiences of violence that establishes an important connection. They share the sense of violation that results from similar patterns of interactions with men in their intimate relationships.

In the case of those who fought, not necessarily the physical altercations connect their experiences. Although an obvious connection can be made on this level, this only tells us that the women fought back. The more important connection is the meaning or the reasons that led up to those fights, which is a sense of violation, which led to their reactions. The fights did not just occur or happen arbitrarily. Instead, their experiences are connected by personal history that shaped the circumstances that made physical violence possible. A critical part of that history was the unevenness of power relations between the women and their male partners. Those relations marked different expectations for women and men; the kinds of privileges the men assumed held important implications for the women's experiences of violence. The ways men assert privilege is not limited to or only shaped by the use of physical violence. And for Mary, Patricia, and Amanda who fought, their experiences suggest that they by no means confuse physical violence with love. Nor did they confuse their own sense of commitment and responsibility with their male partner's attempts at dominance. As a result, conflicts were created that were negotiated through physical violence.

For those who did not experience physical violence in their intimate relationships with men, there are important points of connection to the experiences of the women who did. Similarly, the women who did not fight did not equate cultural and social expectations for being "good wives" and "good lovers" with surrendering their sense of self to the will of their male partners. Unlike Barbara and to a lesser extent Sara, the other women did not totally reject the established expectations or the meaning given to such identities. Instead, in many ways they accepted at least in part the meaning that was imposed as they acquiesced or attempted to manipulate those identities. Only when their husbands or lovers attempted to assert dominance over the meaning of those identities through the abuse of male power did the women reject the limitations that such identities offer. It appears that in their own ways, they entered those relationships wanting to be "good wives" and "good lovers," but they eventually rejected the surveillance, infidelity, forced sex, and lies that became a part of those identities. Similar to those women who experienced physical violence, they, too, would not confuse abusive male privileges with love. Nor would they confuse commitment and responsibilities with their partners' attempts to impose their own meaning over their lives as "good wives" or "good lovers."

In the process of living their lives, the women moved beyond broken marriages and failed relationships. In that process, however, they struggled in their attempts to once again create identities for themselves that allowed them to maintain and sustain a sense of self; some struggled to create lives as single women; others struggled as single mothers; and several struggled as they confronted the ravages of alcoholism and drug addition in their attempts to regain their sense of self.

DRUGS AND ALCOHOL ADDICTION

Substance abuse had a significant affect on the women's lives and was a big part of their experiences during the decade of the 1970s. Even though some women stopped using drugs and drinking alcohol or never abused substances of any kind, they were not immune from the impact drug and alcohol abuse imposed on their lives and the violence that sometimes accompanied it.

Several women were forced to respond to the substance abuse and addiction of family members. Mary said that she "never had the urge for drugs or alcohol," but her husband was an alcoholic, and her youngest son was a drug addict. Increasingly, Mary was concerned for her youngest son's life, and one night he "almost died right here on my sofa":

> He was beat up by drug pushers. I was downstairs in my apartment building at a tenant meeting. Somebody came and got me, and a friend of mine went with me to my apartment. The drug pushers were there to collect money, and I just passed right by them and called an ambulance. It was startling to see him in so much pain. He was just dripping blood. You know how they break your elbows and the bones were all sticking out and he was beaten real badly. While we were waiting on the ambulance, I was trying to stop his bleeding because he was in such pain. I was trying to make him comfortable, and I was scared that he was dying on the sofa.

Mary did everything that she could to encourage her son to go into drug treatment. He went in and out of drug treatment programs and later served time in prison, but his addiction continues. In addition to her youngest son's addiction, Mary also coped with crises that occurred at her mother's house from drug and alcohol abuse. Mary's only brother died from a heroin overdose, and she partially blames her parents for his death.

> I blamed my mother and my father because they knew he was having problems with not going to school and drugs. Once I got married, nobody else took an interest in what he was doing. So he died. Somebody had shot him in the back of his hand with a needle five times. They shot him up with heroin. They found him on the stairwell in an apartment building. My parents didn't stop him from the drug activities when he was in high school. He was into drugs then; he was using; I don't know if he was selling drugs. I blamed them for my brother's death, and I told them that. I worried over him. But he came to me one night after he died, and he told me not to worry because he was all right.

Following her brother's death, Mary's relationship with her mother and other family members became "more estranged," and she tried to have as little contact with them as possible. Although Mary was growing increasingly concerned about her younger sisters, for they too were using drugs and alcohol, she stopped going to her mother's house when she learned that it was becoming known for excessive drug activities.

> My mother started hanging out with people using a lot of drugs, and all of that would be part of her normal environment. So the kids were exposed to that. Whoever were in the house would experiment with drugs, including my mother. She was taking drugs, and she started to drink real bad after my brother died. The remaining kids, my four sisters, all of them were exposed to drugs and experimenting with alcohol. I was afraid that my mother's apartment would be busted at any time, not that anybody was selling out of there, but there was an acceleration of the drug activity in the family, and it was volatile for me in terms of their activities. So I didn't go around my mother a lot.

Mary was not the only woman who was forced to respond in some way to the ravages of substance abuse and the crises it created in families. As they witnessed what was happening to family members, several of the women began to moderate or stopped using substances. This was the case for Amanda. She knew the affects that drugs could have and did not take her drug use serious. She said, "I grew up with people who were using heroin and saw them die and stuff, and because of that I was never really interested." Amanda recalled what happened to a favorite male cousin to whom she was extremely close:

> My cousin and I were like just a few months apart in age, and we were more like brother and sister. After he came back from Vietnam, he had opened up a little store in the neighborhood. He had saved up money from when he was in Vietnam to open the store, and that was his dream. He had been approached by organized crime to use his store as a drug place. At some point he decided that he didn't want to do that anymore. So he gets set up by his friends that he grew up with, and he was murdered. My cousin's death was very, very, painful. To this day, even when I go up in that area, I think about him. It seemed like such a waste.

Anne too confronted the devastating and wasting effects of drug addition in her family. She discovered that her only brother, while he lived with her mother, was addicted to cocaine. Following her father's death in the 1970s, Anne was living in New York, but she commuted on a fairly regular basis to her hometown in an attempt to help her mother out with household chores and errands. On an errand to the bank, she discovered that her brother had been forging her mother's name on checks and making withdrawals from her account. "He was stealing from my mother," she said. Anne confronted her mother who "refused to discuss it, she was in total denial, and said I was invading her privacy." With apprehension Anne also confronted her brother:

> My brother was extremely hostile and he was extremely dangerous. He was physically dangerous, life threatening, gun stuff. He would have pulled a gun on me if I had a chosen to escalate the situation beyond the yelling and the screaming we did. I wasn't afraid of him in the beginning. But I became afraid. I confronted him over a period of time. He became threatening. The fact that my brother could swagger in to my mother's house anytime he wanted, and take

whatever he wanted from the house as though he was entitled to it, disturbed me. I was willing to confront him, willing to help him get drug therapy and go through rehabilitation. But, you know you cannot make people change their behavior; they have to be willing participants. My relationship with my mother and my brother deteriorated over this. I decided that I could not fix the breakage. The form of madness that I stepped into between my mother and brother had gone beyond just dysfunctional behavior.

Following her divorce, Patricia's relationship with her former husband also deteriorated into a form of "madness" because of his selling of and using drugs. She said "he had this idea that he was going to be this great drug dealer, and he knew that there was no way in hell that I was going along with that." Patricia grew increasingly concerned about the effects of her ex-husband's drug activities on her young son. There were long periods of time when he did not visit, and sometimes "when he would show up" Patricia would not allow him to see their son. She explained:

> One time I tiptoed to the door because I knew it was him. I looked through the peephole, and I couldn't believe what I saw. I didn't even bother to open the door. He was really messed up on drugs, and I didn't want my son to see him. Usually when he did something like that I wouldn't hear from him until years later. But he came back during the week. He knocked, and this time I let him in because my son wasn't there. I couldn't believe what I saw. He looked emaciated, he was thoroughly unkempt, and he had a disgusting odor about him. I talked to him. I told him, you know I had told you before if you're messing with drugs that I don't want you around my son. I said I don't even want you knocking on this door. I don't know who you're dealing with, I don't want them following you to my house. I said, now apart from me getting hurt, which I knew he could've cared less about, your son is here and I can't have that. I told him that if he comes to my door again, I'm not going to bother calling the police. I would put him out of his misery myself. He stayed away for eleven years. Somewhere in that drug haze, I guess, I was able to get through to him that you don't want to do this to your son.

Drug and alcohol addiction by family members created different challenges for the women. But it was the challenge that addiction had on the actual lives of loved ones that was more significant. In recalling their family members' experiences with addiction, the women's accounts were usually accompanied by incidents of violence and self-destruction. But the reasons for their relatives' substance abuse and addiction are unknown. What is known is that the women were drawn into those experiences out of crisis, but they were powerless to prevent, stop, or alter the destruction that was occurring. Often in their powerlessness and out of frustration they became detached from certain family members. As a result of abuse and addiction family members went through their own experiences. But Mary, Anne, Amanda, and Patricia found that they could not avoid the violence and destruction that sometimes accompanied those experiences.

At various periods, from the late 1960s through the middle 1970s, seven of the nine women used drugs and/or alcohol. They started using substance recreationally when they were young women working or going to college. Toward the end of the 1970s, several of the women had either moderated their intake or stopped taking drugs and drinking alcohol altogether. They did not view their use of drugs and/or alcohol as an addiction; rather, they saw their use of substance as part of their youth culture, and as mature adults they moved on.

But Sara, Barbara, and Patricia were unable to move on. They had become addicted to substances. Prior to getting "clean and sober," they lost important pieces of their sense of self for which their addiction played an important role. As they gradually succumbed to the ravages of addiction their gauge as to their needs, interests, and aspirations was seriously compromised. Consequently, through their actions they actively participated in self-abuse; this abuse was tantamount to self-violation; and by not caring about the consequences of their actions for their own personhood, self-abuse became a part of their experiences of violence. Through their struggle to regain a sense of their own self-value, they got "clean and sober." Sara and Barbara sought drug and alcohol treatment primarily through faith-based programs, and through her interactions with other black women Patricia gradually stopped drinking on her own.

Sara said "a lot of my stories are about getting high, and what drugs and alcohol did for me. I drank a lot. I was one of the people who did both. Most people I know drank or they would do drugs. And there was a crew of us that did both. I was always impaired, I was always not completely there, and not remembering what happened, being apologetic, being a big mess, tearing my dress, or my hair coming down. You know how you dress-up to go out and you come home, and you're a big ugly mess because you were in a blackout." When Sara separated from her husband, she had gone south to take care of her younger brother and sister following the death of her mother, during that period she received a telephone call from a good friend:

> She had called me and said that she had gone to AA (Alcoholics Anonymous). I said, thank God because you are a terrible drunk. We used to drink together. It was horrible. So I was so glad that she stopped drinking, cause child she couldn't drink no liquor. So when I went back to New York, I went with her to AA. But I didn't stop drinking right away. I just sort of listened. I wasn't committed to it. I was just like I'll go and see what this is about. I started going in the beginning of January, and I stopped drinking in February. I stopped getting high the following August. And I began to see how scared I was.

Initially, staying sober was a tremendous challenge for Sara. As she said, "There's a lot of grief with giving up drinking." In recalling some of her experience as she tried to stay "clean and sober," Sara said:

> I remember once walking by a liquor store, and they were having a sale, and I was just paralyzed outside this door looking at this big old bottle of vodka for eight dollars. I felt like, you're probably going to drink again, you're not going to do this for the rest of your life, you're going to drink again, so why don't you just go on and do it now, why don't you go and buy this bottle. It's a good price. I went and called somebody, and then I went to a meeting, but I didn't drink. . . .
>
> I remember that I got angry when I got sober. I was in a rage. The rage was like—I just can't explain it. I would walk into people in the sidewalk cafes because it was summertime, and I would want to turn tables over. I was like a complete lunatic. I was yelling at everybody. One morning I woke up, and it was gone. I had not done anything. Nothing had changed—I didn't have a boyfriend, job,

money—everything was exactly the same as it was, and the rage was gone. I kind of understood something I never knew, that you didn't have to fix everything. Sometimes it's just about a pendulum. That things change. Everyday is a different day. And I wasn't responsible for bringing the sun up.

Sara said "in getting sober, you're giving up the old self." She has been sober and drug-free for nineteen years. In her reflections, she acknowledges that her substance abuse and dependency evolved from attempts to cover up her sense of personal inadequacies and the resulting fears. "I was afraid of being found out that I'm not smart enough, being found out that I was not able to produce, to deliver, to get the job done. I was ashamed of being weak; being that crazy." Sara's fears created a sense of "feeling needy, feeling paranoid, feeling like everybody hates me, feeling I'm ugly, and feeling I'm stupid." Substance abuse enabled Sara to move beyond her fears and her feelings of inadequacy. It also gave Sara permission to be angry. She said, "I only got angry when I was drunk." But getting "clean and sober" enabled Sara to reclaim her own sense of value; "I'm very proud of the fact that I have come to my own strengths."

Like Sara, Barbara has been sober for years. But prior to getting sober, Barbara said, "I would drink everyday." For a time Barbara was a "functional alcoholic," who didn't think that she had a drinking problem "because I didn't drink in the morning. But I would always drink after work." Additionally, Barbara had Valium prescribed to her for a medical condition and became addicted to them. During her drug and alcohol addiction, Barbara describes herself "as such a phony person, living in a phony world too. And I performed, and performing made me look like I was an outgoing person. But I was like in a totally white world, and I still was fighting to be this black person. I had no idea who I was. It just got to a point that I felt like I was slowly, slowly, slowly losing my mind." She was "drinking heavily" and "doing unbelievable things," when a close girlfriend who would usually tolerate her "outrageous behavior" asked Barbara to leave her house one night:

> I was at her house, and she was having a big dinner party for the Christmas holidays. At the time I could be the most loving and sweet person, and then the next minute I could be pissed off, and I would

curse everybody out. Usually she could put up with me, but I was cursing her friends out because I thought that they were just bourgeoisie, and I hated that. Coming from me to hate this kind of stuff was like unbelievable. So she was sitting there, and she just said get out of my house. Get out of my house. I can still see her face saying that. I left, and I was saying to myself, they must have said something to me. Why would I just go and start cursing people out? They had to have said something. The anger, the rage, that I had then when I was drinking was the same kind of rage that I had when I was a child when I couldn't get what I wanted or something didn't go the way I wanted. I couldn't drink then, but what I would do was to go into the basement, and I would stay up all night, and I would just clean, and I would go into the attic and clean. So when I left the party, a very close friend of mine said to me, I'm an alcoholic and you're one too. I looked at him, and I almost choked. It was how dare this man say this to me? But that's when I made the conscious decision, when I said maybe something is wrong with me, and I wanted to stop drinking.

Barbara believes that "getting sober was the hardest thing that I have ever done in my life." Initially, to cope with her anxiety, she used to go to a Catholic church and "pray, oh please Lord don't let me go crazy today, please don't let me lose my mind today." Later Barbara also turned to AA for help. She described her efforts to stay sober:

What I had to do was get honest with myself. I had to be who I was. I had to tell the truth. It was so hard. When I started going to AA there was hardly any blacks going, and it was like, oh here I go again. But I knew at the time I had to go. I knew I couldn't play games anymore. In other words, I couldn't go in there and perform. I knew something was really wrong with me. I got sober, and all of my emotions were out there. My life became a living hell, and I didn't have the crutches anymore. I was this person that needed a crutch in order to communicate with people. Then all of a sudden I was out there by myself with nothing to protect me. . . .

I coped by going to AA, it just sort of opened my eyes. I didn't trust AA, even when I first went there. I'm not an organizational kind of person. Even when I first went—it was right after the Jim

Jones massacre—I was saying I refuse to drink the Kool Aid. I wasn't going to sit there and spill everything. I like my freedom, and I don't want any kind of thing changing that. . . .

I would cry every morning; every morning my eyes would be swollen out to here. I looked like a monster. And I would put those pads on my face to try and get my eyes down, and I would cry in the shower, and I would be on the subway crying and saying my life is totally over. It's a disaster; everything is horrible. But I realized my true self the second year of sobriety. I can even say that I always knew that it was there, but I just didn't know how to get to it. That second year I saw that there was hope, that there was a possibility that I could be who I am and be accepted, that I didn't have all of these hurdles in front of me. I could just be me. But I still had low self-esteem; I didn't have confidence.

Barbara like Sara realized that she needed help in order to stop abusing substances.

This was a much more gradual realization for Patricia. She admits that she abused alcohol. After separating from her husband for the last time, she said, "I was drinking sometimes heavily but most times not. I knew that I didn't feel really good about myself at the time, and if I was drinking I really didn't have to think that hard about myself, I could just be somebody else. But I really didn't like myself very much. I was trying to drown out and obliterate a lot of things, and on some level it seems that I was trying to drown out and obliterate myself. I guess I was drinking because I was floundering, actually. And I was trying to retrieve something."

On reflection, Patricia said, "One of my major regrets was all of that heavy drinking I did. I regret not treating myself better, and all of that drinking was a part of that." It took Patricia some time to finally grasp the fact that she was an alcoholic like her father. A woman confronted Patricia and told her that she was an alcoholic. As a result, Patricia said, "I began to look at myself and the things I was doing and think maybe that is what I was, an alcoholic."

In her attempts to get "clean and sober," Patricia began to write. She said, "I just had this need, I guess to express myself in some way." She wrote poetry and admits that "actually I wasn't very good, but I was writing it anyway." Patricia decided to join a writer's workshop and started to gain some confidence as she developed her skills as a poet. But her interactions with other black women in the workshop gave her the courage to gradually stop drinking. She attributes the positive relationship that she developed with them as instrumental to her eventual sobriety. Patricia discussed this experience:

> I began to look at the women that I was beginning to come into contact with. I saw that they didn't have any problems with who and what they looked like. I said, you know the more sisters that I'm around and brothers too, but in particularly the sisters, I was getting a lot of good energy. There was some negative stuff out there, but the positive energy far and above outweighed the negative. I've never been a huggy kissy person. I always kind of stood back and surveyed the surrounding to get a read on things. These sisters would just come up spontaneously and just embrace you. I was like real tense for a while because I was not used to people I didn't know touching me. It took a while for me to get used to that, but I saw that it was genuine, so I kind of relaxed a little with that. They were very encouraging and that meant a lot to me, because growing up, even with the females that I would hang out with, there was more competition than encouragement. I saw that these women genuinely encouraged each other's work no matter what it was. They helped me to change my life. I was searching. Here I am, and I've found these women, this wonderful thing that I didn't know that I could do, and now I'm a little timid because I don't know what to do with all of it.

The thread that appears to run throughout and connects Sara's, Patricia's, and Barbara's stories of substance abuse and dependency is woven within and against their need to escape the pain, frustration, and disappointment of their lives. Their experiences suggest that initially drugs and alcohol were used as attempts to alter and mask their sense of inadequacy as measured within and against cultural and social expectations. Although the circumstances and the ways they functioned within those expectations differed, important similarities exist between their experiences of addiction.

Initially, it appears that Sara's and Barbara's use of substance helped to mask their sense of inadequacy while enabling them to disregard cultural and social constraints imposed on their lives in their attempts to feel

worthy. Although expressed differently, it seems that alcohol assisted
Patricia in her efforts to prove that she was worthy as she tried to adhere
to social and cultural expectations. Even though they functioned, they
would falter, for in the process of trying to exercise a degree of control
over their lives aided by substance, they were drawn deeper into the
constraints that addiction and dependency imposed on their lives. As
such, self-medication was no longer an antidote that could help to mask
their sense of inadequacy. Self-medication turned into dependency. And
in that dependency these women began to lose a grip on their reality and
their sense of self within it; they began to feel as if they were either "losing their minds" or "going crazy."

Somewhere in the midst of their dependency, their anger became
useful to them as they decided to try and become "clean and sober." In
return for their struggle they received a renewed sense of being. As Barbara said "I came to realize my true self." She came to realize:

> I couldn't be a victim anymore. I started getting better when I saw
> that I was not unique. Prior to sobriety I definitely saw myself as a
> victim. I would blame my father being blind, growing up in an im-
> poverished family, feeling resentment for being black, and it seem
> like everything around me proved that I was a victim. I would always
> go back to my childhood, and I used all that as my marker. I was a
> poor black girl from Michigan. I don't put myself into little boxes
> anymore. I've learned how to live life on life's terms. I still go through
> the pain, and I grow from the pain, and it takes what it takes. But I
> still have my anger. I prefer being angry rather than fearful. When
> I'm angry I can function, I can defend myself. But fear totally para-
> lyzes me, I feel like I'm handicapped, crippled, I'm not a function-
> ing person. Anger still makes me really crazy. But I know now what
> it means and I've learned how to deal with my anger. It's both my
> strength and weakness.

Drug and alcohol abuse enabled Sara, Barbara, and Patricia to mask their
sense of disvalue from themselves, but it also freed them to express their
anger. Retaining a sense of anger was critical in their efforts toward self-
recovery.

Self-recovery meant finding ways to mange their addiction while also
finding ways that would allow them to reclaim their sense of personhood

in the process. Their anger, as a part of that process, allowed them to rid themselves of the many fears they harbored about "not being good enough." They continue to be angry about those things that they should be angry about. Anger provides an important gauge for how they are treated, what they will and will not tolerate, when they will and will not fight back, and how to establish authority over their sense of self. Barbara explained, "My anger allows me to know how I'm treated in certain situations. It is about not allowing myself to be attacked or stepped all over. It's about defending myself and standing up for me and for whatever I really believe in. I know now that my anger is about respect. And respect is basically how you treat yourself, and how you allow others to treat you, and what you will stand up for, and what you will do when you feel threatened."

CHAPTER 5

She Works

"What Are We Worth?"

> *A Voice from the South,*
> Anna Julia Cooper

AS WORKERS, the women were among the first gener-
ation of African Americans to seek job opportunities under federal affirmative action strategies that were designed to redress past patterns
and practices of race and gender discrimination. As a result of black political protest, legal advocacy, and electoral pressure, civil rights legislation was passed by congress to ensure federal protections for equal access
to society's resources. In the area of employment, the federal government
implemented policies and programs that increased as well as provided
equal job opportunities for African Americans, in both the public and
private sectors of the American economy. Those policies and programs
focused on three major areas of equal access: job opportunities through
affirmative action hiring and promotion, job training and placement in
traditional and nontraditional work, and neighborhood-based job programs that strengthen the human capital of local communities.

Affirmative action strategies are intended to eliminate discriminatory employment patterns and practices. However, as strategies they do
not eliminate deep-seated ideas and beliefs upon which discriminatory
patterns and practices are based, and for which blacks are presumed
inferior to whites and women unequal to men. These ideas continue to
germinate in employment, even with the presence of affirmative action
policies and programs. Nevertheless, the women had to earn a living
for themselves and their families. They took advantage of affirmative action opportunities. Some entered the private sector under affirmative
action hiring policies. Others worked in black communities through
various government-sponsored programs. And, as working artists, several

took advantage of government grants that could aide the making of their art.

In a climate where employment opportunities and barriers coexist, work was an essential part of the women's adulthood experiences: whether it was paid employment, unpaid community and political work, or a combination of both these areas of work. The nature of the women's experiences differed, depending on the types of jobs, expectations, and environments in which they actually worked at any given point in their employment histories. Linking their work experiences are cultural and social constraints that impose discriminatory conditions on their working lives. All the women engaged patterns and practices of racial and gender discrimination that forced them to make important compromises. Sometimes those compromises threatened and jeopardized their sense of self. Unique among their experiences of violence is the lack of physical violence they experienced in the violations. This chapter focuses on the women's paid as well as the unpaid work experiences and the value given to their labor.

A JOB

All the women worked in some capacity as teenagers and received pay for their labor, but they did not start working full-time jobs until they had either completed high school or college. Jackie, for instance worked a part-time job after school at Woolworth's, where she was a sales clerk. Following high school, her "dream was to make money." In this pursuit, Jackie said, "I went downtown and got one of those everybody-got-to-hire-a-black-person jobs on Wall Street. I was probably the third black person that was hired in the whole building." Jackie described how she got the job:

> One of my friends said "they're looking for black people at this firm. Just go and fill out an application and take the test." I went and I took the test, and they told me I was overqualified, and that scared me. I said how could you be overqualified for something you know nothing about? I didn't know what that meant, and I was kind of upset behind that. But then, the next day, it was pouring rain, snow-ing, sleeting; it was doing everything. I had a Kelly green coat, and I had my hood on, and I was soaking wet. I was walking up the hallway

of the firm, and I heard this squishing and dripping all over the place. And these white people were sitting there, and they were looking at me, and there was nothing but big puddles of water. They interviewed me, and I got hired. I went straight to the research department. I made eighteen thousand dollars a year, which was a lot of money in 1965, and I was just eighteen years old.

Working at a firm that was a member of the Stock Exchange, Jackie loved her new job. She worked in the research department, where she had to keep detailed records on the movement of particular stocks that were bought and sold each day. She said, "I knew what the stock opened and closed at. At that time there were no computers. I learned everything. I had a memory. Even if I looked at the paper during the morning, I knew what the stock opened and closed at." Although she loved her job, Jackie had difficulties adjusting to the corporate culture. She recalled her experience:

I was almost too stupid to know how I was treated. I was pretty much a blazer and pleated skirt kind of person. I should have gone to a prep school because I was dressing that way. But when I got there, I had to change my style of dress because they wanted you to dress a certain way in that office. You couldn't come there in skirts and blouses. You had to wear dresses with the heels, which was a whole different attire from what I had. I had to wear my hair back, so I had this long ponytail in the back of my head. I would wear it back or put it up, but basically that was it because they didn't want your hair on your shoulders. They taught me how to speak, so they thought. If I would use any slang language, I would have to pay the pot five-cents. I used to hate that. It was for everyone, but it was only me who was using the slang language, so it was for me. I got tired of them going out for lunch on my money because I did have a small slang problem. But I did know the English language as well. My boss hated me because he would call me by my first name, and I would call him by his first name, too.

Jackie encountered racial tension on the job. She recalls an incident where she had worked closely for three years, over the telephone, with a coworker who was at the firm's Chicago office site. Jackie described the demise of their relationship: "She was coming to New York, and we were going to have lunch and the whole thing. When she walked into the office I heard her, but I was in the back, and this other girl told her I was back there. When she walked back and saw me, she stood there and looked at me and then kept on walking. She never spoke. She had to pass me to get by; it just looked like I was invisible to her. Never spoke to me again on the phone, nothing. That was like the deepest part of racism that I had felt at that job." Jackie continued to work at her job for five years and then quit because she was "on the verge of having a nervous breakdown":

> The breakdown was with the job because my computer was on overload. It got to a point that everything I looked at, I computed. Everything in the world belongs to some kind of stock, a cab goes by, a bus goes by, anything on television, and everything made my computer replay. What happens during that day, that week, that year, what was sold and what was bought. I'm talking about the computer in my head. It was on total overload. I didn't know any other way to unload it other than to leave the job, which was upsetting me. But I mentally couldn't take it anymore.

After high school, Patricia also got a job in the private sector. She said, "After I got my high school diploma that's when I started working a real full-time job." When she started working at her first full-time job as secretary in a bank around 1968, Patricia was still wearing a wig, but shortly thereafter she decided to wear an afro or natural hairstyle.

> When I went into work—they were used to seeing me with the wig on—the manager looked at me and said oh no, no, no, no. I like your hair the other way. He happened to be white, of course. I told him, you like my hair the other way, when I come in here tomorrow I will give it to you, and you can have it because it's not mine. This is mine. At the job I do what I got to do, I'm one of those people who's not talkative at work, telling them your entire life history. But he became very watchful of me. I find a lot of white folks are that way if you're black. He became very leery, watchful, and distrustful. The manager called me over to his desk one day and said he had some dictation for me to take. I got the pad and pencil ready to take dictation and he whips out this paper, *Mohammad Speaks* (the Black

Muslim paper). I'm looking at this paper, and I'm looking at him. He said, "Is this yours?" I said, "No, I don't know whose it is, why?" He was like turning fifty shades of purple because he was so outraged at what was in the paper. I had no idea whose it was. I started to see that in certain situations when I was around white folks, I could be in some kind of potential danger. I was automatically looked at as a militant because I chose not to straighten my hair and then I wasn't that talkative.

The "potential danger" that Patricia refers to are unfounded accusations of wrongdoing based on how others perceived her, as she went about doing her job. She realized that it is not her perception of self, but the perceptions of others, which could threaten or jeopardize her livelihood, her job. So, at work Patricia was ever-guarded.

Patricia got this job by "just walking into the bank and asking who do I see about getting a job"? She was hired as a secretary in a branch office, "Where there were other blacks working, but they were mostly tellers," and all of the people in decision-making positions were white. Patricia worked at the bank branch for three years, but realized early on in her employment that "the branch manager did not want me there and he was trying to push me out. So I left before they could find a reason to fire me." Of this work experience, Patricia said, "In that three-year period that I was there, I didn't get not one promotion; nothing. I remember I was making one-hundred and ten dollars a week, which to me was an insult. I got raises, but they would find everything that they could find wrong and would give me the smallest raise possible. This is what they were doing to me. From there I went to another bank. I worked in a variety of banks, and I was bouncing around all over the place, going to one bank to another."

After arriving in New York City from the rural South, Mary's first full-time job was in the service sector, she worked at a small hotel. At the hotel, Mary said, "I was cleaning bathrooms, making beds, vacuuming and doing whatever had to be done in the hotel. I guess you call it janitorial stuff." Mary kept the "cleaning job" until "the hotel got robbed." Explaining what happened, she said:

The hotel got robbed on the first of the month. I later learned that it had been robbed one year prior to that. I guess on the first of month is when everybody paid their bills. I was in the office when the robbery occurred. I recognized one of the guys because I pulled the mask off his face. I recognized the boy because he used to live in the hotel and I guess he came back to robbed it. They took this cord and cut it up and tied my hands behind my back. They tied up this old man too. But they beat the old man in the head with a gun. The guy said, "You didn't tell me that she looked so good. We ought to take her with us." And then the guy I recognized said, "Naw don't bother her. We don't want to get involved in no kidnapping." So after about a month, the old man wouldn't give me a gun to protect myself, so I wouldn't work for him any longer.

The danger that Mary experienced on the job was different in kind to the one Patricia identified. For the danger posed to Mary was bodily injury and harm. This would be the only incident where one of the women was physically threatened or jeopardized while at work. Mary left this job and "went and got a job at the dry cleaners." While working there, she "signed up for night school. I started taking business courses I guess you call it secretarial course back then." These courses proved instrumental when Mary later attempted to build a career and advance in the corporate sector.

After college, Sara decided to enroll in a special journalism program that had been established at a university in New York City. She decided to go into journalism for two reasons. First, "I wanted to come to New York, and I knew my parents would have a problem with it, and I was sort of afraid to come here without a hook." And second, "I decided to go to J school right after the Kerner Commission Report: the Kerner Commission had decided that more black journalists were needed," and this college established a special summer program that was different from its degree program to train minority journalists.

Sara struggled through the program because she "would get high and get drunk and hang out, and then I would miss my morning appointments." And by doing this, she eventually got caught in "a big fat lie." On one occasion, Sara "wrote the story as if I had been there." But she did not go to her interview, and her professor caught the fact that her story was fabricated. They did not expel Sara from the program, but she said this experience made her more aware of the "ethics in journalism and in life."

After completing the requirements for the program, Sara said, "You didn't end up with a degree, you ended up with a job, which was what I liked about the program." She worked her first full-time job as a journalist for a city newspaper in 1969. Talking about this experience, Sara said she "took her job seriously' and "felt that I was on a mission":

> It was a mission for me to keep these white folks from running these stereotypes on black folks. My first commitment was being a black person. I took all that stuff very seriously. I didn't feel like I could really tell the truth in the system. I wanted to write about the TRUTH. I wanted to tell the truth. I was there standing guard to keep these white people in check. There were some fights. The minority journalists, the black journalists, had a big meeting. There were a lot of activities. A lot of it was trying to make some kind of difference because it was obvious that we needed to do something about the way the news was reporting on black folks. I believed in all that stuff.

Although Sara "believed in all that stuff," she could not be depended on to follow through on work assignments or produce, "for the simple fact that I was getting high and drinking." Sara said, "I didn't feel authentic somehow." She worked as a journalist for about a year and then decided to quit: "I felt like I was writing about other people's lives; I felt like a voyeur; I felt like I wasn't actually living my own life; I felt like I had to distance myself from things." Through her ongoing drug and alcohol abuse, Sara continued to distance herself from things, and this became a consistent pattern in her employment history, as she went from one job to another.

Going into her senior year at college, Amanda got a summer job that was "really an eye opener." It was as a model with a major company that published various white women's fashion magazines in New York City. One magazine put out an annual college edition that would showcase female college students. It was decided that a special black college edition would be published as well. The magazine held a contest at various historically black colleges to find women for this special edition. Amanda's friends talked her into entering the contest, and she won: her prize was to work as a model for the magazine company during the summer months. Of this experience, Amanda said:

I was supposed to be a model, but it was more like I was a go-for. I was sent around to work with the different magazines. It was interesting, but I didn't get paid very much. And then I had to model in the showroom. It's the kind of modeling you do in a showroom for buyers who come from the various stores to decide what they were going to buy for the fall season. Everybody was really into this real thin stuff. I saw that you could become very neurotic, so preoccupied with every little thing about your body. Then there was this cosmetics firm that was going to show for the first time black make-up. So I was sent on this shoot, and I thought that I was in another world. I eventually ended-up sitting on the side talking to this white photographer because the women were like barracudas. These were all black women. They were very catty and insulting to each other, and they were trying to seduce the photographer to get selected. I just felt that this was all real stupid, and I didn't find it a good experience.

Although the nature of their first full-time jobs differed, several of the women were hired under affirmative action policies. Like Amanda, they did not see these jobs as the start of professional careers but viewed them simply as jobs. During the late 1960s, the women's first full-time jobs were generally in predominately white work environments at entry-level positions. During a period when companies were beginning to diversify or integrate their work force. With the exception of Mary and Faith who pursued different areas of work, all the other women initially entered the labor force through the private sector as low-level clerical workers. Usually, they were often one among a few blacks that worked in the same place. They clearly understood how they were positioned: Anne said that she was "a novelty," while Jackie admits to being "a token hire." Isolated in corporate cultures for which they were not fully familiar, they were expected to adhere to different dress, language, and behavioral codes of conduct in order to fit in, perform, and to keep their jobs. The women perceived and responded differently to those expectations. This difference depended on how they defined their needs, interests, and aspirations, on whether they were simply trying to maintain employment or attempting to establish a professional career.

A Career

By the mid-1970s, Mary and Anne were attempting to establish professional careers. They entered the world of white corporate America through entry-level or clerical positions, and, in this highly hierarchical culture, they did not have college degrees. Over the years, Mary progressed in banking to become a part of management, and Anne became an associate editor in fashion publishing. As they pursued professional careers, they came to understand the value of their labor in corporate America and its meaning for how they saw themselves as workers.

Following the break up of her marriage, Anne realized that she wanted as well as needed to work. She went to the Urban League for assistance because the organization was assisting corporations in identifying blacks for their affirmative action recruitment and hiring programs. Anne said, "At the time the Urban League was the major referral route for black people to get hired at the company." They referred her to the same publishing company where Amanda had worked some years earlier as a model. The company published a variety of women's fashion magazines, and Anne was told "that I had been hired because I seemed to be the kind of individual that they were looking for. I didn't realize that there had to be special criteria for blacks to be in that environment. I was ignorant of that. But I also knew that there wasn't much I could do about the corporate structure."

Initially, Anne was hired as a temporary secretary, but she "thought that it was a full-time job." And when the woman whom she was replacing returned to work, the company offered her a permanent clerical job. Anne was employed at what she called "the Tiffany of the magazine publishing world" for nine years. Anne discussed the different phases of her employment at this company:

> In my first job there I reported to the senior fashion editor. My responsibility was to do her clerical work, which required the typing of some reports and her expense account. I was the only black woman in the fashion department. From her, I went to work with the shoe and accessory editor. She was the terror of the office. I worked for her like seven or eight years. It was great. I got promoted to an associate fashion editor, whereby my name went on the masthead. Eighteen months after I was there my salary increased but

magazine publishing paid paltry sums for salary. I would tell them I wanted a raise. I'm sure I was so naïve that it was pennies and peanuts I guess, to a certain degree, I was humored, and I didn't exceed the boundaries.

With a promotion to associate editor, Anne's primary responsibility was "to maintain the shoe closet. The shoe closet was a room with floor-to-ceiling shelves filled with shoes on three walls. I had to know all of the manufacturers; I had to know all of the sizes; I had to know what was there, because you had photography shoots coming and going." Technically, with this promotion, Anne was no longer a secretary. However, she was "still doing the clerical work for the shoe and accessory editor." But gradually Anne assumed more and more responsibility on her own because she loved her job. Anne describes herself as a "natural fit into this environment, both in terms of personality and the ability to execute the job." She eagerly performed her job; however, she was acutely aware of the contradictions between her work environment and her private life:

> I fit in the work environment during the confines of the workday. But I was very clear that I was living a schizophrenic existence. Schizophrenic is my way of describing the split. I was aware of the fact that I worked in a much more plusher environment than the one I lived in. I was very aware of the fact that I had to keep a balance between the two. I could not buy into the luxury of the magazine business without suffering the consequences of alienation from my own private lifestyle. There were compromises; the compromise was one of time, of association with friends being curtailed, there was a compromise in terms of lifestyle, and there was a compromise economically.

Along with what she considered to be compromises, Anne was also aware of the unique benefits she received from the job. As she said, "I got exposure to do more and more and more. I would do fashion shows, I would travel around the country, I would do television, I would do radio, and I would do commercials. I wouldn't ask for it, but if an opportunity presented itself I wouldn't turn it down. I'm a firm believer in the value of experience. I was very aware of that because I didn't have a college diploma that said okay we know that she can count beyond five."

Anne saw herself as a "spokesperson representing the magazine." But she concedes that "there was always a white female counterpart and we worked together doing the same things." Nevertheless, she enjoyed the visibility that her job afforded her. Anne understood that as an associate editor with her name on the magazine masthead she was in a unique position at the company.

During this period, Anne saw herself "as a very fortunate black woman. I saw myself as fortunate because I knew I had somebody's job that had studied to be this, and I just fell into it. I understood that I recognized opportunity when it knocked. I understood that there were other black women who had worked at this magazine and who, for whatever reason, did not survive it." Anne felt that she was appreciated by the company. Given her growing expertise and increased responsibility at the magazine, she began to apply for positions within the company that were of "higher status and pay." But she quickly found that:

> I was being constantly let down indirectly. I was allowed to interview for these positions, so seemingly it was equitable; it was fair. But I would find after the fact that these jobs that I had applied for were being given to other people. They would be people with less experience, people who belonged to very important families, people who had another piece of education, or not necessarily education but had money. These were still the days when magazine employment was a rite of privilege, a right of class. By this time, the few blacks may have been around in other departments, working at other company magazines, had now dwindled. I'm the highest ranking black fashion editor, the highest ranking editor that's black, who had her name on the masthead, whose name has been on the masthead for close to nine years.

Anne was ambitious. She "wanted to be somebody at the company. I knew that I was good at what I did in that environment, that I could hold my own. I worked hard, and I should've been promoted." Initially thinking that she fit into the company environment, Anne had a change in attitude, and she became angry. She attributes "not being promoted primarily to racism." She eleborated, "I was very conscious of being black, of being different. I didn't fit. I didn't fit the mold that was acceptable. I think that I was too brown. I wasn't paid what I was worth. I'm aware that I hit that proverbial glass ceiling." Angered by a lack of both promotion and an increase in pay, Anne submitted her letter of resignation, and "they were stunned that I would have gall enough to resign from this great and wonderful job."

As a result of what she perceived as discriminatory treatment, Anne felt violated. In her best efforts, she had not only attempted to fit into the corporate culture but also gave it the benefits of her growing knowledge and expertise. In return for the nine years she worked at the publishing company, she received only one job promotion and small periodic raises in salary. Although she had the title of associate editor and limited prestige as a result, Anne knew that she was extinguishable. It was not the day-to-day work that provoked a sense of violation, for Anne enjoyed her job immensely; rather, it was the lack of recognition, a lack of value, given to her as a worker. Anne believes that the denial of job advancement, increased pay, and corporate status, which she had rightfully earned, was due solely to racial discrimination.

Mary's experience would be similar to Anne's, as she attempted to establish a professional career in banking. Mary worked in banking for twenty years. Through the years, in the absence of a college degree, Mary had taken special courses and night classes in an effort to learn about the banking business and enhance her potential for job advancement and pay increases. From an initial clerical position, Mary had advanced to a supervisory job, when a former boss who was working at another bank asked her to come and work with him at what she describes as a "union bank." At this bank, Mary was "in charge of the night shift operations of the computer room. The computer room was a big old cold icy place, where you had people using an IBM keypunch machine. I would have to train them or show them how to do the keypunching and the other work." Mary recalled her early work experiences at the "union bank":

> When I moved over to the union bank, I was the only black that was in a supervisory position, because that was a new department. Whites ruled all the other areas. The day shift supervisor would always leave all the work for us to do on the night shift. I would complain and try to explain to them why it wasn't fair. What were they doing during the day if they were leaving everything for the night shift? You could see how much work had come in, and you could see how much

work had been done. I don't know what they were doing during the day, but they certainly weren't working. I had to keep going in and proving that they were not completing their jobs.

Mary described herself as "straightforward and outspoken" on the job. "People always knew that I was fair and I knew what I was talking about." She saw herself as a "fair supervisor" but admits that she "was a little prejudiced." She said, "I'm being prejudiced with whites because some of them would try and tell me what to do or try to intimidate me." Mary continued to work the night shift, but she wanted a promotion to management, then she found out, "you had to be at the bank for ten years before you got your first promotion." But this did not seem right to Mary because she saw other people getting promoted with less than ten years' experiences: "the guys but not the women." So she decided that the best way to get promoted was to transfer to the dayshift: "Once I got on the day shift and I excelled and I made them promise that I could go to every department and learn every crook and cranny of banking. Eventually I got promoted. I went there in 1968 in 1978 I got my promotion: ten years after I started. I think that there was one other black person that was an officer before me. My promotion was to assistant manager. That's the first introduction to what you would call the administrative level."

But Mary's promotion was not necessarily obtained through merit. To get a promotion she had to make an important concession:

> I had to come out of the union. I was the union representative from the time I got there in 1968 until 1978. They wanted to get me out of the union because I was too strong for them with negotiations. They couldn't intimidate me. They would try to harass me, and I would just bring them up on charges all the time. I was a shop steward, which means I represented all of the unionized workers at the bank. They had asked me earlier to come out of the union, but I didn't. I knew why they wanted me to come out. They asked me to vote their way on contracts. They promised me all of this stuff that I could get if I did it, and I didn't do it, so they saw that they were wasting their time. . . .
>
> But then they offered me $7,500 to become an officer, at that time if they gave you a promotion it didn't mean money. They thought that the promotion was going to do so much for your ego,

but I didn't see the reason for changing a title for no money, so I said, okay, for $7,500, yes I will become an officer. But I saw that as just a salary adjustment probably that I was deserving of anyway for all the hard work that I was doing. So, yeah, I came out of the union then. I had trained some union people very well, and I taught them about how to get around in the politics of the bank. But they didn't listen; they were more vulnerable. Whatever management would ask them to do they would do it. The union went down fast after I left.

Mary was disappointed that the union "was not as productive as when I had managed it," but she said after ten years, "It was time for me to move on. Once you've made a choice to move on then you can't really feel bad about it." With the promotion, Mary was responsible for establishing minority accounts for the bank. She said, "I recruited all of the major black organizations, 'cause I was a member of all of those organizations: the National Urban League, United Negro College Fund, the NAACP and many of its branches. I recruited them to open up accounts at the bank."

In addition to bringing in new accounts, Mary also started a chapter of the National Association for Women in Banking in an attempt to "strengthen and empower the women" she worked with. Through this association and other activities at the bank, increasingly Mary became known as a "trouble maker," and she had to deal with the implications this held for her:

If racism or gender discrimination was blatant I would be confrontational with management about it. The bank was afraid to really mess with me, but they would do things to other people, and other people would bring it to my attention, and I would still go to management and try to rectify the problem. I knew that I was in a unique position. So what they would do in contrast to me was to keep me from getting other promotions. As long as I was getting bonuses for the work that I was bringing into them, that helped me personally to be able to take care of my children, and take care of all my basic needs, I didn't need a title. I wasn't the highest ranking black in title, but in action and in responsibility I was. Sometimes you can be a clerk and be more powerful than a vice president in a given situation, and that was always my contention. I didn't need a title in order to be empowered. I would do things based on what was right or what was needed.

Mary believes that "even without realizing it" she had "created a power base," and this was important because management was constantly trying to find ways to get rid of her. The pressures and stress of the job took a toll. Mary realized that she had worked at the bank for twenty years and could take an early retirement. In reflecting upon her twenty years of banking and her contributions, Mary said:

> By 1988, I was pretty well known in the banking community. I had like maybe 1,300 clients when I left that I had recruited on my own. I brought in 33 million dollars in business to that bank. This was supposed to mean that I would get at least $7,500 if not $10,000 in bonuses each year. But they would give me like half of that, maybe $3,500 as a bonus. When I left the bank, I was making $1,300 a week, and when I started there as a supervisory I was making $137 a week. In all fairness I didn't do to bad. But comparing males verse females I should have been doing maybe $2,000 a week instead of $1,300. Since I retired early, that's what my retirement is, one fourth of what I was making, so I now get $1,300 a month. Women usually get about 65 percent of what the men were getting paid. But I liked what I was doing, so that was the compromise—a mental compromise to offset not getting paid what I should be getting.

Right after she submitted her retirement papers, Mary filed a race and gender discrimination lawsuit against the bank. She explained her decision: "I decided to sue for discrimination, and I had itemized about twenty-five different incidents where it was so obvious. My case is still pending. I've gone through four lawyers, and the last one is making tiny bits of progress, but it takes a long time. I'm not in it for the money. You see I don't live high on the hog here. I don't have high aspirations for material things. It was the right thing to do cause of the way they treated me." At the union bank, Mary received only one job promotion over her twenty-year employment and deeply resented not having received the bonuses she merited due to job performance. Unlike Anne who walked away because of her anger over discriminatory treatment, Mary's anger led her to take action against her employer. However, Mary's attempts to get redress through her lawsuit occurred when her job and economic security was no longer on the line.

For those who pursued professional careers in corporate America, the violations they experienced occurred primarily in three related areas of employment: first, in the corporate culture that inhibited self-expression and self-presentation; second, in the interactions with coworkers that was deemed insulting, humiliating, or demeaning; and third, in discriminatory patterns and practices that limited opportunities for job advancements and salary increases. The women's experiences suggest that corporate culture requires at least a degree of assimilation, adoption of established norms and role behavior, and adherence to expectations. Within this context, unfair or uneven treatment may not be blatant or obvious. Sometimes, discriminatory patterns and practices are masked within the hierarchical culture making it difficult to discern, owing to what appears to be normal for those environment. At other times the insidiousness of racism and sexism may appear in the absence of definable patterns and practices, but is conveyed by personal attitudes or even through humor that goes unchallenged and becomes tolerated or acceptable in the environment.

In their attempts to make a living in predominately white working environments there are similarities in the experiences of the women who pursued professional careers and those who viewed their employment simply as a job to be performed. To varying degrees, they both expressed a sense of disappointment, disillusionment, and resentment in the face of persistent challenges that limited their employment needs, interests, and aspirations. Whether the corporate cultural norms were subtle or blatant regarding uneven race and gender relations, after having worked primarily in clerical positions, Patricia concludes that such work environments are generally oppressive and often humiliating for black women: "It hard work just to be a black woman at work, no matter what the conditions are, we are only perceived as work horses, as mammies." Patricia recognizes that with a high school diploma she has had few alternatives or options for employment. She worked in a particular job until she could not longer tolerate it, and then she moved on to another clerical position, usually at another bank. Patricia offered her reflections on her work experience as a secretary in white environments:

The white folks generally don't see you as a human being. They know that you're there to perform a job, but women in my position are as dispensable as a paper clip. I've never gotten the sense that they see you as a full-fledge human being. They see you simply as a servant, and they treat you as a servant. I have a problem with that. I have a problem when they speak to you in a very disrespectful manner. I have a problem when they expect you to call someone Mr. or Mrs. so and so, yet they feel that it's all right to call me by my first name. I have a problem that if I'm sick and I call in and I tell you I'm sick, you want me to bring a doctor's note like I'm some child in school. You work hard, and it's not appreciated. And you get paid less simply because you're not white and male. That's why I would stay on a job for about three years and then leave. There's no such thing as my having loyalty to a job. A job is a job, it something you do to make a living.

Based on their work experiences several women wanted a job to be more than a job. They wanted the work they performed to have value. They wanted to derive a sense of satisfaction from their labor. As such, they decided to work for themselves.

WORKING FOR MYSELF

Initially, Barbara bounced around from one clerical job to another with different advertisement firms. She said the culture of the advertising business was such that "you go from agency to agency." As she moved from job to job, Barbara gradually worked her way up to various positions in advertising, and eventually she became a publicist. For Barbara "if racism was around, I didn't see it at all" because she was afforded the opportunity to advance. However, when she became a publicist things started to change, and Barbara found that she had hit a ceiling. As such, she began to see that "racism was around." She recalls an incident where she was "really enraged." At an office party, a white female coworker, whom Barbara believed to be a racist, "dressed in black face." Barbara's boss dismissed her sense of violation over this incident, and she described her reaction: "I had to tell him in no uncertain terms that I know what racism is. I said, I know what it is, and you can't tell me what I think I'm supposed to know, should know, or could know. I know what it is and you know what it is, so lets don't play this game. What she did was racist. I aint going to pretend it wasn't. I told him I refuse to eat the watermelon and dance like Steppin Fletcher, I aint going to do it." Soon after Barbara was laid off from her job as publicist. After her failed marriage and amidst her efforts to get "clean and sober," Barbara needed to find work. Unable to do so, Barbara made a decision: "I'll create a job. I'll make my own job." Having worked as a publicist promoting artists, she decided that this was something she could do on her own. Barbara drew on her advertisement experience and the network of people she had developed over the years, and along with a partner she started her own publicity firm.

Barbara describes the eight years that she worked for herself as "the best time of my life. It was so rewarding, and that's when I got my self-esteem back." Her partner "was like my mentor. He's like eighty years old," and she primarily looked to him for guidance. But she was "the one who really went out and got the business." Recalling her "love" of this experience, Barbara said:

> That's when I had more courage than I ever had in my life. I learned how to trust myself, trust my instincts. It gave me the courage to say, you know I can do things that I didn't think that I was capable of doing. I did publicity. I did major campaigns. I did a campaign for the first East Europeans who came into the country to play different basketball teams. I did a campaign for a major black pop singer. I had this one artist, this woman who was a therapist, and she had this thing Therapy To Go, and I got her on all of these television shows. She was like in a limousine, and these were busy people, so you just called her and she would go to where you were. I did a television station's fifth anniversary. Whatever it was I figured out a way to do it.

But Barbara reached a point when she could no longer figure out what to do, and her business gradually started to decline.

> You're constantly looking for business, and it just got to a point that it was to difficult. You had to fight to get paid from clients. At one point I had about fifteen accounts. It was a lot, because you had to try and get them something, because if you had like a no-name

person, you had to get them publicity, you had to get them something to show them, hey this is warranted money. Then you could work like crazy and they would come to you and say I have to pay my rent. My thing was I have to pay mine too. So it got to the point where it was too difficult to make a living.

To make ends meet, Barbara started working freelance two days a week with a large music company. Impressed by her work, they said, "Why don't you come and work with us?" Barbara did. But she found that she was the first black professional woman to work at the company. In the seven years she worked with this company, Barbara has "only been promoted once." She described her frustrations and dilemma:

> My instinct told me that I shouldn't go to work there because I knew that I would lose a part of myself, but then again my bank book said, yes, take it. I thought that I could cope with it. In my first year there I wasn't doing nothing, just doing like little press releases. No major stuff. Nothing where I was using my brain, not going to work and saying I've accomplished something, I've done something good; my first year, my second year, my third year, and my fourth year. My position is coordinator, and in a sense a coordinator is a glorified step above a secretary. It's not something that is challenging. That's the thing that's a real problem for me. And then of course being forty-five years old, so you can't do anything anymore. I feel just the opposite because I'm a person where the first years, I was just floating around. In a sense I'm ready mentally and physically to do the things I could not do years prior. And forty-five is like a cut off point that says, oh you can't do it. I gave a major presentation and they said, thanks for being creative. But they just ignored it. People say, well you're limiting yourself. If I could find something to leave there for, I would be gone. But I don't have anything to take to go somewhere else. You got to have something to show if you go somewhere else, you got to have products, but I don't have anything to take.

Similar to Barbara, Anne was also in need of a job. After resigning from the women's fashion magazine where she had worked for nine years, Anne drew on contacts she had established while working in the "industry" to become a freelance consultant. This allowed her to "stash some money aside for investing in my own business." Even as a child, Anne was interested in designing and making clothes. So she teamed up with a designer, an attorney, and a Chinese manufacturer in Hong Kong to start a clothing business. She wanted to move into the "plus-size clothing market" because this reflected who she was at this period in her life, and besides she "had now become a mini expert on plus-size fashion." Anne thought that there was a growing "trend that was not starting then, but people were beginning to mumble about." Anne recalled this experience:

> All of the team members had a fashion background. The designer illustrated my concepts and would buy the fabric, and I would stitch the design. Some friends of mine would also sew. It was a mom-and-pop operation. We wore as many hats as it took to do what we had to do. It was long hours. Some days we wouldn't sleep for two days. We shared the showroom with the manufacturer. We sold 300 thousand dollars worth of confirmed paper orders to Macy's, Harrods, and a bunch of other stores. I got all kinds of publicity. I got national publicity. When the samples came out people were stunned. They were clothes that they wanted to wear. We knew that we had a good product. But the backer gave us no warning, and pulled the rug from underneath us. We were expecting our shipments, some stores got their clothes, so we are calling trying to find out where's the rest of the shipment. That's when we found out that nothing had been made.

In an attempt to avoid humiliation and to save the company, Anne got a design contract with a "very big manufacturer: it was separates and accessories." Her team developed the designs, but the manufacturer decided "they weren't going to spend the money to develop the line." So they gave her a "big check" for her work, and she, in turn, "paid off everybody" who she owed. This experience left Anne "stunned." She said. "I was just stunned that they could pay me for the designs and then just treat them like old Kleenex." But it was also an experience that left Anne immensely satisfied: "I've been a risk-taker for a very long time and I did what I felt I should be doing with my life." Similar to Barbara's perspective, Anne viewed her efforts as "successful," even though the business failed. It was successful because "I didn't necessarily have to use the same measuring stick that other people used for success. I could see my own efforts manifested in what I did. I could express myself. I felt empowered by going though the process of creating something new, by taking the risk on myself, by going after what I wanted, and doing it. I felt good about me."

Barbara and Anne created their own sense of value though the work they did for themselves. As entrepreneurs, both point to these experiences as the best and most productive of their working lives. They encountered financial constraints generally experienced by small businesses and were unable to sustain their efforts. Even though such constraints may have been influenced by race and gender relations, neither Barbara nor Anne perceived this to be the case. As such, other than their constant concerns about cash flow, they felt a certain freedom from cultural and social expectations which allowed them to explore their creativity as well as new possibilities. It was not the struggle of running a business that is of importance to their experiences, rather it is what they gained in the process of establishing those businesses. In other words, they gained a sense of their own value that was reflected in the ways they viewed themselves during those periods of self-employment.

THE ART OF WORKING

Three of the women—Sharon, Faith, and Patricia—worked as artists, and in their own ways they too were entrepreneurial. Sharon had practiced the piano for most of her childhood, and later she received a bachelor of arts in music. She moved to New York City to pursue a singing career. In the meantime, to make ends meet, Sharon worked a series of temporary clerical jobs. Sharon said that she was not making money off of her art, "so I was working just like anybody else." But, while she was trying to establish a career singing, Sharon joined a large black choral group that sang Negro Spirituals. "Almost every weekend we had jobs singing. It was just like being in a glee club," she said. With other members of the group, she began "hanging out and meeting people on the musical scene." Along with two other women, Sharon decided to start a singing group. Although she was also trained as a classical singer, the group performed "rhythm and blues and pop music." Through connections, the group hired managers, "but things never quite jelled, so we signed them to be our songwriters." Describing her attempts to make a career out of singing, Sharon said: "We were being paid for some things and for other things not. But we were determined. I was still singing in the choral group. I was going to a vocal coach. The group would go and audition for anything and everything. I knew I wasn't an actress, but I would go in and read just in case I got a part. It was an exciting time for me. This was like the middle 70s, and I was singing all over the place. This was the best time of my life. But my mother died. She just dropped dead in 1977." Sharon was "devastated, totally devastated" by her mother's sudden death from a heart attack. She returned to her midwestern home town to make funeral arrangements. As she said, "I had to handle everything." She stayed at home for several years, and when she returned to New York City discovered that the "singing scene had died." During this period, Sharon tried to rejuvenate the group, but "a lot of things went wrong, and there were a lot of disappointments."

> If you are not in the business, it's hard to understand how many auditions you go on, how many people you meet, how many people tell you lies. All the things that happened to me are really just incredible. The group sort of broke up. The songwriters let us out of the contract because they couldn't fulfill their end. Me and another girl in the group did backup work on stage and in the studio. We got a record contract, and six months into the deal we were working on our own album, and we found out that this was a whole mafia sort of thing. We were under contract for about a year, and then they put our project on the shelf, and the whole deal sort of died, and we got out of the contract. We had a whole album that we did with them. Meanwhile we did background singing with their other artists. The gigs we got after that weren't paying the rent; we were only doing background stuff here and there. I was working temporary clerical jobs to make ends meet. It's not necessarily the thing that you work really hard for that you get. But things have a way of evening themselves out. So that's what happened to my singing career.

When Sharon stopped singing professionally, she said "it wasn't painful because by then I was totally fed up with the business." She reflected:

> You know how you work really hard, and it still doesn't mean anything. You may or may not succeed. By that time I was nearly forty

years old, and I noticed that the girls coming behind me were much skinnier and younger. You would be dense not to notice that your time is over in the business. That if you haven't become a star by a certain age, that you can pretty much wrap it up. And my friends who were models and opera singers that didn't make it big, we were all seeing the same thing, and it was time to move onto something else. After a while you get tired of the bullshit. You're putting out money, and you're getting nowhere, you're putting out money for pictures, you're putting out money for postage, you're putting out money for tapes. It's like having your own business. It's a lot of stuff that you have to put into it, and you're getting no returns on it, so what's the point? After you've had so many disappointments you come to grips with the fact that hey, I'm not meant to be a big star. Always in my mind, I said, I came from a small town in the Midwest, and I got to run with the sharks. I did get a chance to really try. I had enough nerves to try. So it was time for me to move onto that other part of my life.

Faith was an actor. And like Sharon, to make ends meet, Faith relied on temporary clerical jobs as she went about the business of becoming a working actor.

For a very long time I didn't have an acting job. I was doing Off Broadway stuff. I was working showcases. Equity, the union, will allow you to do a certain number of performances where people are paid damn little so they can try and see if they can get backers for their show. I was doing the showcases. If I had my SAG (Stage Actor Guild) card, then I was probably doing some extra work, but nothing really substantial. I was trying to find an agent. What I was doing to put food on the table, I might have been doing temp work. I was not by any means a great typist. I was taking classes. During this period I was trying to sharpen my skills.

But Faith soon realized that sometimes acting skills were not as important as having a "look," in getting a job. She said "somewhere along the line it's probably better to have a craft, but initially it's better to have a look." Faith found that especially for films "it's better to be a type"; therefore, she "needed to be browner cause they wanted to be sure that there was no confusion that they had cast somebody black. But I wasn't interested in developing a look. I was trying to be a craftsman."

But Faith also found that even more important than developing a certain "black look" was developing business contacts. Of her art she said, "I don't know if there is anything that I enjoy doing more than acting." But of the business of art she said, "I don't know that there is anything that I hate more." Faith explained her comments:

> What I discovered was that if you wanted to be a working actor you had to have a look, but it was definitely much more important to develop business contacts. Who you know is probably more important than what you know. But I just never could quite figure out the agent thing. All the agents offices said don't come in. But you went in anyway. The whole thing was that you went in hoping that somebody was going to be coming out of the office, or casting for somebody where you had the right look, and they would take two minutes to talk to you. Well ninety-five percent of the time that did not happen. What did happen is that they would usually curse you out for coming through the door. I found the business unbearable. I thought that casting people and agents who were a very necessary part of any success that you had, were rude and ill-mannered. They seem to do everything they could to undermine your confidence in yourself. And if you didn't deal with them you could never get to the work.

Given her experiences with the business of art, Faith started to "really question" whether she wanted to continue acting. She took time off to reflect on her acting career, and while doing so Faith decided to develop a character that she could possibly sell to educational markets as a one-women performance. Faith thought that if she was successful this could give her some financial independence and allow her to continue acting. The character she developed for her performance was based on Sally Hemmings, the slave mistress of Thomas Jefferson. But in the early 1980s, Faith said, "It never crossed my mind that Sally would be controversial." Describing her attempts to bring Sally Hemmings to the stage, she said:

> I didn't think there was anything controversial about it, but for most people just the fact that Jefferson had this thirty-eight-year relationship

with this black woman was enough. She was hardly black. She was a quadroon. In fact, I'm too dark to be Sally. People thought that I was denigrating one of their founding fathers. The booking agents would ask me if I could prove the relationship, I said, yeah the oral history. They said oral history is not proof. I said depends upon what culture you're from. I said, white people write thing down. Booking agents find you jobs to perform, so they have to accept the piece, and then they would try and find gigs for you. I could not get anybody to accept the piece and during that time I wasn't even saying slave wife. Later on I just really decided to call it what I thought it was: The Story of Jefferson Slave Wife, not mistress. Like I said, I couldn't find a booking agent, and that's definitely not anything that I do well. So I just chalked it all up to experience and put Sally in the corner.

Both Faith and Sharon enjoyed their art and took enormous pleasure from performing. But they both realized early on in their careers that to be considered successful they had to treat their art as a business. The business of art required that they represent their interests by finding jobs, which were often temporary, and manage their careers in the highly competitive cultural environment in New York City. As black women artists, race and gender relations influenced the opportunities and options available to them as they pursued their art and the business of art.

Their art was rooted in black cultural aesthetics. As such, Sharon expressed general agreement with Faith's contention that "it's important for black artists to have a venue that allows them to present their own voice." But given the business of art, often they would take wherever work they could find, regardless of the venue or their ability to give voice to what they deemed important. To be full-time working artists, Sharon knew that she had to have a particular "sound and have a manager who would promote me in the right way," and Faith knew that she needed a particular "look" and an agent that would help her to gain access to acting jobs. Not having these essential things, they both were unable to make a living solely off of their art; they worked other jobs, usually temporary clerical jobs, in order to make ends meet. Although they had disappointments, neither Sharon nor Faith regrets pursuing their art.

Patricia's experience as a working poet and writer was different from Faith's and Sharon's experiences. She had participated in a number of writers' workshops to develop her skills as a poet. By the early 1980s, she along with other poets started to give public poetry readings. By the mid-1980s, she was feeling comfortable enough with her skills and progress as a poet, so she decided to self-publish her first book of poems. Initially, Patricia tried to get a company to publish her work and sent her work "out to a variety of places, and the majority of those places were white-owned publishing housing, and what people had told me proved true—if you are not already a name, your work wasn't going to be considered by them." There was one publisher who accepted her poetry: "a small press, but they wanted to edit my work, change it. I said that's totally unacceptable. Thanks, but no thanks." Given her experience in trying to get published, Patricia came to a realization:

> The large publishing concerns could care less about publishing you, in particular African American poetry or African American writers who write poetry because it relates to their experience. To me, it's like a mind-set that the work is too black, whatever that means, or it's too ethnic whatever that means. It was always too something when it came to black folks work. I decided that this almost struck me like begging; please publish my work. So I decided that I would look into publishing my own work. I said, well you know on the one hand I would have control over what goes in the book. I would have control over what the book looks like; I would have control of the book entirely. So whatever positive or negative comes out of it, it's on me if I publish my book myself.

Patricia did research on self-publishing and discovered "it wasn't as difficult as I thought that it would be." She learned what "camera ready and type-setting fonts and all that kind of stuff was." To pay for publishing her first book, Patricia said, "My mother loaned me some of the money, I had saved up some on my own, and part of it came out of my income tax return." Following the publication, Patricia gave herself a book party.

Becoming more self-assured and reliant, Patricia said that she was "actually feeling really good during this period." She decided to start her own writer's workshop, called "Ngoma's Gourd." She wanted to organize poetry programs through her writer's workshop that would focus on the writings of black women poets, but she also thought that this could be a useful way to market her book of poetry. Patricia was confident that she could start the workshop, but she was uncertain about the programming. Drawing on relationships that she had forged over the years and her female friends, she said, "I'm going to try":

> So what I did is call on people whenever I wanted to do a program. There's one girlfriend that I knew that no matter when I called on her if she were capable of helping, she would be there for me. I knew a couple of other women writers and singers who told me that they felt the spirit and the energy was right in what I wanted to do, and they didn't mind helping me out. I was fortunate because I had worked with other writers' groups. I knew how to get money from Poets and Writers, a small funding source for artists. I would organize and make up the programs; you know, get out the flyers and mail them out. My girlfriends would help me with the mailings. I always made certain that I did some programs specifically around women. I'm not saying that there weren't a lot of programs for black women, but there weren't enough of them around for me, so I figured I would try and add some. I didn't think that enough was being said about African American women experiences in particular: discussing our problems, discussing our standards of beauty, discussing sisterhood. There simply weren't enough of that for me. I felt that it was important for me as a woman to do that kind of stuff. I was fortunate that the programs did go off pretty well, but it was also my way of bringing other women together so that they could interact and network together and hope something could jump off from that.

Of her experience as a poet, Patricia said, "I was deliriously happy and felt an enormous sense of pride and accomplishment." She elaborated: "I'm proud of the fact that I can say I'm a writer. And I'm a damn good writer actually. I'm proud of the fact that even though I didn't have an agent or a well-know publisher, I published and sold my own books. I'm proud of the fact that people seen to appreciate my work. I'm proud of the fact that I accomplished something in my life. All of this changed my life and my way of looking at myself." Patricia took control over her art and the business of art. In her reflections, Patricia said the important lesson that she has learned is that "you can't wait around and let other people place their limitations on you and determine the outcome of your life. When I think back on my life and the struggles I've gone through, it could have happened to me. But now I appreciate the fact that when I want something, I find a way to do it, to make it happen."

In their maturity, similar to Patricia, several women refused to accept the limitations placed on their lives and adopted a "can-do" philosophical stance as they engaged in community and political work. They were drawn into community/political activism out of a sense of conviction about what was culturally and socially right and wrong. Their activism was usually aimed at institutional change that would allow blacks to have greater access to decision making and a louder voice in the distribution of resources.

COMMUNITY AND POLITICAL WORK

Working full-time jobs, several women also worked in the black community as a way of expressing their political commitments to racial and social justice. This largely unpaid work required many hours of active involvement. They did not view their community/political activism as separate and apart from other aspects of their working lives; rather, they saw their activism as essentially work that had to be done.

Jackie was looking around to find "something different to do," and a parent she knew invited her to a housing conference. "I said sure, why not." She went to this "housing conference at a monastery and started to listen to things that were going on out in the world." Jackie wanted to learn more about "what was going on in public housing," and this conference proved to be invaluable to her learning. At the conference, Jackie was "impressed with what people were doing in public housing: they were showcasing a lot of black women who were doing things in their particular projects, and they were from all over the country." As a member of the tenant association at her public housing development, Jackie wanted to know how to get tenants more involved, but being pragmatic she was especially interested in:

Figuring out how to get people to respect each other when somebody is talking, and letting people complete sentences. Because honey, we used to have some knocked out, dragged out battles at the tenant meeting. And if we had a process in which people could be able to talk to one another, a lot of stuff would have probably been accomplished much sooner and better without so much bad feelings. People get real sensitive when you criticize their shit. I get sensitive, too, but I get over it. Some folks never get over it. So I wanted training; I wanted to learn the process the other black women at the conference were using.

When she left the conference, Jackie had ideas about what could be accomplished at her own housing project and began to look at her development "in a different kind of way from just being a resident there." She said, "You don't think about what it takes to run a place: where does the water come from and how it is getting to your apartment? What makes the heat come up when it does come? Why is that noise coming from the pipes? So you need to know the daily operations of the place. And then you start to run into, well, why don't we have programs here? Where's the money for programs? And you just try to figure out how to make things happen for the residents." Jackie decided to try and make things happen for the elders and youth in her complex, and with a small grant from the Public Housing Authority she started an intergenerational program at her public housing site. But first she had to establish a new identity:

> In the very beginning it was hard living and working in the same place because now you have to build a different relationship with people. I was my grandmother's granddaughter. I was my mother's daughter. So I had no identity of my own. I was seen as somebody's child. And my first task was to work with elderly folks who knew my grandmother and knew my mom. My name is Jackie. Just getting that point across to them, that was kind of hard with folks whose children I hung out with. You just had to walk softly around some areas. And then the folks that I didn't know, it was okay to be as direct as I wanted to be. But there were always some folks that I tipped around. The first thing that I did was get the confidence of the elders that lived there. I knew the youth would come around.

Jackie won the trust of the seniors and the youth trusted her as well, largely because at this time she was the mother of two adolescent children and knew all of their friends in the projects. People started to "hang out" at the Elders and Youth program, which was located in the basement of one of the public housing complexes. Seniors and young people were becoming involved in her program, and Jackie felt a sense of accomplishment.

But there was a disturbing aspect of the job that Jackie had not anticipated. By the mid-1980s both elders and youth in the project were dying, and this had an effect not only on her program but also on Jackie.

> Some of the folks that I had grown up with were starting to die because they were elderly. That was the hard part for me. There're a lot of things that I learned from the seniors, and when they started to die that was the most painful thing for me. I just couldn't believe that I was making friends with these people and really enjoying their friendship, and we were getting stuff accomplished. They were like really supportive, and then they started dying. So, for me, this was really a terrible time because not only were seniors dying, the young people that I had known through my children were also dying. They were being killed. The drug wars were killing them off, and old age was killing off the seniors. It was really a bad time. I was going to so many funerals I couldn't stand it.

During this period, as Jackie said, her public housing development was in the midst of a drug war. She described what this meant and its complexities:

> The folks that are selling the drugs lived with us. They're in our own home. You know their parents, their uncles, aunts, and their cousins. The drug war started playing out because of territory. Territory meant who was whose corner—but nobody didn't own nothing in the projects. Fighting to be top dog—who was going to be top dog on the corner—and there were just senseless shootings that were going on. Different from when we were running around in the 50s with guns. It got so bad here, I knew at least three kids who got killed because they looked at somebody. Each one of the young men that got killed were going away to school on scholarships or working. A lot of these kids were kids I was working with. I tried to address their problem, and their problem was economic.

By living and working in the projects, Jackie could not avoid the drug war even if she wanted to; she described the difficulties:

> Every week I was going to a funeral, every single week. I saw families die off. I'm talking about the middle 1980s, when crack (cocaine)

hit the streets. But the people that I'm watching getting killed are not because they are users, they were selling the stuff. I haven't been to no users' funerals, to this day. I saw whole families getting killed who were living in my projects and the surrounding developments. When I say family, I mean the brother, the cousins, the nephews or the uncles. People in my projects were very concerned. And we almost had a riot at my projects one day. It was the first time I probably came face to face with a shotgun. One of our young people, over the drug thing, killed another young person. And he went to jail, and he left two young ladies pregnant. They had gotten into a street fight with each other. And the fight escalated because their brothers got into it. So someone called the cops, and cops came, and all the kids watching got real wild and crazy. One of the mothers came over to ask what was going on, and the cops threw her down on the ground and handcuffed her. Everybody was like saying to the cop, are you crazy? . . .

The cops called for backup. All I heard was all these sirens, and the next thing I knew the place was flooded with cops. When they got there all I could hear after that were clicks going on. Right at that particular time the kids had more guns than the cops. The only thing that I could do was stand in front of one cop and say y'all need to put your guns away. Tell your sergeant to call these guys back. Let's not have a war here for real. Let this woman up, and let her go. He was talking about her mouth. How do you arrest people because of their mouth, because of what they say? And there was this other cop, this little Puerto Rican cop. She was going off on me. She was calling me and the other women all kind of "fat black bitches." But we got it calmed down. The cops pulled off. They took away who they needed to take away, and we followed them down to the precinct to file a complaint.

Gradually, Jackie began to change her focus; she wanted to "address some of the living conditions in public housing." As president of tenant association she now represented the more than five-thousand residents that lived in her public housing development. From her position as president, Jackie started to make demands on the Public Housing Authority to make some structural changes to the buildings at her housing project. On behalf of the tenants, Jackie submitted a "wish list" to the Housing Authority:

> I was basically thinking about this utopian kind of thing in my mind. I really wanted to change the quality of life. I was really convinced that people wanted change; that stuff really could happen if we all worked at it together. I was really on that American dream thing. What burst my bubble was, we developed a plan, got the right kind of information, put it into the right kind of package, and took it to the people down at the Housing Authority, and they laughed at it. It was like, "What are you doing? Why did you bring this stuff to the Housing Authority? You're not going to get none of this stuff done."

Jackie did not believe that the plan the tenant association submitted was unreasonable, and she was unwilling to "let the Housing Authority say no. There's going to have to be a bit more to it than no." She became a public housing activist. Jackie realized that "everybody got a boss. And we went through all the channels. We couldn't get to meet with the main person at the Housing Authority. He wouldn't even talk to me." But from the contacts she had made through her involvement with white women's organizations, Jackie and members of the tenant association were able to meet with the secretary of Housing and Urban Development (HUD) in Washington, D.C. which funds and monitors Public Housing Authorities across the country.

After getting support from federal officials at HUD for her development plan, Jackie said, "The Housing Authority is like what the hell is going on here?" As a consequence of her actions, Jackie's tenant association got some important building renovations completed at her public housing site. She said, "We got about thirty-three million dollars to redesign the bathrooms in all the units, and interior and exterior renovation to buildings. The grounds were redesigned. We got a six foot fence all around the place. We were building our own prison but trying to make it look as nice as possible. The Housing Authority had just never really dealt with residents and residents' ideas and residents' participation." However, the Housing Authority resented Jackie's activism and initiated a backlash against her:

They tried to discredit me. There was this whole thing in the paper about how I had stolen money from the Housing Authority. Well you can't steal money that you got to sign for, and you can't get no more until you turn in all of your receipts. They figured if I was the head and they cut me down to size, then everybody else would stop functioning. My credibility was at stake. This is my neighborhood. I don't come here to work and go home; I work and live here. I had to get attorneys. It took me about five months before I got out of the hysteria. I was hysterical, too. I said, God, if I knew hit people, I would have all of them bumped off; they would have been just killed. I felt like I was assaulted. I felt like I was just beaten up and bloodied.

Jackie said that she realized what the "real issue was," for which she had been politically "beaten up and bloodied: I said, okay, I really see what this is all about; it was about power. The Housing Authority thought that I had too much power; they thought that I had so much power that I wanted their power. But I didn't want that kind of power. That wasn't what I was about. I was trying to do one little thing; I was trying to improve where I was living." Jackie reflected on this conflict:

They saw us as troublemakers. I really didn't understand that, but what I did understand is that they figured if we made changes to our projects then the other projects were going to want to make changes as well. At the time I didn't feel threatened?, I was too stupid to feel threatened?, because I was feeling empowered, things were moving along, we were moving forward. I said look this is what the residents want, and this is how we want it to happen. So they laid out the stuff that they were going to give us. And that's when I started critiquing all of the stuff. I had learned how to read blueprints, I knew as much as they knew, and things they didn't know. They perceived me as a pain in the ass. I became more and more militant. I would be sitting down at the table with twenty-three white men; the rest of my tenant board would just sit there and not speak at all, so I had to do all of the negotiations. I felt the biggest task was to follow the money like it was my own. There was a lot of scandal at the Housing Authority, corrupt contractors stealing money and incomplete renovations because they always run out of money. After the renovations,

I wanted to get into economic development and more sustainable programs for the residents. What does it take for you to lift yourself up by your bootstraps? Jobs. The Housing Authority said we couldn't do that. But we started businesses anyway. That's when they decided they got to chop the head off, and it was my head. They felt that I had become to powerful. They figured if I were cut down then everybody else would stop demanding stuff. That's when they said I stole money from the Housing Authority, and they shut down my Elders and Youth Center.

Following her anger over what happened, Jackie went into a "deep depression." Jackie's sense of violation was almost total, and she simply stopped functioning as a human being. She was devastated by the attacks on her integrity, and, unlike her more pragmatic approach to a physical fight, Jackie found herself foundering in the face of personal and social abuse. Even though she attempted to legally fight the allegations made against her, Jackie said, "Every time I moved one step forward, they would push me two steps backward with all their lawyers. And to bring it to an end I said y'all do whatever y'all want to do." Jackie had by no means anticipated either the consequences her activism would have in confronting institutional power or the toll it would take on her sense of self. Gradually, she regained her sense of being and is now able to appreciate the accomplishments she made in attempting to improve the quality of life for the residents of her public housing development. As such, Jackie continues to be a public housing activist.

Similar to Jackie, for Amanda there was often a thin line between her paid employment and her unpaid political and community work. After obtaining a graduate degree in social work, Amanda's first full-time job was at a Model Cities program, where she developed and managed a "comprehensive day care program," which served low-income black parents.

Amanda was excited about the possibilities this job held: "It was like doing something from scratch and creating a whole child care network that included a daycare center, family daycare homes, infant care and training women to be service providers." She thought "it was really a good experience and liked the job," but discovered that "Model Cities was so full of shit." She believed that the director of the Model Cities

Program was "owned, bought and sold by Standard Oil." Additionally, she thought, "he was taking money that was supposed to go for youth programs, and was using it to build a shopping mall out in the white suburbs." After completing the project for which she was hired, Amanda decided to change jobs; she was hired to direct a similar daycare initiative. A black consulting firm had received a federal contract to develop daycare services for low-income families around the country, and Amanda administered this initiative. In addition to this full-time job, she became involved in several political organizations.

> I worked with several political organizations. In the beginning my work was very peripheral. I worked with Black People United for Prison Reform. We went to the prisons. We hooked up with this group called the Lifers, and they had a newspaper. I got sort of turned off at one point because all these white women started getting involved, and their thing was just screwing the brothers. Anyway, we were doing a lot of stuff in the community. It was going crazy with the police brutality. The cops were killing people in the precincts and everywhere else. One night we were coming home late from a meeting, there was a group of us, and we saw this cop take this brother and slam him up against the car. This might have been right after another brother had just gotten shot, handcuffed, walking up the steps to the precinct, and the cops said that he was trying to get away. That's why they shot him in the back. So when we got out of the car and went over to try and find out what was going on, the cops didn't want to talk to us, so we just stood there and watched them.

Through her increasing activism, Amanda joined the African Liberation Committee that later evolved into the Revolutionary League, and she worked full-time as a "community developer" and part-time at a local hospital where she helped to unionize workers. After the birth of her daughter, Amanda curtailed some of her political activities but not her political views. Amanda decided that she wanted to "work in a working-class job and not use my Master Degree." She enrolled in a job-training program targeted at women, it was a "tool and dye program." She recalled her experience:

This was right up my alley because then I could get a job being a steel worker and really be a proletariat. My mother, of course, thought that I was a total lunatic, she just couldn't understand why I was doing all of this. I started working at this factory where they made pumps and parts for pumps for all across the world. It was one other woman, an older white woman, and me. All of the other people were young boys or kids that had dropped out of high school. And here we are these two old biddies. But both of us had some kind of aptitude for it, and I enjoyed the work. There was this whole thing going on at the factory when we started; it was being sued by former women workers in a class action lawsuit. It was being charged with sex discrimination, and they saw the handwriting on the wall, so they hired us.

In this all-male working class environment, early on Amanda began to experience harassment, which she described:

I went through a lot of craziness when I got there. I worked in the evening so I would follow the man who had been there during the day. You had to use a blueprint, and you had to set the tools up a certain way. If you're following somebody everything is supposed to be set-up when you come in. You just have to run the job. But they would change the set-up, so I would end up scraping pieces because they wouldn't have the right dimensions set. Then I would have to spend all this time resetting everything myself. So I had that kind of harassment, and then there was the sexual harassment. They would put up pictures and say sexist stuff. I stayed there for about two years, but I got fired. I filed charges against them and also raised the issue of racial and sexual discrimination against management. I went to the union to get support, and the union gave me no support because they saw the workers in that particular shop as being in opposition to the union leadership. So I filed charges against the union with EEOC (Equal Employment Opportunity Commission) because the company had all these government contracts.

After she was fired from the tool and dye factory, Amanda "filed for unemployment. And when my unemployment ran out I applied for welfare.

I didn't get it." So out of "desperation," Amanda "applied for another job as a social worker in a day care center," and she got the job. The day care center focused on children who had "special needs," and Amanda was responsible for doing home visits with the parents. "I really enjoyed the job, going to people houses and helping them to sort out the issues around their kids." Amanda was interested in trying to figure out "how to empower the parents" by increasing their involvement in decision making at the day care center. But the director saw Amanda's efforts at empowerment as a way of "trying to undermine her authority." Amanda quit the job, and she said, "That was the last social work job that I had for a while. I knew I shouldn't have gone back into social work."

Amanda's political activism was broadly focused around issues of racial and social justice. Through her community/political work, more than the other women, Amanda at various times encountered violence and experienced violations to her physical, personal, and social self that are too numerous to recount. In one incident, the police removed protesters from abandoned city-owned buildings. Amanda was a part of this protest and recalled her arrest:

> They dragged me out of the building, bumping my head on the cement, then they handcuffed my wrist so tight they were like raw, and threw me into the back of car. On the way to the precinct, they talked about black folks living in the jungle, and the bitches with their children. All of this, of course, was to provoke me, enough for me to say or do something, and I would wind up dead on the highway, and they could say I was trying to escape. When I got to the precinct, because I said I weren't going to answer any questions other than my name until I had a lawyer, they stripped searched me, body cavity search, and then they put me in a room where there was blood everywhere; they were trying to intimidate me. I didn't deserve this kind of behavior. It was on a Friday, and because I insisted on still not answering their questions, the seventy-two-hour rule went into place and I was taken to central booking and stayed in jail over the weekend.

Amanda tried to put this and her other experiences of violence and violation into perspective: "I think when I was younger I didn't understand violence from the standpoint of being a woman. But with my own

experiences over the years, I think I've really started to get a better understanding. Being violated and being a black woman has crystallized it
more and more for me. I'm living in a society that resolves issues through
violence, and too often black women are on the short-end of the stick.
It is the indignities, physical or otherwise, of being a black woman, and
not just a black person or a woman that been my struggle. The indignities are something that attacks black women's being, and everyday it just
eats away at you. It's amazing that more of us are not completely and totally dysfunctional. I think that all of us have some insanity because you
can't live in an insane society and not be touched by violence. But that
we can function everyday and take care of our families and still find
something to laugh about and enjoy life, is also an amazing thing."

Conclusion

Knowing Violence and Violation

In returning to their past, I followed along as the women traveled uncertain paths. From their early journey through childhood to their lives as mature adults, I listened and watched as they re-created their life histories. In the telling of their stories, I heard what happened to them and could not help but notice what they thought and felt. But I also saw what they did as they engaged their cultural and social worlds. In the process of living, they walk with a sense of self-assuredness and purpose. But sometimes they stumbled over barriers that were in their way. Some only lost their balance, but a few actually fell. Yet they all gathered themselves. They took deep reflective breaths, drew upon the lessons learned, and, for those who had cuts and bruises, allowed their wounds to heal. Each of the women figured out how to proceed. And, now, they have continued on in their own particular journey of becoming the person they see themselves to be.

The women have moved on with their lives. But they leave behind rich and compelling stories of their struggles to maintain, sustain, and in some instances regain a sense of their own humanity as interwoven in their particular versions of what it means to be black-and-female in America. In the women's struggles the perceptions, decisions, and actions of others were significant in shaping their experiences. However, their self-perceptions, decisions, and actions on behalf of their own needs, interests, and aspirations provide a starting point for a different kind of dialogue on women's experiences of violence.

I began this inquiry knowing that if we are to better understand the role that violence plays in women's lives, then a different conversation is needed; the starting point for this discussion must be rooted in women's experiences. In asking that we shift our gaze, I argue that, rather than focusing exclusively on women's relationships to men, we must broaden our inquiry to explore women's relationships to their cultural and social worlds to see what is revealed about their experiences of violence. In so doing, I propose that we explore the complicated interplay of what happens in women's interactions when agency collides with cultural and social constraints: when women's needs, interests, and aspirations are in conflict with cultural and social arrangements under which they live their lives; and by which physical, personal, and social constraints are imposed on their experiences. When this conflict arises, violence is sometimes insinuated into women's lives and becomes a part of their experiences. What happens as a result? Women experience this violence as a violation to their sense of personhood. To varying degrees, that violation and the disrespect that is engendered constitutes an assault to their sense of self-integrity and affects how they come to view their own human worth.

My approach allows me to avoid positioning women as either "passive victims" or as agents acting solely on free will. Instead, it allows me to look at the tensions, dilemmas, and contradictions of women's lives as they engage the process of living. Women do not simply stand around in the world waiting for something to happen to them. The course of women's lives is neither predetermined by cultural and social conditions and practices, nor do women fully control their lives through independent action or will. Rather, both dimensions of life—predetermination and individual will—are present and intersect to make women's experiences. Therefore, it becomes critical that we continue to examine the context of women's lives and closely analyze what is done, by whom, and for what purpose. But this provides only partial responses to the answers we seek. For along with those responses it is also essential that we explore what women think, feel, and do in relationships to their cultural and social worlds. Such a dual reference provides critical insights and allows us to develop deeper and enriched perspectives on gender-based violence.

I offered the conversations that I had with nine African American women about their varied life experiences as a way to begin our dialogue. In exploring the nature and scope of their experiences, a critical question is posed: Are their experiences too particular to form the basis for our conversation? Precisely the particularities of their experiences provide the reference point for a broader dialogue. Their experiences move beyond the narrow boundaries of the current discourse on violence and allow us to consider issues that are often avoided or not talked about. The disconnection between their experiences of violence and the exegesis of the current government-sponsored discourse on violence against women is apparent. As you have discovered while reading about their lives from childhood through adulthood, experiences do not fit neatly into this discourse. And any attempts to make this so, to be inclusive, requires distorting, fragmenting, and ultimately marginalizing the meaning of violence in women's lives.

The women's experiences described in this study have much to offer our understanding of gender-based violence, beyond that which is offered by the current discourse. In exploring the relational context of violence and violation, their experiences raise a fundamental issue regarding the meaning of violence against women itself. We cannot avoid the issue of human value, the worth of women's lives, for value lies at the center of their experiences and at the crux of the critical dialogue. Their experiences provide ample evidence of what happens when agency collides with social and cultural constraints. Their needs, interests, and aspirations might be disvalued in ways that can be injurious and harmful to their sense of personhood. This important contribution allows us to understand how women most frequently experience violence: it is through violation. However, an even more significant contribution might be found in the stories of their experiences to clarify the aim of our dialogue. The lack of human value and its affects on women's lives should not be the focus; rather, the complete opposite focuses this discussion. Therefore, we should focus our discussion around the question: What does it mean to value women lives?

I recognize that the importance of human worth is both essential to and also transcends women's particular experiences, but so do the issues and problems engendered by violence. Precisely the narrow and broader implications of human worth make it critical to our discussion. A dialogue on human value in the context of women's lived experiences allows us to explore what is essential for women to live in a just and humane society.

Some important groundwork for this exploration has already been done by international feminists and other anti-violence advocates from around the world. They have expanded the meaning of gender-based violence to include forms of injustices to women. They recognize the direct as well as the indirect impact of injustices that are associated with physical and psychological force, economic deprivation, political exclusion, social denial of needed goods and services, and cultural traditions and customs. In general their focus is on securing and guaranteeing women's human rights as largely embodied in the United Nations' Convention on the Elimination of All Forms of Discrimination Against Women (CEDAW). International conventions, laws, and covenants are important tools for holding nation-states responsible and accountable for the ways women are treated—or to be more exact—mistreated. However, as with VAWA, words on paper and even strategies, monitoring and resources albeit important, do not secure or guarantee women's lives are valued in society.

To place women's human worth at the center of the dialogue on gender-based violence requires that our discussion embrace radical cultural and social change. I do agree with and support the call for women's human rights and believe that such a framework offers important contributions toward ending gender-based violence. But our challenges in many ways are quite different and in some ways particular; for we must engage our own complicity, we must engage ourselves. As members of this society we are important stakeholders in violence, for, in general, we are all vested by our own complicity. Violence and its disvaluing effects on people's lives are pervasive in our society, and gender-based violence is only one of its manifestations. In historically chronicled events as well as in contemporary life, our society has derived enormous privileges and wealth through the violent destruction of life. As such, even if tacitly, we decide that some form of physical, personal, and social violence is acceptable to us, as long as cultural and social benefits are derived from its existence. It appears that the benefits outweigh the injury and harm until violence in its most cruel and brutal manifestation touches our individual lives. And even in those instances we often retain an important stake because revenge and retribution can become powerful motivations for reproducing violence at its most basic and fundamental dimensions.

In a society where violence intersects our most basic needs, interests, and aspirations, I find it difficult to isolate women's experiences of violence and the significance it holds for their lives from the experiences of their children and the men that they love. We cannot divest ourselves of our complicity in violence if our aim is focused solely on the worth of only one component of the human family: women. It becomes an impossible task, in terms of meaning and practicability, to seek to eradicate violence from women's lives in the absence of attempts to end all manifestations of violence in our society; for all forms of violence are knotted together whether we acknowledge it or not, and the disvaluing consequences connect our human experiences. This presumes that we cannot envision nor would we want to live in a world where only women's lives have value. By this I am not suggesting that we fold women's lives into some large humanistic umbrella where their experiences are lost in its creases. Women must be the focus of our attention, for their instructive experiences provide models upon which to ground radical cultural and social change.

To divest ourselves of the current stakes we now have in violence, exploring human worth in the context of women's lived experiences will demand of us that we probe deeply into the character of our society to determine what is essential for "human flourishing." In our critical probing of the conditions and practices that disvalue women's lives, we immediately bump into ourselves. What does it mean to divest ourselves of our stakes in violence? On the one hand this means that we challenge not only our own beliefs, attitudes, and values that make any violence acceptable, but also our participation in the reproduction of relations of power that devalue some women's lives according to gender, race, and class distinctions while our actions affirm the worth of other women's lives. On the other hand, divesting ourselves means that we critically engage the cultural and social institutions that reproduce on a daily basis conditions and practices in our names, which place constraints on women's needs, interests, and aspirations. To give up the benefits that we derive from violence requires that we not only think about the world differently, but also act differently as a result, and demand that our cultural and social institutions do the same. Only then will our discussion of human value in the context of women's lived experiences sow the seed for radical change in the conditions and ways in which we live our lives, and by which we define our needs, interests, and aspirations.

A dialogue on the issue of human value in the context of women's lived experiences is the starting point for a different discussion on gender-based violence. It is a critical dialogue that must be had. As we engage the ten-year anniversary of the passage of VAWA, it is essential that we pause to consider the issues that have been raised as a result of the women's experiences in this study. By inviting you to engage in this important conversation, I too have been invited to dialogue. I have just received an invitation entitled "Learning From the Past, Shaping the Future" that was sent to me by the Department of Justice Office on Violence Against Women asking that I "join a select group of law enforcement, prosecutors, judges, advocates, survivors, community leaders, and others as we commemorate the Violence Against Women Act of 1994."

I choose not join this particular discussion, for I know that there will be no space for or a tolerance of the issue of human worth, the value of women's lives, for these crucial issues do not fit within this discourse. The agenda is set, and fingers will be pointed at bad male behavior toward women. It is most appropriate to point fingers in their direction, but it is neither the only nor even the major target at which finger-pointing must be aimed. Listening to the women's experiences of this study will no longer allow me to be complicit or to participate in the reification of women's experiences of violence, to position their experiences according to established paradigms and models regardless of the fit and consequences thereof.

Thirty years have now passed since the inception of the anti-violence movement, a movement based on women and their experiences, especially those of physical violence. Over time, the tremendous changes in the ways our society responds to violence against women stand out. As a result of women-led advocacy, we now have a "coordinated system of response" that includes battered women shelters, safe homes, and other havens and sanctuaries for physically battered and abused women and their children in every state in the country. This system also consists of victim referral hot lines, mediation and violence intervention programs, and rape crisis centers. Also, the "helping professions," specifically in the areas of social work but also legal advocacy and health services, provide meaningful assistance to female victims of violence. Nowhere is change more obvious than in the responses that have occurred over the years in the criminal justice system, in the ways police respond to *female victims* and how prosecutors charge defendants, and in the manner in which courts sentence *male perpetrators* for violence against women. These changes are accompanied by established laws and public policies that are supported by an enormous and diverse body of scholarly literature, which provide both the ideological and the political rationale that says this system is needed.

But along with progressive trends are serious regressive tendencies that continue to shape the government-sponsored discourse on violence against women. From all documented accounts and common sense awareness, domestic violence and sexual assault are major *problems* faced by many women in our society. However, the critical question is whose needs, interests, and aspirations are currently served by this vast and interlocking system of response? Amidst enormous structural and programmatic changes as well as concentrated effort and resources, the most that can be said with assurance of the impact, influences, and implications of the crime-and-punishment model, as introduced by VAWA, is that a "coordinated system of response" has been and continues to be developed. The most basic and fundamental question that formed the intent of VAWA is: Are women safer? This question remains unanswered. We can only hope that this is the case, but who knows? This is not a question that will be raised in commemoration of VAWA's tenth anniversary.

Along the way, women have gotten lost in the transition that has bureaucratized and publicly resourced the *issue* of violence against women. As a result, women and what they know to be *true* about their experiences of violence and the *problem* they face in their daily lives appears to be even less of a concern to those who frame, guide, and direct funding to the "coordinated system of response." Even though advocates continue to play an important role in legitimizing and reproducing this system, they generally do not participate in the process of needs' interpretation that establishes the complex bureaucratic guidelines under which service provision is conducted and by which women's experiences are included and marginalized. Nor do they participate in the funding decisions where resources are unevenly distributed and often awarded to large public and semipublic institutions that rarely look at women beyond images of victimization, or engage women's needs, interests, and aspirations in ways that are not predetermined. The only tension frequently introduced into the discourse by advocates seems to evolve around inclusivity and the lack of adequate services to different populations of women. Meanwhile, women and their experiences of violence continue to be reified within the workings of the government-sponsored discourse; they have become yet another good, though a public good, in a market economy that is now the government-sponsored discourse on violence against women.

The workings of the government-sponsored discourse at best provide a minor backdrop and at worst a disconnection from the real women's experiences of this study. The nature and the scope of their particular experiences of violence and violation are not validated by the system. Yet based on what the women know to be *true* about their lives they validate their own realities. Listening to and thinking about these women's experiences has allowed me to shed my contradictions, ambiguities, and frustrations about participating in the government-sponsored discourse. I do not want to commemorate the passage of VAWA. Instead, I want to end the physical, personal, and social destruction that violence begets, especially in women's lives, for this is the contribution that the women of this study has given me and the contribution that I in turn share with you.

References

Abel, Elizabeth, Barbara Christian, and Helen Moglen, eds. 1997. *Female Subjects in Black and White: Race, Psychoanalysis, Feminism*. Berkeley: University of California Press.

Alcoff, Linda. 1988. "Cultural Feminism versus Post-Structuralism: Identity Crisis in Feminist Theory." *Signs: Journal of Women in Culture and Society* 13, 3: 405.

Alcoff, Linda Martin, and Eduardo Mendieta, eds. 2003. *Identities: Race, Class, Gender, and Nationality*. London: Blackwell Publishing.

Alcoff, Linda, and Elizabeth Potter. 1993. *Feminists Epistemologies*. London: Routledge.

Allen, Richard L. 2001. *The Concept of Self: A Study of Black Identity and Self-Esteem*. Detroit: Wayne State University Press.

Allen, Robert L. 1970. *Black Awakening in Capitalist America: An Analytic History*. New York: Anchor Books.

Ammons, Linda L. 1995. "Mules, Madonnas, Babies, Bathwater, Racial Imagery and Stereotypes: The African-American Woman and the Battered Woman Syndrome." *Wisconsin Law Review* 1995: 1001.

Appiah, Kwame A., and Henry Louis Gates. 1995. *Identities*. Chicago: The University of Chicago Press.

Aptheker, Herbert. 1973. *The Education of Black People by W.E.B. DuBois: Ten Critiques*. New York: Monthly Review Press.

Austin, Regina. 1992. "Black Women, Sisterhood, and the Difference/Deviance Divide." *New England Law Review* 26: 877.

Bell, Derrick. 1987. *And We Are Not Saved: The Elusive Quest for Racial Justice*. New York: Basic Books.

Belenky, Mary F., Blythe M. Clinchy, Nancy R. Goldberger, and Jill M. Tarule, eds. 1997. *Women's Ways of Knowing: The Development of Self, Voice, and Mind*. New York: Basic Books.

Benowitz, Mindy. 1990. "How Homophobia Affects Lesbian' Response to Violence in Lesbian Relationships." In *Confronting Lesbian Battering*, edited by P. Elliott. St. Paul: Minnesota Coalition for Battered Women, Lesbian Battering Intervention Project.

Berger, Peter L., and Thomas Luckmann. 1966. *The Social Construction of Reality: A Treatise in the Sociology of Knowledge*. New York: Doubleday.

Blackman, Julie. 1989. *Intimate Violence: A Study of Injustice*. New York: Columbia University Press.

Blumer, Herbert. 1969. *Symbolic Interaction*. Englewood Cliffs, N.J.: Prentice Hall.

Bolton, Ruthie. 1994. *Gal: A True Life*. New York: Harcourt Brace and Company.

Bozzoli, Belinda. 1991. *Women of Phokeng: Consciousness, Life Strategy, and Migrancy in South Africa, 1900–1983*. Portsmouth, N.H.: Heinemann.

Brown, Angela. 1987. *When Battered Women Kill*. New York: The Free Press.

Brown, Elaine. 1992. *A Taste of Power: A Black Woman's Story*. New York: Pantheon Books.

Brown, Elsa Barkley. 1989. "African American Women's Quilting: A Framework for Conceptualizing and Teaching African-American Women's History." *Signs: Journal of Women in Culture and Society* 14, 4: 921–929.

———. 1995. "Negotiating and Transforming the Public Sphere: African American Political Life in the Transition from Slavery to Freedom." In *The Black Public Sphere: A Public Culture Book*, edited by the Black Public Sphere Collective. Chicago: The University of Chicago Press.

Bunch, Charlotte. 1991. "Gender Violence: A Development and Human Rights Issue." New Brunswick, N.J.: Center for Women's Global Leadership.

Burt, Martha R., Janine M. Zweig, Cynthia Andrews, and Ashley Van Ness. 2001. *2001 Report: Evaluation of the STOP Formula Grants to Combat Violence Against Women*. Washington, D.C.: The Urban Institute.

Burns, Mary Violet, ed. 1986. "The Speaking Profits Us: Violence in the Lives of Women of Color." Seattle: The Center for the Prevention of Sexual and Domestic Violence.

Butler, Judith. 1990. *Gender Trouble: Feminism and the Subversion of Identity*. New York: Routledge.

Campbell, Jacqueline C. 1992. "If I Can't Have You, No One Can: Power and Contro in Homicide of Female Partners." In *Femicide: The Politics of Woman Killing*, edited by J. Radford and D. Russell. New York: Twayne Publishers.

———. 1992. "Wife Battering: Cultural Contexts Versus Western Social Sciences." In *Sanctions and Sanctuary: Cultural Perspectives on the Beating of Wives*, edited by D. Counts, J. Brown, and J. Campbell. Boulder: Westview.

Carbado, Devon W. 1998. "Black Male Racial Victimhood." *Callaloo* 21, 2.

Chisholm, Shirley. 1970. *Unbought and Unbossed*. New York: Avon.

Chrisman, Robert, and Robert Allen, eds. 1992. *Court of Appeal: The Black Community Speaks Out on the Racial and Sexual Politics of Thomas vs Hill*. New York: Ballantine Books.

Coles, Robert. 1971. *The South Goes North*. Boston: Little Brown.

Coley, Soraya M., and Joyce O. Beckett. 1988. "Black Battered Women: A Review of the Empirical Literature." *Journal of Counseling and Development* 66: 266.

Collins, Patricia Hill. 1990. *Black Feminist Thought: Knowledge, Consciousness, and the Politics of Empowerment*. New York: Routledge.

———. 1998. *Fighting Words: Black Women and the Search for Justice*. Minneapolis: University of Minnesota Press.

———. 1998. "The Tie That Binds: Race, Gender, and US Violence." *Ethnic and Racial Studies* 21, 5: 917–938.

Cooper, Anna Julia. 1892. *A Voice from the South: By a Black of the South*. Xenea, Ohio: Aldine Printing House; reprint, New York: Oxford University Press, 1988.

Crenshaw, Kimberle W. 1994. "Mapping the Margins: Intersectionality, Identity

Politics, and Violence Against Women." In *The Public Nature of Private Violence*, edited by Martha A. Fineman and Roxanne Mykitiuk. New York: Routledge.

Crenshaw, Kimberle, Neil Gotanda, Gary Peller, and Kendall Thomas, eds. 1995. *Critical Race Theory: The Key Writings that Formed the Movement*. New York: The New Press.

Crooms, Lisa A. 1996. "Don't Believe the Hype: Black Women, Patriarchy, and the New Welfarism." *Howard University Law Journal* 38: 611.

————. 1999. "Using a multi-tiered analysis to reconceptualize gender-based violence against women as a matter of international human rights." *New England Law Review* 33, 4: 881–906.

Davis, Deirdre E. 1997. "The Harm That Has No Name: Street Harassment, Embodiment, and African American Women." In *The Public Nature of Private Violence*, edited by Martha A. Fineman and Roxanne Mykitiuk. New York: Routledge.

Davis, Angela Y. 1981. *Women, Race, and Class*. New York: Random House.

Davis, Dana Ain. 2004. "Manufacturing Mammy." *Anthropologica* 46, 2.

De Lauretis, Teresa. 1984. *Alice Doesn't*. Bloomington: Indiana University Press.

————. 1986. *Feminist Studies/Critical Studies*. Bloomington: Indiana University Press.

Dietz, Tracy. 1997. "Disciplining Children: Characteristics Associated with the Use of Corporal Punishment and Non-Violent Discipline." Durham, N.H.: Family Research Laboratory, University of New Hampshire.

Dill, Bonnie Thornton. 1988. "The Dialectics of Black Womanhood." In *Feminism and Methodology*, edited by Sandra Harding. Bloomington: Indiana University Press.

————. 1988. "Making Your Job Good Yourself: Domestic Service and the Construction of Personal Dignity." In *Women and the Politics of Empowerment*, edited by Ann Bookman and Sandra Morgen. Philadelphia: Temple University Press.

Dinnerstein, Myra. 1992. *Women Between Two Worlds: Midlife Reflections on Work and Family*. Philadelphia: Temple University Press.

Dobash, R. Emerson, and Russell Dobash, eds. 1979. *Violence Against Wives: A Case Against Patriarchy*. New York: Free Press.

————. 1992. *Women, Violence and Social Change*. New York: Routledge.

————. 1998. *Rethinking Violence Against Women*. London: Sage Series on Violence Against Women.

DuBois, William E. B. [1903] 1961. *The Souls of Black Folk*. Repr., New York: Dodd Mead.

DuCille, Ann. 1994. "The Occult of True Black Womanhood: Critical Demeanor and Black Feminist Studies." In *Female Subjects in Black and White: Race, Psychoanalysis, Feminism*, edited by Elizabeth Abel, Barbara Christian, and Helene Moglen. Berkeley: University of California Press.

Edleson, Jeffrey L., and Zvi Eisikovits. 1985. "Men Who Batter Women: A Critical Review of the Evidence." *Journal of Family Issues* 6, 229.

Erikson, Eric. 1963. *Childhood and Society*. New York: Norton.

Feagin, Joe R. 2000. *Racist America: Roots, Current Realities, and Future Reparations*. New York: Routledge.

Ferguson, Kathy E. 1980. *Self, Society, and Womankind: The Dialectic of Liberation*. Westport, Conn.: Greenwood Press.

Fields, Barbara. 1982. "Ideology and Race in American History." In *Region, Race and Reconstruction: Essays in Honor of C. Vann Woodward*, edited by J. Kousser and J. McPherson. New York: Oxford University Press.

Fineman, Martha A., and Roxanne Mykitiuk, eds. 1994. *The Public Nature of Private Violence: The Discovery of Domestic Abuse*. New York: Routledge.

Foucault, Michel. 1977. *Power/Knowledge: Selected Interviews and Other Writing 1972–1977*. New York: Pantheon Books.

Fraser, Nancy. 1989. *Unruly Practices: Power, Discourse and Gender in Contemporary Social Theory*. Minneapolis: University of Minnesota Press.

Garfinkel, Harold. 1967. *Studies in Ethnomethodology*. Englewood Cliffs, N.J.: Prentice Hall.

Giles-Sims, Jean, Murray A. Straus, and David B. Sugarman. 1995. "Child, Maternal and Family Characteristics Associated with Spanking." *Family Relations* 44, 170.

Gelles, Richard J., and Suzanne K. Steinmetz. 1980. *Behind Closed Doors: Violence in the American Family*. Garden City, N.Y.: Anchor Press.

Gelles, Richard J., and Murray A. Strauss. 1988. *Intimate Violence: The Causes and Consequences of Abuse in the American Family*. New York: Simon and Schuster.

Giddings, Paula. 1984. *When and Where I Enter: The Impact of Black Women on Race and Sex in America*. New York: William Morrow and Company.

Gilkes, Cheryl Townsend. 1994. "If It Wasn't for the Women . . . African American Women, Community Work, Social Change." In *Women of Color in U.S. Social Change*, edited by M. Zinn and B. Thornton Dill. Philadelphia: Temple University Press.

Goffman, Erving. 1959. *The Presentation of Self in Everyday Life*. New York: Doubleday.

Gwaltney, John Langston. 1993. *Drylongso: A Self-Portrait of Black America*. New York: (The New Press, Vintage).

Hampton, Robert L., ed. 1991. *Black Family Violence: Current Research and Theory*. Lexington, Mass.: Lexington Books.

Harding, Sandra. 1987. *Feminism and Methodology*. Bloomington: Indiana University Press.

———. 1991. *Whose Science? Whose Knowledge? Thinking from Women's Lives*. Ithaca: Cornell University Press.

Harley, Sharon, and The Black Women and Work Collective. 2002. *Sister Circle: Black Women and Work*. New Brunswick, N.J.: Rutgers University Press.

Harris, Angela. 1997. "Race and Essentialism in Feminist Legal Theory." In *Critical Race Feminism: A Reader*, edited by Adrien K. Wing. New York: New York University Press.

Harris, Trudier. 1982. *From Mammies to Militants: Domestics in Black American Literature*. Philadelphia: Temple University Press.

Hawkesworth, Mary E. 1989. "Knowers, Knowing, Known: Feminist Theory and Claims of Truth." *Signs: Journal of Women in Culture and Society* 14, no. 3.

Higginbotham, Elizabeth. 2001. *Too Much To Ask: Black Women in the Era of Integration*. Chapel Hill: University of North Carolina Press.

Higginbotham, Evelyn Brooks. 1992. "African-American Women's History and the Metalanguage of Race." *Signs: Journal of Women in Culture and Society* 17, 251.

Hill, Susan T. 1985. "The Traditionally Black Institutions of Higher Education 1860 to 1982." Washington, D.C.: National Center for Education Statistics.

Hine, Darlene Clark. 1994. *Hine Sight: Black Women and the Reconstruction of American History.* Bloomington: Indiana University Press.

hooks, bell. 1984. *Feminist Theory from Margin to Center.* Boston: South End Press.

———. 1989. "Black is a Woman's Color: An Essay." *Callaloo* 12, 382.

———. 1989. *Talking Back: Thinking Feminist, Thinking Black.* Boston: South End Press.

———. 1995. *Killing Rage: Ending Racism.* New York: Henry Holt and Company.

Honneth, Axel. 1995. *The Fragmented World of the Social: Essays in Social and Political Philosophy.* Edited by Charles W. Wright. Albany: State University of New York Press.

Hurston, Zora Neale. 1978. *Mules and Men.* Bloomington: Indiana University Press.

Jewell, K. Sue. 1993. *From Mammy to Miss America and Beyond: Cultural Images and the Shaping of US Social Policy.* New York: Routledge.

Jones, Jacqueline. 1985. *Labor of Love, Labor of Sorrow: Black Women, Work and the Family from Slavery to the Present.* New York: Vintage Books.

Jones, Lisa. 1994. *Bulletproof Diva: Tales of Race, Sex and Hair.* New York: Doubleday.

Jordan, June. 1981. *Civil Wars.* Boston: Beacon Press.

Kaschak, Ellyn. 1992. *Engendered Lives: A New Psychology of Women's Experience.* New York: Basic Books.

Kauffman, Linda S., ed. 1993. *American Feminist Thought At Century's End: A Reader.* Cambridge, Mass.: Blackwell.

Kelly, Liz. 1996. "Beyond Victim to Survivor: Sexual Violence, Identity, Feminist Theory and Practice." In *Sexualizing the Social: The Social Organization of Power,* edited by L. Adkins and V. Merchant. London: Macmillan.

Kelly, Liz, and Jill Radford. 1996. "Nothing Really Happened: The Invalidation of Women's Experiences of Sexual Violence." In *Women, Violence and Male Power,* edited by M. Hester, L. Kelly, and J. Radford. UK: Open University Press.

Kluger, Richard. 1975. *Simple Justice: The History of Brown v. Board of Education and Black America's Struggle for Equality.* New York: Vintage Books.

Ladner, Joyce. 1972. *Tomorrow's Tomorrow: The Black Woman.* New York: Doubleday.

Leidig, Michael W. 1992. "The Continuum of Violence Against Women: Psychological and Physical Consequences." *Journal of American College Health* 40: 149–155.

Lockhart, Lewis. 1985. "Methodological Issues in Comparative Racial Analyses: The Case of Wife Abuse." *Social Work Research Abstracts* 21: 35–41.

Lorde, Audre. 1984. *Sister Outsider.* Trumansburg, N.Y.: The Crossing Press.

Mahoney, Martha R. 1994. "Victimization or Oppression? Women's Lives, Violence, and Agency." In *The Public Nature of Private Violence: The Discovery of Domestic Abuse,* edited by Martha Albertson Fineman and Roxanne Mykitiuk. New York: Routledge.

Mahoney, Maureen A., and Barbara Yngvesson. 1992. "The Construction of Sub-jectivity and the Paradox of Resistance: Reintegrating Feminist Anthropology and Psychology." *Signs: Journal of Women in Culture and Society* 18: 44.

Maynard, Mary, and June Purvis. 1994. *Researching Women's Lives from a Feminist Perspective.* Bristol: Taylor and Francis.

Mead, George H. 1962. *Mind, Self and Society: From the Standpoint of a Social Behaviorist.* Chicago: The University of Chicago Press.

Mendieta, Eduardo. 2003. "Identities: Postcolonial and Global." In *Identities: Race, Class, Gender, and Nationality*, edited by Linda Martin Alcott and Eduardo Mendieta. London: Blackwell Publishing.

Merry, Sally Engle. 1994. "Narrating Domestic Violence: Producing the 'Truth' of Violence in 19th and 20th Century Hawaiian Courts." *Law and Social Inquiry* 19, no. 4.

Meyer-Emerick, Nancy. 2001. *The Violence Against Women Act of 1994: An Analysis of Intent and Perception.* Westport, Conn.: Praeger.

Messerschmidt, James W. 2000. *Nine Lives: Adolescent Masculinities, the Body, and Violence.* Boulder Colo.: Westview Press.

Minh-ha, Trinh T. 1989. *Woman, Native, Other: Writing Postcoloniality and Feminism.* Bloomington: Indiana University Press.

Mohanty, Chandra T., Ann Russo, and Lourdes Torres, eds. 1991. *Third World Women and the Politics of Feminism.* Bloomington: Indiana University Press.

Mohanty, Satya P. 2003. "The Epistemic Status of Cultural Identity." In *Identitites: Race, Class, Gender and Nationality*, edited by Linda Martin Alcott and Eduardo Mendieta. London: Blackwell Publishing.

Morris, Aldon D. 1984. *The Origins of the Civil Rights Movement: Black Communities Organizing for Change.* New York: The Free Press.

Morrison, Toni. 1992. *Playing in the Dark: Whiteness and the Literary Imagination.* Cambridge: Harvard University Press.

————, ed. 1992. *Race-ing Justice, En-gendering Power: Essays on Anita Hill, Clarence Thomas, and the Construction of Social Reality.* New York: Pantheon Books.

Morton, Patricia. 1991. *Disfigured Images: The Historical Assault on Afro-American Women.* New York: Praeger.

Mullins, Leith. 1997. *On Our Own Terms: Race, Class, and Gender in the Lives of African American Women.* New York: Routledge.

Omi, Michael, and Howard Winant. 1994. *Racial Formation in the United States from the 1960s to the 1990s.* New York: Routledge.

Omolade, Barbara. 1994. *The Rising Song of African American Women.* New York: Routledge.

Pleck, Elizabeth. 1987. *Domestic Tyranny: The Making of American Social Policy Against Violence from Colonial Times to the Present.* New York: Oxford University Press.

Pierce Baker, Charlotte. 1998. *Surviving the Silence: Black Women's Stories of Rape.* New York: W. W. Norton and Company.

Rasche, Christine. 1986. "Minority Women and Domestic Violence: The Unique Dilemmas of Battered Women of Color." *Journal of Contemporary Criminal Justice*, 4: 150.

Richie, Beth. 1985. "Battered Black Women: A Challenge for the Black Community." *The Black Scholar* 16: 40–44.

————. 1996. *Compelled to Crime: Gender Entrapment of Battered Black Women.* New York: Routledge.

Riley, Denise. 1989. *Am I that Name? Feminism and the Category of 'Women' in History.* Minneapolis: University of Minnesota Press.

Rothenberg, Paula S. 2001. *Race, Class, and Gender in the United States.* New York: Worth Publishers.

Schechter, Susan. 1982. *Women and Male Violence: The Visions and Struggles of the Battered Women's Movement.* Boston: South End Press. New York: Worth Publishers.

Schneider, Elizabeth M. 2000. *Battered Women & Feminist Lawmaking.* New Haven: Yale University Press.

Simmel, George. 1971. *On Individuality and Social Forms.* Edited and with an introduction by Donald N. Levine. Chicago: The University of Chicago Press.

Spelman, Elizabeth. 1988. *Inessential Woman: Problems of Exclusion in Feminist Thought.* Boston: Beacon Press.

Spillers, Hortense J. 1997. "All the Things You Could Be By Now, If Sigmund Freud's Wife Was Your Mother: Psychoanalysis and Race." In *Female Subjects in Black and White: Race, Psychoanalysis, Feminism,* edited by E. Abel, B. Christian, and H. Moglen. Berkeley: University of California Press.

Stanko, Elizabeth. 1985. *Intimate Intrusions: Women's Experience of Male Violence.* London: Routledge.

Stark, Evan, and Anne Flitcraft. 1985. "Woman-Battering, Child Abuse and Social Heredity: What is the Relationship?" In *Marital Violence,* edited by N. Johnson. London: Routledge.

Stewart, Julie H. 1998. "Pro-Violence Attitudes and Approval of Corporal Punishment." Durham, N.H.: Family Research Laboratory, University of New Hampshire.

Straus, Murray A. 1983. "Corporal Punishment, Child Abuse, and Wife Beating: What Do They Have in Common?" In *The Dark Side of Families: Current Family Violence Research,* edited by D. Finkelhor, R. Gelles, G. Hotaling, M. Straus. Beverly Hills, Calif.: Sage Publications.

Straus, Murray A., Richard Gelles, and Suzanne Steinmetz. 1980. *Behind Closed Doors.* New York: Doubleday.

Straus, Murray A., and Anita K. Mathur. 1996. "Social Change and Change in Approval of Corporal Punishment by Parents from 1968 to 1992." In *Family Violence Against Children: A Challenge for Society,* edited by D. Frehsee, W. Horn, and K. Bussmann. New York: Walter de Gruyter.

Straus, Murray A., and Julie H. Stewart. 1999. "Corporal Punishment by American Parents: National Data on Prevalence, Chronicity, Severity, and Duration, in Relation to Child, and Family Characteristics." *Clinical Child and Family Psychology Review* 2 (2): 55.

Strauss, Anselm. 1979. *Negotiations: Varieties, Contexts, Processes, and Social Order.* San Francisco: Jossey-Bass Publishers.

————. 1990. *Qualitative Analysis for Social Scientists.* San Francisco: University of California Press.

Swigart, Jane. 1991. *The Myth of the Bad Mother: The Emotional Realities of Mothering.* New York: Doubleday.

Violence Against Women Act, Title IV of the 1994 Violent Crime Control and Law Enforcement Act of 1994 (P.L. 103-322).

Walker, Alice. 1983. In *Search of Our Mothers' Gardens.* New York: Harcourt Brace Jovanovich.

Walker, Gillian. 1990. *Family Violence and the Women's Movement.* Toronto: University of Toronto Press.

Walker, Lenore E. 1979. *The Battered Woman.* New York: Harper and Row Books.

————. 1984. *The Battered Woman Syndrome.* New York: Springer.

Wallace, Michele. 1978. *Black Macho and the Myth of the Super-Woman.* New York: The Dial Press.

Wray, Matt, and Annalee Newitz. 1997. *White Trash: Race and Class in America.* New York: Routledge.

Watson, Lawrence, and Maria B. Watson-Franke. 1985. *Interpreting Life Histories.* New Brunswick, N.J.: Rutgers University Press.

West, Carolyn M. 2002. *Violence in the Lives of Black Women: Battered, Black, and Blue.* New York: Haworth Press.

West, Traci C. 1999. *Wounds of the Spirit: Black Women, Violence, and Resistance Ethics.* New York: New York University Press.

Westra, Bonnie, and Harold Martin. 1981. "Children of Battered Women." *Maternal Childnursing Journal* 10: 41.

Websdale, Neil. 2001. *Policing the Poor: From Slave Plantation to Public Housing.* Boston: Northeastern University Press.

White, Evelyn. 1985. *Chain, Chain, Chain: Change for Black Women Dealing with Physical and Emotional Abuse.* Seattle: The Seal Press.

Wilson, Margo, and Martin Daly. 1993. "An Evolutionary Psychological Perspective on Male Sexual Proprietariness and Violence Against Wives." *Violence and Victims* 8: 271.

Williams, Patricia J. 1991. *The Alchemy of Race and Rights: Diary of a Law Professor.* Cambridge: Harvard University Press.

Wing, Adrien K., ed. 1997. *Critical Race Feminism: A Reader.* New York: New York University Press.

Wolak, Janis. 1996. "Pattern of Parental Control and Sibling Violence." Durham, N.H.: Family Research Laboratory, University of New Hampshire.

Wyne, Marvin D., Kinnard P. White, and Richard H. Coop. 1974. *The Black Self.* Englewood Cliffs, N.J.: Prentice-Hall.

Yanow, Dvora. 2003. *Constructing "Race" and "Ethnicity" in America: Category-Making in Public Policy and Administration.* Armonk, N.Y.: M. E. Sharpe.

Zinn, Howard. 1995. *A People's History of the United States: 1492–Present.* New York: HarperCollins Publishers.

ABOUT THE AUTHOR

GAIL GARFIELD was a founder and executive director of the Institute of Violence, Inc. For the past twenty years, she has been a researcher, activist, and leader on the issue of violence against women. She holds a Ph.D. in sociology from the Graduate Center of the City University of New York.